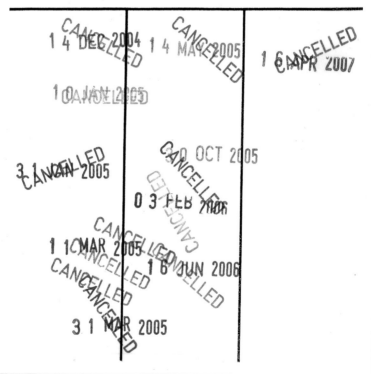

Communication and Society
*General Editor*: James Curran

# Media Moguls

Jeremy Tunstall and
Michael Palmer

London and New York

First published 1991
by Routledge
11 New Fetter Lane, London EC4P 4EE

Simultaneously published in the USA and Canada
by Routledge
29 West 35th Street, New York, NY 10001

Reprinted in 1993

© 1991 Jeremy Tunstall and Michael Palmer

Set in 10/12pt Times by Selectmove Ltd
Printed and bound in Great Britain by
T J Press (Padstow) Ltd, Padstow, Cornwall

*British Library Cataloguing-in-Publication Data*
Tunstall, Jeremy
    Media moguls.
    1. Media
    I. Title   II. Palmer, Michael
    302.2340922

*Library of congress Cataloging-in-Publication Data*
Tunstall, Jeremy.
    Media moguls / Jeremy Tunstall and Michael Palmer.
        p. cm. – (Communication and society)
    Includes bibliographical references and index.
    1. Mass media-Europe.   2. Mass media-Biography.
    3. Communication, International.   I. Palmer, Michael.
    II. Title.   III. Series: Communication and society (Routledge (Firm))
    P92.E9T8 1992   91–16744
    302.23'09224–dc20

ISBN 0–415–05467–2
ISBN 0–415–05468–0 pbk

# Contents

# Acknowledgements

This is the third product of a collaboration initially financed by a 1983–6 grant from the (British) Economic and Social Research Council (ESRC). Of the previous books, the first dealt with the United States – Jeremy Tunstall, *Communications Deregulation* (Blackwell, 1986). The second volume was a comparison of France and Britain – Michael Palmer and Jeremy Tunstall, *Liberating Communications* (NCC Blackwell, 1990).

In particular, of course, we want to thank Gianpietro Mazzoleni and Hans Kleinsteuber, who have written the excellent Italian and German chapters in this book. In editing their contributions, we have greatly benefited from regular discussions with both of them and with other colleagues from across western Europe in the Euromedia Research Group. We also especially thank Els de Bens and Mario Hirsch for valuable background help. Any errors that occur in this transnational, European and frequently updated project are our own.

The editorial staff at Routledge have been both competent and supportive. We thank Maria Stasiak for struggling so effectively with a heavily amended manuscript. Finally we have also been dependent on the typing skill and support of Ruth Newton and Maggie Brough, who have deciphered our handwriting through successive drafts.

# List of figures and tables

**Figures**

**Tables**

# Chapter 1

# Introduction

A small number of media moguls in a few western European nations are the sole subject matter of the second half of this book. But the phenomenon of media moguldom is only one important aspect of a European media industry of almost endless complexity.

Looking at individual media moguls is one way of getting a handle on the wider complexity of European media. In the first half of the book we present case studies of selected industrial themes across the European media. We first consider the case of western European television in the transatlantic context of imported Hollywood programming.

Second, we discuss the international news agency – the type of media organization which first established a pattern of media global hegemony. In the late nineteenth century the British and French agencies (Reuters and Havas) established an effective global cartel for *fast news*, based on their imperial telegraph networks. We describe how in the 1970s and 1980s the British agency (Reuters) became transformed into a *fast data* agency, offering financial data-on-screens as well as currency transactions; Reuters' media news became the visible tip of a data iceberg. The French agency (Agence France-Presse) had difficulties with both news and data.

Our third case study also shows how other previously powerful media industrial forces have adapted to the new political realities of European politics and commerce. The newspaper and advertising industries around Europe have often been powerful interests and successful lobbyists. We show that at the international level of Brussels, Strasbourg and Luxembourg the Press and advertising lobbies have been extremely diligent. These lobbies have seen national and European policy moving in directions favourable to newspaper and advertising interests; in particular there was a large increase in the 1980s in the number of available TV channels, with newspaper ownership and advertising finance in the driving seat.

These are only three industrial media case studies among a much larger potential total. But the European media industry defies simple analysis or even tidy mapping. There are indeed many different maps of Europe; in 1989–90 there was much talk of the eastern European nations as potential new members of the western European media club. But there were several different 'media Europes' potentially available for joining. The smallest of these was the twelve of the European Community based in Brussels and stretching only from Denmark to Greece; in between was the twenty-four of the Council of Europe, based in Strasbourg. There was also the still wider grouping of Eurovision, based in Geneva, stretching from Iceland to Jordan and engaged in daily television news exchanges.

Apart from these uncertainties of map and membership, media Europe offers several other dimensions of uncertainty. Much media policy discussion in Europe is primarily about television; but the Press in most countries still attracts more advertising revenue. There are often separate national policies for radio and film while advertising and recorded music tend to lack policy salience. And whether or not one includes book publishing makes a huge difference as to how important major book publishers (such as Bertelsmann or Maxwell) appear in the media industry.

The media also exist in Europe on many different levels, from the international to the local – and there are radically opposed definitions of what is meant by international and what is meant by local.

## GOING HOLLYWOOD–GLOBAL AS WELL AS GOING LOCAL–ETHNIC

During the 1980s most Europeans found themselves receiving an increased number of video channels. Most countries increased the number of conventional TV channels; and some countries – such as Belgium and its small population neighbours – became very heavily cabled; cable in turn offered conventional TV channels from neighbouring countries as well as new satellite channels from afar. Video-cassette machines offered additional new choices. This increase in channels (and in the number of hours of transmission per channel) typically led to an increase in the proportion of American content. In absolute terms – the available hours of American material per week – the increases were much greater. Italy, for example, began around 1980 to take virtually the entire prime-time output of Hollywood television.

Was this, then, not clear evidence of Europe being on the receiving end of an American-led global media industry? American rhetoric about the 'technological inevitability' of more channels and less regulation drifted across the Atlantic after 1980 and became, in some respects, a self-fulfilling prophecy. This 'inevitability' was somewhat naively accepted in western Europe and not least in Brussels. Governments competed to launch satellites and to encourage the cabling of streets; new conventional channels were created and Hollywood imports duly increased.

Yet towards the end of the 1980s, it also became evident that there was a contrary trend – the prophecies of more channels and of 'television without frontiers' were in some respects self-disproving. Foreign language material in general remains unpopular. The great popularity of *Dallas* in Europe around 1980 had no television equivalent by 1990. Popular channels required extra advertising revenue, while both popular viewer demand and regulatory pressure persuaded those channels to invest in more domestic programming. Some of this domestic programming was Italian, French, German and Dutch copies of American game show formats. American programming by 1990 still occupied a vast number of scheduled hours, but increasingly these were at low audience times like 3 a.m. or 3 p.m., or on new channels, often with very low audience shares.

Europe also saw in the 1980s some increases in media output at various levels below the national. 'Local' – like 'global' or 'international' – is another level which lacks any agreed European definition. In most European nations there is a distinct *regional* level – especially noticeable in television and newspapers and in Germany, Belgium, Spain, and several eastern European countries. There is also a distinct *city/urban* area level; and finally (we suggest) there is a *community* level of the small town, rural area, or single suburb. In the 1980s most European nations saw major developments at all three of these sub-national levels, especially in radio and newspapers.

In this book we do not seek to sustain a consistent conceptual framework covering these levels. We are merely attempting here

to point out the lack of agreed definitions of these various levels
across even western Europe.

There is evidence not only that European media are becoming
more global as well as more local (or regional), but that these
apparently contradictory tendencies are often interdependent. This
happens in many ways. Belgium, for example, seems to be an
extreme case of internationalized media; its nearly complete cable
system imports entire TV channels from France, Luxembourg,
Holland, Britain, Germany and Italy. Among the material most
attractive for Belgium viewers is a vast array of Hollywood films.[1]
The international character of Belgian television is linked to the
highly regionalized character of Belgium; this is a small country,
whose two distinctive language communities nevertheless insist on
two separate (and hence weak) domestic television systems.

There are many other local–international connections and alliances within European media. Minority language ethnic areas
such as Wales and the Basque country exchange programming.
French language regional broadcasters in Quebec, Belgium and
Switzerland share costs through co-production. And so on.

If both the supra-national and sub-national levels of broadcasting
and media have been growing stronger, does this indicate a
weakening of the national media level in Europe? Broadly speaking, this appears true. But the weakening is most noticeable in the
smaller population countries.

National media industries are subject to severe competition from
both above and below. However, the bulk of political power and
cultural-linguistic loyalty remains at the national level. In European
media then, we see international economics and technology in
opposition to national politics and language.


## THE TRIUMPH OF NEW TECHNOLOGY AND OLD MEDIA

As in other fields, so also in the media; new technologies, once
invented, have to wait two or even three decades to achieve – far
from certain – market acceptance. Three key 'new' technologies
of the 1970s were cable, satellite and the domestic video cassette
machine. Cable was an updated version of a technology used in
radio in the 1930s across Europe, east as well as west. Even the
high-powered satellite, capable of transmitting direct to a domestic
roof antenna, was potentially available in the 1960s and still was not
very successful by 1990. The first fully operational direct-to-home

satellite system in Europe was Rupert Murdoch's Sky offering, first available to the British public in 1989.

But cable-and-satellite's quite modest growth in 1980s Europe was perhaps less significant than the indirect impact on conventional television policy and operation. France, for example, went almost nowhere with cable-and-satellite in the 1980s, but this spectre on the horizon and across the border contributed significantly to a doubling of France's number of conventional TV channels, and where France went, Germany, Spain and Britain broadly followed – although via quite different detailed routes.

Consequently we have the paradoxical result that the main impact of the 'new media' was a strengthening of the conventional form of television. However, since newspaper owners (in several countries) finally achieved their long-time ambition to buy into television, the old medium of newspapers also benefited. All three of these new media – cassette recorders, cable and satellite – were, to a greater or lesser extent, mechanisms for getting more of much the same television programming onto the same old television screen.

## STALKING CASH COWS ON THE AUDIO-VISUAL LANDSCAPE

In the United States, established daily newspapers (which are typically monopolies) and established TV stations (especially network affiliates) are widely regarded as 'cash cows' – high in profit, and low in risk. The same is broadly true in Europe, where, of course, until recently most television was controlled by public non-profit corporations.

But on the 'media landscape' (*paysage*) not all properties are cash cows. We tentatively suggest a distinction between 'one-off' and 'cash flow' media. The main cash flow media, newspapers and television, have customers who typically use the service on a daily and continuing basis. The one-off media are all the others; these are media services which the customer typically purchases on an irregular basis – one cinema visit, one magazine or book purchase, one record or audio tape or disc. The one-off media suppliers typically attempt to routinize the purchasing behaviour – by mail subscription, book club membership and so on – but even here customer turnover is typically very high.

In Europe the cash flow media have traditionally been owned by state corporations or, in the case of newspapers, by established (often politically aligned) families. New entrants to the media industry – apprentice or 'baby' moguls – have often entered via the more volatile and risky one-off media. A common progression has been from magazines into newspapers. In recent decades the ultimate destination has typically been television.

There are other distinctions between the cash flow and the one-off media. The cash flow media are not only the most established, they are also the main news media and have a special political salience; they are thus the subject of policy, legislation and regulation. In Europe, as elsewhere in the world, foreign ownership of major newspapers and television is uncommon.

On the other hand the one-off media are much less politically salient, less regulated, and much more open to commercial purchase by moguls and companies, whether domestic or foreign.

## MEDIA DIPLOMACY, LOBBYING AND REGULATION – LEARNING A NEW GAME

Perhaps the most celebrated media lobby in the world is the Motion Picture Association of America (MPAA) which has over the decades adopted an aggressive, indeed bravura, lobbying style, especially in Washington. In Europe, and around the world, Hollywood – with State Department assistance – has also long engaged in cultural lobbying on a country-by-country basis. In recent years the MPAA's export wing (the Motion Picture Export Association, or MPEA) has been especially active in persuading friendly governments to take tough measures against video piracy.

But national media industries in Europe also have a long history of successful lobbying in their own countries. Major newspaper owners in Europe have had quick access to Presidents and Prime Ministers throughout the twentieth century. State broadcasting corporations have also been engaged in continuous negotiation with incumbent politicians about the details of broadcasting policy and finance.

Media lobbying has in recent decades acquired a new dimension – a European dimension. We discuss below the operation of the newspaper and advertising lobbies in Brussels. Certain media industries, nations and individuals seem to have been especially adept at learning this new game of media lobbying. The most adept media entity is the advertising industry – possibly because it is the most international (and American) element of European media; the Brussels advertising lobby has shrewdly focused upon one very clear long-term target – a Europe with more advertising and with less national regulation.

The nation which has taken most successfully to media lobbying and diplomacy must surely be France. Where France has gone, others have followed, and yet France seems to have mastered the high-wire act of pursuing both European and French goals at the same time.

Finally the greatest individual exponent to date of media lobbying and diplomacy has been the Italian TV mogul, Silvio Berlusconi. An individual mogul personality probably has some advantages in the new European media world of numerous different regulatory regimes. Berlusconi first practised these skills in his relationships with Italian politicians; he then applied the same skills in Paris, Madrid and Bonn and – not least – in Brussels.

# Part I

# Western European media industry case studies

# Chapter 2

# Western European television and the North Atlantic setting

Throughout the 1980s European policymakers in Brussels confronted what they saw as an unstoppable wave of new media technology and multiple new video channels. They saw this inevitable channel explosion as leading to a vacuum in available programming, which might have to be filled with cheaply imported American material.

Seeking to avoid such an American media invasion, European policymakers accepted the 'inevitable' growth of new channels but attempted to encourage European nations to fill the programming vacuum by importing from each other. 'Television without frontiers' would lead to a flowering of the European television production industry, which incidentally would help to increase European – rather than simply national – consciousness.

What happened in the 1980s was rather different. Channels did increase – if not as fast as, or in the way, anticipated. But western European nations continued largely to ignore each other's media output. Direct imports from the United States expanded not only in absolute quantity but as a percentage of all material offered. In addition there was a large increase in domestic national production of American-style formats such as cheaply made soap operas and quiz-game shows. During the 1980s France for example went from a three-channel television system with heavy overtones of national culture, education and public service to a six-channel system with much more entertainment in general and much more American entertainment in particular, financed by much more television advertising.

Around 1980 (it seems clear in retrospect) Europe misunderstood the nature of the 'challenge'. Perhaps the key event was the 1979 decision of the French and West German governments jointly to finance a direct broadcasting by satellite (DBS) project. This decision led to Britain also deciding to pursue its own separate DBS project.[1] In this way the French, German and British governments committed themselves to a high technology – indeed international space-race – approach to new media and broadcast deregulation. Meanwhile, when entering this hardware contest, the European governments failed to understand the much more cautious approach which the entire American continent, North and South, had adopted at the 1977 World Administrative Radio Conference (WARC) in Geneva. A common assumption of the US, Canadian, Mexican and Brazilian broadcasting industries (all of them more commercial than any European broadcast system) was that direct broadcasting by satellite was unlikely to be viable for some years yet.

Not only did the Brussels policymakers exaggerate the prospects for DBS, they also greatly exaggerated the likely growth of cable TV. The location of the European Community (EC) in Brussels may accidentally have contributed to the misunderstanding of cable. Belgium – whose cable systems imported broadcast channels from several neighbouring countries – may have seemed to indicate the inevitable and nearly complete cabling of Europe. It was the combined examples of cable television in the United States and in small European countries like Belgium which seemed so convincing.

The Brussels policymakers, however, failed adequately to analyse the probable responses of consumers in the larger population countries, where the majority of Western Europe's population lived. And the Brussels bureaucrats, in particular, ignored the Italian explosion of unregulated commercial television which was to prove the largest and most decisive 1980s break with the various European versions of 'public service broadcasting'.

The first full account of the Brussels television policy, *Television Without Frontiers*, was published in May 1984, and this initiated a five-year debate, leading to a Directive finally agreed in October 1989. But the early thinking in the EC Commission was already indicated by a 1983 'interim report' – *Realities and Tendencies in European Television: Perspectives and Options*.[2] In retrospect it is easy to see some key errors. This document considers the 'inevitability' of a channel explosion mainly in terms of cable and satellite. The document assumes that European countries will by the end of the 1980s have, on average, thirty cable channels, three

DBS channels, and three traditional TV channels. These channels will require 500,000 hours a year of 'films and similar productions', although the four largest countries of western Europe in 1983 together only produce some 1,000 hours.

The 1983 EC document failed to see the significance of the then recent Italian expansion of conventional channels from three to six or more. The document also saw the problem too much in terms of industrial competition and the growth of the space industry. Its discussion of consumer demand was superficial in the extreme. There was little attempt to think through the implications of new advertising-financed channels. Finally the 1983 EC document already gave high priority to an EC Europe-wide television channel. This was briefly realized in the form of a 'European' channel called EURIKON, made available via a Netherlands satellite slot; it quickly collapsed due to lack of support from viewers, broadcasters and advertisers. The ambition for this TV channel detracted from EC objectivity and went along with lack of commercial insight.

The EC, in seeking to extend its trade and commercial remit into the area of broadcasting was attempting to steer between two powerful forces. On the one hand it was attempting to avoid increased United States programming sales into Europe. On the other hand it had to steer clear of the traditional predominantly public service national broadcasting systems; each nation had its own (mainly license-financed) state-sponsored inward-looking broadcasting system whose protective walls nurtured national culture and encouraged national eccentricity and taste.

The EC policy in effect was to avoid both American hegemony and national public service broadcasting, by encouraging new national channels funded by advertising which would rely upon importing programming from each other and would attract a cross-frontier audience via satellite and cable. In retrospect this attempt to leap clear of both European national tradition and dependence on Hollywood imports was a highly improbable scenario. Much more probable was some marriage of the European national traditions with some expansion of importing from Hollywood and other faraway places.

## TELEVISION WITHOUT FRONTIERS, POLICY WITHOUT CLEAR GOALS

The EC Commission document *Television Without Frontiers*, published in May 1984, reflected both seven years of DBS debate since WARC 1977 and the two years of satellite-to-cable since Sky's European launch in April 1982.

But European policymaking and activity in transborder television dates from much further back. Four bodies have had important influences: the European Broadcasting Union (EBU); Eutelsat; the Council of Europe (COE); and the European Community.

The EBU dates from 1950. Its major activity of exchanging television programmes expanded rapidly after the advent of the video-tape recorder in 1958. The daily news exchanges between western European public service broadcasters became its main activity; in 1962 three items per day were exchanged and by 1982 this had risen to twenty-one news items per day. The other major activity was the exchange of sporting events. By 1981 these EBU exchanges accounted for some 5 per cent of total programming output in the average country. Nevertheless EBU was unable to move out of live (or same-day) news and sporting events. It was performing a fairly modest role, much of it of a video news agency character. Indeed the largest contributors to the EBU news exchanges were indeed the three major newsfilm agencies (two based in London).[3]

Eutelsat was a second European club which affected transborder video. Eutelsat was established by the European telecommunications authorities to coordinate communications satellite activities. Eutelsat oversaw the Orbital Test Satellite (OTS) series in the late 1970s, and the subsequent ETS series. These satellite activities were intended for European telecommunications traffic which, however, largely failed to materialize. So Eutelsat sold its spare satellite capacity at rather low prices to the new breed of satellite-to-cable adventurers. Satellite Television (later renamed Sky Channel) began its initial service from London to Malta, Finland and Norway in April 1982 on OTS-2. British Telecom played a significant role here; since control of Eutelsat was on the basis of international telecommunications traffic, British Telecom International was Eutelsat's largest shareholder.

The two major bodies which did seek to identify and implement a coherent policy were the Council of Europe (Strasbourg) and the

European Community (Brussels). The then twenty-one-member Council of Europe made most of the running in the 1970s; it concentrated on questions of content, copyright, piracy and the like. The main European Community effort occurred in the 1980s and – most notably in its 1984 document *Television Without Frontiers* – it focused on television across borders as an economic and trading activity, which, as such, fell within the Treaty of Rome.[4]

Towards the end of the 1980s there was much evidence of both rivalry and co-operation between the (significantly weaker) Council of Europe and the EC in seeking to establish a European broadcasting policy. In 1986 and 1987 the policy moved forward more quickly. The Council of Europe and the EC each had its own legislative, executive and judicial branches – with all three branches (in both cases) involved in the policy evolution. And in addition to the national memberships, there were major industrial interests (such as press and advertising) organized both nationally and Europe-wide.

The difficulties of extracting an agreed policy from all of these conflicting pressures were very considerable. So much so, that when the agreed policy began to emerge in the late 1980s, it was a policy without clear goals. The EC draft Directive of March 1986[5] included these major points:

*advertising* to be limited to 15 per cent (nine minutes per hour) of broadcasting time;
a *minimum quota* of 30 per cent of programming must be made within the EC, rising later to a 60 per cent quota;
*tobacco advertising* banned, alcohol advertising restricted;
*copyright* holders' right to withhold material for transborder transmission to be limited, but procedures to ensure fair payment;
*satellite transmissions* to be 'MAC packet' incorporating D2–MAC as well as C–MAC standards;
*independent* programme producers to receive European financial support.

Each of these measures had its own history of negotiation and argument; each was a compromise between opposing positions.

The advertising limit of 15 per cent (nine minutes per hour) was a compromise between 10 per cent and 20 per cent. There was much argument about the placing of advertising within feature films. More significant in revenue terms was an ultimate decision that while nine minutes per hour must be the average, the maximum for any single hour would be twelve minutes of advertising.

The quota of EC programming rising from 30 per cent to 60 per cent was designed to accommodate initially the heavy importing, small population, nations and to encourage them to import more from their EC partners. News and sports programming, game shows, advertising and teletext were to be excluded. These exceptions would allow American news and sports channels (such as CNN) to transmit in Europe with little or no European programming; or a channel could provide perhaps half of its programming in the form of American sport, news, ads and game shows; a 60 per cent quota for the remaining half would mean a total of only 30 per cent European programming.

The tobacco and alcohol restrictions were simply an acceptance of the commonly existing European restrictions. The 'MAC packet' technology was also another compromise between at least two rival versions of MAC, at a time of uncertainty concerning high definition television.

The copyright semi-compulsion was designed to prevent particular copyright holders (such as an actor) vetoing the transborder transmission of, for example, a whole television series. Nevertheless many other copyright problems remained (and the entire copyright proposal was later dropped).

The support for independent producers was another point in line with practice already strongly emerging in 1985-6 in a number of western European nations. The overall impact of this encouragement was likely to be fairly modest.

Crucially, these proposals were unlikely to support the strategy, or to achieve the goals, behind the policy. The emerging strategy seemed to indicate these goals:

1  to impose barriers on United States programming entering EC countries;
2  to endorse increased trade in programming between conventional broadcasters within Europe;
3  to endorse the emergence of new channels in general and of transborder channels (especially by satellite and cable) in particular;
4  to endorse advertising as the prime source of funding for new channels;
5  to encourage the expansion of the total advertising expenditure going to television channels across Europe.

These points overall were likely to increase, rather than decrease, US imports into Europe. New channels financed by advertising appeared in plenty in the 1980s and they raised dependence on US programming to new heights.

The policy deliberately attempted to avoid confrontation with established forces such as the dominant major networks of the larger nations. There was also an avoidance of any attempt to specify how existing national ratios of home/EC/US production should, or could, be altered. Was the central objective to reduce the *proportion* of imports from the US? Or was the real objective to increase the imports from the EC, so as to match an inevitable increase in US imports?

After very protracted discussions within and between the Council of Europe and the European Community, the EC at last in October 1989 agreed on a Broadcasting Directive. Most of the later contention focused on the permitted quota of imported programming. A maximum import quota of 50 per cent was agreed (to apply mainly to imported feature films and TV series) but the 50 per cent quota was also agreed to be voluntary, not compulsory.

The Directive, then, which finally emerged from the 1984–9 negotiations, lacked teeth. But the somewhat irrelevant nature of the policy was already evident at the start of the marathon five years of negotiation. 1984, the year of the original *Television Without Frontiers*, was also a year of events which indicated how the document was already being superseded.

In April 1984 the London-based Sky Channel (now Murdoch-owned) obtained access to the rich cable market of the Netherlands; but although Sky had by 1988 reached the screens inside fifteen million households across mainly northern Europe, it continued to lose money. The very widely scattered audience did not appeal to advertisers. Moreover the local politicians in the Netherlands (and elsewhere) were sensitive to the overwhelmingly American and British programming on Sky. They gradually raised their demands for Dutch content; this meant that Sky's costs would always rise fast enough to increase its losses. Early 1989 indeed saw the cessation of Sky's transcontinental ambitions and its relaunch as a multi-channel service (on a Luxembourg SES–Astra satellite) aimed solely at the British national market.

Already in 1984 there were indications of the likely evolution of satellite television as a mainly *national* service aimed at a single language market. In January 1984 RTL in Luxembourg launched its German-language television service in which the major media company Bertelsmann had just acquired a 40 per cent interest. This RTL Plus service became a key element in the rise of German-language advertising-funded television backed by print-based companies. The RTL launch led the conventional German public service networks (ARD and ZDF) to protect their future by buying up the German TV rights to hundreds of Hollywood films. This 1984 development itself followed a pattern already familiar from Italy; it showed that an early beneficiary of European satellite TV was Hollywood – whose archives of old films would henceforth attract higher prices across western Europe.

November 1984 also saw the launch of Canal Plus in France – a new conventional TV service available on subscription and specializing in feature films. One major beneficiary of Canal Plus was the French film industry but the other main beneficiary was again Hollywood. Only two months later – in January 1985 – President Mitterrand announced the launch of private commercial television in France – to take place by the end of 1985; a fifth advertising-financed channel was indeed awarded to a consortium (Seydoux–Riboud–Berlusconi) in November 1985 and a sixth to another consortium.

Meanwhile in 1984 there were fresh developments to Italian commercial television which further emphasized that the *Television Without Frontiers* analysis was at best too little and too late. In 1984 the leading commercial channel in Italy – Berlusconi's Canale-5 – claimed that it had for the first time passed the leading public channel (RAI-1) in audience share. The Italian channels in 1984 were showing virtually the entire Hollywood production houses' fresh output of television series; and, of course, they were also showing Hollywood films. Much of the remaining time was taken up with Italian versions of American television game shows. All of this was well known in Brussels.

But the US–Italian connection went further still. There was a wholesale reorganization of Italian television which involved massive borrowing of American industrial practices. For example all three of the New York networks were involved in consultancy relationships with Italian networks and were advising on such key issues as scheduling. CBS and ABC were working with commercial networks and NBC with the public service RAI.[6]

## 1989: 'WORLD MEDIA TOP TEN' THINKING EMERGES

1989 was not only the year in which the European Community agreed on a broadcasting policy for Europe, complete with non-binding import quotas. It was also a year of mega-mergers. Two mergers in particular seemed to highlight the emergence of a small media league of world players.

The Time–Warner merger involved two of the largest American media companies; it marked the emergence of an American audio and video company larger than any previous Hollywood company and larger also than any New York TV network. Time–Warner would be strong in the production and distribution of films, TV series and recorded music; strong as a satellite distributor of entertainment (Home Box Office); strong in local cable systems; and immensely strong in magazines.

1989 also saw the Sony takeover of Columbia Pictures. Sony already owned, in CBS records, the world's leading music company; it now acquired a major Hollywood production house, especially successful in television series. This obviously was a marriage of Japanese hardware with American entertainment and it had strategic implications for future developments in high definition television as well as in digital audio tape.

In Europe these mergers were seen by some as evidence of an American–Japanese alliance – comparable to those in micro-electronics and computers – whose intention was to dominate markets in Europe. Meanwhile a growing European–Japanese challenge was quoted in Congressional hearings by Time and Warner as a justification for their mega-merger.

There was perhaps an element of self-fulfilling prophecy in fashionable talk about world players and top ten companies. The construction of a media Top Ten league occupied much space in trade publications in 1989 and the selected players varied quite radically from list to list. This derived largely from the vagueness of the term 'media'. The claim of the low-profile German company Bertelsmann (previous to the Time–Warner merger) to be the world's largest media company depended heavily on its strength in book and record clubs, printing and publishing. Similar questions arose about Hachette in France.

Nevertheless media Top Ten thinking not only seemed by 1989 to be reflected in company acquisitions but also involved certain common assumptions about the identity of the leading players. These Top Ten players were seen as all being based in the US, Japan and western Europe. The US companies, in addition to Time–Warner, included News Corporation (Murdoch) and companies owning national networks such as ABC and NBC. The Japanese companies were less well known on the world scene – and especially in Europe – but after 1989 Sony could no longer be ignored as a media giant; other obvious Japanese candidates for the world top ten included the TV network/newspaper combines such as Fujisankei (which in 1989 was showing an interest in British films and music).

American selections for the media Top Ten invariably included the German Bertelsmann and the French Hachette; Bertelsmann already owned the old RCA music companies while Hachette had major US interests, including magazines. Maxwell Communications (of Britain) was another favourite American selection. The Italian Fininvest company was perhaps a more obvious candidate, not least because the successes of its transnational controller, Silvio Berlusconi, included in 1989 his acquisition of a stake in a Spanish channel, Telecinco.

There were clearly many other candidates, some of which had ambitions to join the world's media Top Ten. There were also many arguments for and against massive size in the media industry. These arguments largely focused upon whether substantial 'synergies' did or did not exist. Some synergy-seeking presumably will be a lost cause; a television network may gain few, if any, programming advantages from owning a book company. But synergy may result from vertical or horizontal integration which enhances market power. In some cases size will bring buying advantages such as bulk discounts. Market power is especially important in some media fields, such as video entertainment. Video material has no 'natural' value in a particular market; the level of competition and the market strength of buyers (such as TV networks, cinema chains, cable system operators and video-cassette distribution chains) determines price. This is partly true also of the price of finance. Big media companies seeking to get bigger have been favourably regarded by the financial world.

The 1989 changes focused heavily upon the United States, indicating that the 'American media challenge' had changed greatly from the challenge which *Television Without Frontiers* was initially designed to address.

The changes of the 1980s derived primarily from the introduction, by the first Reagan administration (1981–5), of deregulation, its general economic policies, and its relaxation of
anti-trust constraints. The later 1980s saw the Time–Warner and
Sony–Columbia Pictures mergers, as well as other mega-mergers.

All of these developments indicate tremendous changes in
the late 1980s in Hollywood, most of which had significant
implications for Europe in the 1990s. These predominantly
Hollywood developments attracted much more attention than
anything – including the EC Directive agreement – which happened
to the European media in 1989. Nevertheless, there were some
important European changes. One of these – the selection of
three consortia to introduce commercial television to Spain –
was somewhat ambiguous in terms of US–European influence.
In some respects this massive infusion of commercial television
in Spain was a major advance for Americanization. On the other
hand it was an advance also for Europeanization – because French
and Italian companies but no American companies were included
in the winning consortia.

## SATELLITE POLICY TUNNEL VISION: MAJOR REALITIES IGNORED

European broadcasting policy of the 1980s – 'Television without
frontiers' – reflected a tunnel vision concern with satellites.
Broadcasting policy was seen as being about 'satellites and other
new technology' or satellite channels and domestic networks.

Relatively little attention was paid to audiences and their
preferences. Some research organizations did indeed throw doubt
on popular demand for new channels. CIT Research (of London)
produced through the 1980s a long succession of highly pessimistic
forecasts about demand for foreign media across western Europe.
These gloomy predictions were proved ultimately to have erred in
the direction of being slightly too optimistic.

The apparent success of cable in Belgium, the Netherlands and
other small European nations was misread and misunderstood. In
heavily cabled Belgium the French-speaking audience was largely
watching programming cabled in from France and Luxembourg;
the Flemish population was tuning to programming in its own first
language from the Netherlands.

Many studies of cable audiences including the multi-national

PETAR studies of the later 1980s broadly supported[7] these general statements about cable.

1 Cable is used to receive the main conventional national channels (better reception, antenna not required).
2 People also tune to programming from neighbouring – usually larger – countries which speak the same or a very similar language. Austrians and German Swiss watch German channels; French–Belgians and French–Swiss watch French channels.[8]
3 There is a smallish audience for foreign-language programming – but this is mainly confined to Scandinavians and other northern Europeans watching English-language material; most of this English-language material is music, feature films or drama series.
4 Of the moderate amount of viewing in foreign languages, much of the material actually viewed is American. For example in Belgium – where Dutch and French are widely spoken – much foreign viewing is of Hollywood films and series. Belgians switched to a German, Italian or French channel are often watching Hollywood products.[9]

Many studies and forecasts in the early and mid-1980s asked interviewees to indicate their own foreign-language ability; even the real remarkably high level of English-language ability in northern Europe was thus probably exaggerated. Part of the appeal of American programming was that its music, its 'production values', its action-adventure themes and its rapid pace could be appreciated without a good knowledge of the language. Incidentally even British audiences probably understand Hollywood language and references less well than they may realize.

Brussels broadcasting policymakers also had to confront national political systems and may not have recognized the extent to which these were already attuned mainly to home-made, or at least own-language, material, topped up with American imports. National audiences which watched the national TV news before switching to Hollywood entertainment were quite convenient for incumbent politicians.

Brussels with its enthusiastic advocacy of the 'inevitability' of 'television without frontiers' helped to give new TV channels a prominent position not only on the European political agenda but upon national political agendas. This heightened interest in new channels in due course tended to transfer national political attention to the fact that the quickest way to introduce new channels to all or most of the populace was to license additional conventional channels. Inevitably some parties – especially those on the political left – opposed the introduction of new channels, the accompaniment of more TV advertising and the importing of more programming. However, once opposed by a party of the left, the contrary policy – more new channels – was likely to be adopted by parties of the right. In some cases (such as France and Spain) socialist governments introduced new channels as pre-emptive moves.

The Brussels' objective of achieving a European television audience and industry might, or might not, have been better achieved by encouraging the retention of 'public service broadcasting'. But *Television Without Frontiers* attempted in effect to by-pass the national public service systems in favour of Euro-commercial broadcasting. Brussels attempted to by-pass the national public service systems precisely because these systems were so embedded in each national political and cultural structure. Some key implications of the *national* tradition of public broadcasting may have been missed.

The 1984 *Television Without Frontiers* document commented on the enormous variety of law, regulation, commercial practice and taste which affected television advertising across Europe. This enormous variety made, and will continue to make, enormous difficulties for standardized trans-European advertising campaigns. But public service broadcasting has also encouraged (across the whole range of programming) national eccentricity, national taste and national mythology. The Netherlands broadcasting system is, for example, based on allegiances in religion and politics, while, by contrast, in neighbouring Belgium there are separate systems for the two main languages. Different European nations handle humour in very different ways; although the British and German TV systems are in some ways quite similar, the British and German approaches to television humour are utterly different.

Paradoxically, also, in some respects European national broadcasting systems in the 1980s grew more national. Extended hours on additional channels had to be partly filled with cheap formats; such formats as studio-based game shows and chat shows were often licensed from the United States. But the production itself was national. Quiz shows present viewers with their fellow citizens;

there is little demand for dubbed or sub-titled quizzes or talk shows.

News, actuality and sport are mixed cases. There is strong demand for imported inserts and for sport in which national teams compete against foreigners. But most of the news and sport and other actuality presented to viewers is national.

All of these factors tended to count against the numerous satellite channels of the 1980s – such as the British-based Sky Channel and Super-channel – which were aimed at cable systems across western Europe; most such channels attracted very modest audience shares and little advertising, thus making losses. At the end of the 1980s there was a trend towards own-language satellite offerings – notably German-language channels aimed at German-speaking cable subscribers. But in May 1989 yet another gloomy report by CIT Research found that 40 existing satellite channels had only a 1.6 per cent audience share in 120 million households across 17 western European nations. So much for satellite television without frontiers.

 **DEFERENCE AND DISDAIN: EUROPE AND HOLLYWOOD**

International trade in film and video entertainment has long involved an element of cultural deference. The larger European nations have since about 1920 paid deference to Hollywood as the mecca of popular culture; the smaller nations of Europe have paid double deference – not only to Hollywood but to their particular big brother neighbours.

Europe's collective (popular) cultural deference for Hollywood has, however, been combined with an opposing strain of disdain. Deference is paid to Hollywood's usually reliable entertainment, its 'production values', and the apparently universal appeal of its silent comedies, its action-adventure shows and its stars; Hollywood has also been seen in Europe as the bearer of the glad tidings about new consumer and social trends. However there has long also been an element of disdain for Hollywood's slickness, superficiality and commercialism. Nowhere has such disdain been more strongly felt than in Europe's public broadcasting organizations; these publicly funded broadcasters were able to use their monopoly position to acquire expensive imported productions at low prices for showing to large television audiences. This enabled public service broadcasters habitually to regard Hollywood as 'cheap' in several senses.

The deference–disdain combination has played its part in Brussels' and Europe's generally weak comprehension of the full extent of the challenge from Hollywood. Certainly while Europe was in the 1980s evolving both Strasbourg and Brussels versions of European policy, Hollywood was strengthening its position.

Indeed in the 1980s Hollywood finally eliminated all other national film industries as serious competitors. At various points in the sixties and seventies the Italian, French, German, British, Australian and Japanese film industries had looked like serious competitors – but to no avail. Between 1975 and 1990 western Europe's film production steadily declined. During the 1980s several of these film industries attracted production finance from their television industries; this turned national film industries into makers of lowish budget films or effectively made-for-TV-movies; these low-budget European movies offered little competition to Hollywood's larger budget offering – especially in cinemas and on video-cassettes.

Since the 1960s Hollywood also reduced its involvement in international co-productions. In addition fewer European films and fewer US–Europe co-productions achieved exhibition access to the US market. In the year 1967 220 films made in Britain, Italy, France and West Germany entered the US; in 1987 these same nations supplied only 83 films to the US market.[10] Hollywood was now the only industry which made over a hundred multi-million dollar films each year. In the 1980s about ten Hollywood major companies were each making about fifteen features per year. These bigger budget American films went on to dominate cinema exhibition around the world and especially in Europe.

But both feature films and cinema exhibition were in the 1980s only minority slices of a much bigger Hollywood picture. In the 1980s Hollywood consolidated its strength not only in making a wider variety of product formats but in orchestrating and sequencing the marketing of these products through a succession of 'windows'. Data on revenue for feature films released through some of the main 'windows' is presented in Table 1.1. The biggest 1984–8 increase was in revenue for films shown on TV/cable, reflecting the price consequences of increased channel competition in Europe.

*Table 1.1*   Hollywood feature film sales to Europe 1984–8 in US $ millions

|              | 1984 | 1986 | 1988 |
|--------------|------|------|------|
| Theatrical   | 111  | 118  | 217  |
| TV/cable     | 39   | 59   | 143  |
| Home video   | 99   | 142  | 201  |
| Total        | 249  | 319  | 561  |

*Source*: *Variety* (22–8 February 1989).

These 1984–8 figures are from the American Film Marketing Association (AFM) and cover only feature film exports. The same set of figures showed that western Europe accounted for 60.4 per cent of Hollywood's film export earnings. Europe with Japan and Australia/New Zealand accounted for 83 per cent.

Hollywood had, of course, a wide range of formats to offer. At the peak in terms of cost and prestige were feature films; next most expensive to produce per hour were made-for-TV movies; then came short series, 'specials' and docudramas; cheapest of the main Hollywood formats were the TV series, several of which by 1989 cost over $1 million per hour to make. A new product format of the 1980s was the music video. And in addition Hollywood was the home of a vast audio-music industry.

All of this amounted to Hollywood's being a diversified recorded entertainment industry. Increasingly during the 1980s Hollywood's diversified industry – and no longer the New York networks – was the core of American entertainment. In this change home video perhaps played a special role as a new way for Hollywood to sell through a window over which the networks had no control.

It was of course Hollywood's status as an integrated industry and as the core of American entertainment which attracted foreign buyers to venture where the New York networks were forbidden to tread. But the main 1980s foreign incursions into Hollywood's video heartland – the major studios – were made by an Australian company (News) and a Japanese company (Sony). Nevertheless, Europe was not so far behind. In addition to CBS music (Bertelsmann), Europeans in the 1980s also bought Technicolor (Carlton) and MTM (TVS of the UK).

As competitive pressures continued to build up in Europe, national television networks continued to face acute cost dilemmas posed for them by Hollywood. In order to compete with imported

Hollywood video fiction – in its various forms – European broadcasters felt compelled in new productions to raise their own production values; home-made drama escalated in cost. Networks thus found their own drama and also the fresher Hollywood output both rising in price. One consequence was to fill out the schedule by reshowing older Hollywood material; thus one could see on French television, for example, 20-year-old American crime series. Or the supposedly up-market British Channel Four during one week in February 1989 showed nineteen American series, mainly ancient westerns and old situation comedies.[11]

## EUROPEAN CO-PRODUCTION – A FALSE HOPE?

Co-production appears to offer a solution to the common European problem of finding adequate finance for making expensive programming, especially the various forms of feature film and video drama. The way to compete with Hollywood's economies of scale is to generate similar economies of scale within Europe. In particular major television networks in two or more European nations should combine together to finance and screen films and drama series.

But co-productions have always faced practical difficulties. Perhaps the core difficulty is the familiar hierarchy which stubbornly continues to dominate the international video market. From a European viewpoint the international hierarchy continues to mean that (with some exceptions) audiences are still only willing to watch productions from their own or from larger nations. The hierarchy is first the USA; second France, Britain, Germany and Italy; and third the 'smaller' European nations. The central problem is that while the four larger nations would be the obvious core of a western European co-production industry, their own publics will only watch domestic or American productions.

This means that the only sure-fire co-productions within Europe are between one 'large' and a 'small' nation – for example Germany and Austria or Switzerland, or Britain with the Netherlands or Sweden. These 'co-productions' are then not between equals; the larger country has the bigger audience and resources and it dominates the production, while the co-producer in fact is a junior partner.

A similar difficulty faces the European–American co-production; the American market might look like the perfect solution because it is so large and affluent. However, in general, American audiences require their video entertainment to be made in (not dubbed into) English, to adopt American conventions of pace and production value (cost) and to use American actors and performers. All of these requirements can mean in practice that European–American co-productions may be American-dominated productions with European participation.

Following from the dilemma of the equal co-production in an unequal international market hierarchy, there is the problem of control: who in fact is in charge? Successful media forms have typically established some well-understood pattern of combining the business and creative sides of the activity. This is so in newspapers, for example, as well as in national television networks. It has also been the case with 'international' movie production; sometimes one individual combines two or more key roles (such as producer-director or director-writer) and in practice becomes the dominant force, the 'film-maker'. Sometimes there is a partnership between a director-writer and an international producer who controls the finance and marketing.

But in general the need for unambiguous control and aggressive management in both the creative and business spheres means that 'international' media undertakings are like most 'multi-national' companies in being controlled from a single national base. 'International' news agencies have been most successfully controlled from a single location such as New York, London or Paris.

It may perhaps be because feature films appear to be a partial exception, that such co-production hopes have been held out for television series. The two are, of course, very different. Feature film projects take much more time and money; the international market for films is more open, and Hollywood films can generate half of their earnings outside the US. Feature films are more dependent on visual production values than are TV series. An international feature film can be packaged by an international producer (or by agents) to include an American–European mix both of locations and of star actors; there is time to rewrite the script several times to please the leading participants. The great majority even of such projects stop at the script stage and the movie is not made.

None of these luxuries of time, money and flexibility exist in the production of television series. American networks (and increasingly European networks) want a reliable predictable product. Time is of the essence and a highly disciplined style of production, firmly controlled by an executive producer, seems essential for television series. Everywhere TV series are part of a schedule. Either these series are made within the hierarchy and production facilities of the transmitting network, or (as in the US) the series is made in a production house but commissioned by a network which insists on the series being tailored to a specific task and audience within the network's schedule.

Consequently it is very difficult for a European television series to be accepted onto a major network either in the US or in one of the larger European nations. Most European TV series which are exported are sold (at low prices) to lesser US networks. British television has a history of selling series to American television but for a long period this was predominantly to the small-audience Public Broadcasting System (PBS); there were also some sales to the syndication market, but none to the New York networks. In the 1980s the BBC switched much of its main sales effort to cable networks such as the Arts and Entertainment Network with even smaller audience shares than PBS. Other American cable networks took substantial amounts of European material – for example sport in the case of the ESPN and children's material on Nickelodeon. But all of this was for very low audiences, and quite small amounts of money.

Within Europe there was a similar trade in children's material and the continuing exchanges of sport and news via the EBU. But there was fairly little genuine co-production. In some fields various kinds of sale, exchange and co-operation were commonplace; but even television programmes with serious musical and art themes – when words and language are less important – continued normally to be made or at least dominated by one organization. In such areas 'co-production' often involved pre-selling of the national television rights and some quite modest pre-consultation. The same is broadly true of documentary and political programming; expensive filming of a distant foreign war may be facilitated by minority financing from foreign 'partner' networks.

In view of the obvious difficulties of genuine television series co-production – either across the Atlantic or across Europe – much interest and many hopes focus upon the mini-series. But mini-series are a television form and hence incorporate many of the same problems as the TV series. In the case of European–American co-productions, the mini-series faces additional problems, not least the fact that American networks have often seen their mini-series as popular ratings ammunition (for example in the special 'sweeps' research months) and were thus unlikely to use foreign reinforcements of doubtful ratings strength.

None of this means that both Euro–Euro and Euro–American co-productions may not increase in the future. Such are the financial pressures that co-productions probably will become more common and more successful. However the lesson from the 1980s seems to be that any growth in co-productions may well be slower than, and over-shadowed by, other changes.

## ITALY AND BERLUSCONI INTRODUCE A NEW BROADCASTING ERA FOR EUROPE

The Commission of the European Community was well placed in Brussels to observe a change in broadcasting policy leadership. The EC policies which evolved during the 1980s both reflected and endorsed the emergence of Italy and France as the leaders in deregulating European broadcasting.

In the period from 1945 to about 1980 Britain had been the policy leader. First the BBC and later the ITV system were models which were not copied precisely, but which did powerfully influence all other nations in western Europe. In particular the Federal Republic of Germany also evolved a public service pattern, based on licence fees with some carefully restricted advertising revenue. Next in line of policy influence came France and then Italy. 'Public service broadcasting' had always fitted less comfortably into the French and Italian political systems. The direct intervention of the state and of the political parties remained stronger in both France and Italy; in the 1960s and 1970s both France and Italy moved awkwardly towards a more BBC/IBA and ARD/ZDF pattern.

The great change occurred around 1980. While Britain was, with Channel 4, completing a decade of argument as to how the BBC/IBA duopoly should be modified, the Berlusconi revolution was occurring in Italy. Within a few years the leadership ranking among the west European Big Four had been reversed. By the late 1980s the new order was: Italy, France, Germany, with Britain now fourth.

Within a few years Italy went from three RAI television channels (with RAI-3 having less than total national reach) to a system of eleven channels (three RAI, three Fininvest–Berlusconi and five others all with at least 65 per cent national market reach). Within an even shorter space of years (1984–7) France went from three public service channels to two public service and four commercial.

Germany and Britain moved in the same direction, but with agonizing slowness compared with Italy and France. Meanwhile the migration of policy leadership from northern to southern Europe was assisted by the EC entry of Spain, Portugal and Greece – all three of which showed signs of following the Italian–French lead. This southern European group of Italy, France, Spain, Portugal and Greece contained over 52 per cent of the total EC population.

Italy in the 1980s itself demonstrated – and to a greater or lesser extent led other European nations towards – a new pattern of broadcasting. Multi-channel competition was perhaps the key innovation; Italy went further in this than did any other western European country. But across Europe there was a marked tendency for governments to launch new commercially-based conventional TV channels. This quickly led to a much greater emphasis on audience maximization.

Increasingly advertising-funded channels achieved audience ratings leadership. In Italy Berlusconi's Canale-5 became the leading force. It was scheduled for audience maximization throughout the day and evening.

Greatly increased emphasis was placed on advertising finance; in Italy the private networks first surpassed the advertising of the (RAI) public networks in 1982; total television advertising surpassed total press advertising for the first time in 1984.

Ownership of newspapers by non-newspaper companies expanded. In Italy the surge in television hit the Press, which experienced a financial crisis; in Italy during the 1980s nearly all of the leading newspapers came to be owned by leading Italian industrial companies, while one major daily was bought by Berlusconi himself.

The film industry also became integrated increasingly into television. The public service RAI had long been involved in film-financing; Berlusconi, however, became the dominant force in the Italian film industry. Firstly he integrated film production into Reitalia, his TV production company, then he set out to become the leading Italian owner of cinemas.

Greatly increased reliance on importing programming from Hollywood was especially evident in the late 1970s and early 1980s. Berlusconi and RAI began to buy up virtually the entire annual prime-time output of Hollywood; as a result prices increased.

During the late 1980s Berlusconi's initial near-total reliance on Hollywood programming was somewhat reduced. Gradually Berlusconi made more of his own programming. But by 1987, for example, only 38 per cent of Canale-5's output was in-house production; 49 per cent was 'acquired' and 13 per cent advertising. And on another Berlusconi channel, Rete-4, the home-made element was much lower.[12]

In addition to direct imports, much of the home-made or in-house programming was based on local versions of American game shows. RAI, like other public broadcasters, had started to adopt some American-format game shows back in the 1950s; the Berlusconi innovation was to schedule on Canale-5 a long daily sequence of Italian versions of such American favourites as *Family Feud, The Dating Game, Blockbusters, The Price is Right, The Newlywed Game* and *Hollywood Squares*.[13]

The new commercial television also became highly politicized. Berlusconi and his early competitors had found a convenient gap in the Italian law. Subsequently on many occasions Berlusconi was threatened with closure by court and by legislative action. But, as in the tradition of serial drama, he always escaped with the help of Italian politicians in general and a few highly placed politicians (such as Bettino Craxi) in particular.

Most of these aspects later appeared in other European nations, although usually in less extreme form. However, in some respects Italy was unique. The scale of the Berlusconi phenomenon was unique within Europe. Few other European nations would allow a single individual to dominate even one national TV channel, let alone three. Berlusconi also, of course, influenced yet other channels, by supplying them with programming and finance and selling their advertising time. To find a parallel to Berlusconi's Fininvest company one had to look to Brazil's Globo and Mexico's Televisa for examples of multi-channel private television companies.

Italy was unusual also in allowing Berlusconi to exercise such a high degree of control over the nation's advertising expenditure. Berlusconi's Publitalia company handled all of the commercial time on his own (as well as other) networks and thus sold the majority of Italian television advertising.

Another Berlusconi diversification involved the buying of Italy's largest retail chain – Standa – which at the time included 255 department stores. This was an example of 'synergy' which some other European nations might have termed a marketing 'monopoly'.

The latter diversifications – even though they might not have been legally approved in other European nations – nevertheless underlined another lesson of the Italian events which did have continent-wide significance. Commercial television – based neither on satellites nor on cable – had become a major commercial and industrial force.

## THE FRENCH–ITALIAN–SPANISH CONNECTION

Much of the importance of the Italian and Berlusconi developments was that a somewhat modified version of the Italian pattern was subsequently introduced into both France and Spain. In both countries these decisions were introduced by Socialist governments.

President Mitterrand announced in January 1985 that France would have additional commercial television channels. Mitterrand's decisions – and some modifications under conservative Prime Minister Chirac – took France in the space of three years from a system of three public channels, to a new system of two public and four commercial channels. The latter included the pay channel, Canal Plus, and two new channels, la Cinq and M6. Meanwhile the former premier public channel, TF-1, was privatized and moved to full dependence on advertising.

The French decisions included two major aspects not present in Italy. Firstly France adopted the idea of channels run by consortia – in which no single interest would control more than 25 per cent and which involved non-French ownership elements. Secondly France showed some signs of trying to retain not only public service channels but a significant continuing element of regulation. Its commercial approach as well as these two modifications succeeded in putting France at the head of European leadership in broadcasting policy, as did government support of a cultural channel, la Sept, with German, and possibly Spanish partners.

Within France much attention was focused upon the partisan aspect of the decisions by both Mitterrand and Chirac, the involvement in the new consortia of businessmen from the construction, water and other industries, as well as the prominent part given to Robert Hersant, the French Press mogul, in la

Cinq. But from a European viewpoint the foreign participation was more significant. Berlusconi himself acquired 25 per
cent of la Cinq; the Luxembourg company CLT acquired 25 per cent
of M6; and Robert Maxwell (of Britain) acquired 12 per cent of
TF-1.

The French approach of consortia – with foreign participation
– was followed by Spain, whose government (after lengthy
delays) finally in August 1989 announced the allocation of
franchises for three new conventional commercial television
channels. Again there was substantial press involvement. Each
of the three winning consortia included foreign participants. In
one consortium a group of foreign banks was involved, while
Berlusconi's Fininvest and the French Canal Plus each had 25 per
cent of a winning consortium.

The second French modification of the Italian pattern was to
place some added emphasis on regulation. This especially took
the form of insistence on French quotas. The new watchdog,
the Conseil Supérieur de l'Audiovisuel (CSA), in 1989 fined
the highly successful commercialized TF-1 for showing too much
American material and also for scheduling French material out
of prime audience times. Another commercial channel, la Cinq,
experienced similar attention.

By such policy changes France clearly became the policy leader
in Europe. The consortium approach (with minority non-French
participation) was the most substantial single step towards
European integration in broadcasting. France's 'rediscovery' of
regulation and reaffirmation of public service also made France
a flag-bearer in Europe. Even though the French preference
for binding import quotas was rejected, the general principle
of limiting US TV fiction imports was accepted as desirable by
almost all western European governments.

The broadcasting policy which emerged from the EC Directive
of 1989 resembled the national policy of France more than that
of any other single nation. France thus was very loosely the
leader of western Europe. However France was in particular
the leader of a southern grouping of Mediterranean nations;
amongst these nations the key initiative had been that of
Berlusconi and Italy. Moreover, the Spanish commercial television
decisions presaged further similar moves also in Greece and
Portugal.

## THE OLDER BROADCAST LEADERS, BRITAIN AND GERMANY: SLOWLY, SLOWLY

In all of these southern European policy changes the old broadcast policy leaders, Britain and Germany, were effectively left behind. Both had stronger traditions of public service broadcasting; both had much stronger newspaper presses and much higher levels of daily press readership. Both nevertheless moved towards broadcast deregulation, more channels, and a greater role for television advertising. But both nations moved extremely slowly in these directions – taking a decade to arrive at more modest versions of what Italy and France each did in a single bound.

West Germany's deregulatory journey in the 1980s was slowed down by opposition from the Social Democrat party and by the location of broadcasting policy at the (regional) *Länder* level. Nevertheless a loose coalition of the Conservative parties, the newspaper press and the telecoms authority (DBP) used the new technologies of satellite and cable with dogged determination in order to bring about policy change. The details of these changes are highly complex, but by the later 1980s German broadcasting policy had been transformed.[14] The Post Office's aggressive cabling policy was accompanied by some eight German-language satellite channels. Two commercial satellite channels, Sat-1 and RTL Plus, were especially important. Sat-1 was largely a newspaper publishers' channel; RTL Plus involved a large minority holding for CLT but German publishers (UFA–Bertelsmann, WAZ, FAZ and Burda) together had majority control of this 'Luxembourg' channel. Both of these channels were lavishly funded (by satellite-to-cable standards) and research indicated steadily growing audiences. However the most crucial change was that these channels started to become available on terrestrial broadcasting systems at the *Länder* level. Thus by a different route, and with very different political detail, Germany was following in French footsteps.

Britain also moved towards a more commercial broadcasting system very slowly. The Thatcher government, elected in 1979, quickly introduced Channel 4 – a new channel with public service goals, sheltered from the full blast of commercial competition. After a decade in power, the Thatcher government still had not made the substantial move towards commercialism, now common on the continent. It did in 1988 declare its intention to make such a move; but the resulting Broadcasting Act of 1990 in fact retained most of the 1980s arrangements.

## GLOBAL MEDIA PRECEDENTS: FILMS, NEWS, BOOKS, MUSIC AND ADVERTISING

Newspapers and broadcasting have long been the most national and least global parts of the mass media. Because newspapers have to be physically distributed in a few hours each day, they cannot easily be sold over long distances. Broadcasting has tended to stay national, especially where – as in Europe – state involvement has effectively resulted in market protection and sheltered finance. When the state systems did step into the market – to acquire foreign programming and entertainment – they did so as monopoly buyers within their national market; this enabled them to acquire Hollywood products at very low prices. When, however, national policy deliberately increases channel competition, much of this special protected status disappears.

The Brussels policymakers seem not to have recognized that, in favouring new channels of commercial television without frontiers, they were in effect advocating that European television should become more like other unprotected parts of the mass media. In most of these a strong global market element already existed by the 1980s, and was being further strengthened.

In film there had been an effective global market since the silent era and Hollywood had led this market since about 1920. International (as opposed to national) news had already been the subject of a world news cartel in the late nineteenth century. By the 1980s the appearance of satellite news feeds had done little to extend competition. Books had always been more competitive, but in the 1980s a series of massive mergers had largely integrated United States and United Kingdom book publishing into a single industry – in which German, Netherlands, Canadian and Australian publishing were also partly involved.

However, perhaps the world recorded music industry is more significant because music is so close to television and so central to radio. By the late 1980s the world music industry was dominated by six companies: of these only two were still US-owned (Warner and MCA); one was Japanese-owned (CBS), one Dutch-owned (Polygram), one German (RCA) and one British (EMI). These six companies accounted for the great bulk of world recorded music sales revenue.

The final field of particular relevance to broadcasting was that of advertising agencies. A number of mega-mergers in the mid and late 1980s led to the emergence of a handful of giant advertising agencies; the largest of these each controlled not one, but two separate world networks of local offices.

## TOWARDS AN INTEGRATED GLOBAL AUDIO-VISUAL INDUSTRY

The late 1980s saw new elements of 'globalization' arriving in the major broadcasting industries in general and in Hollywood in particular. Europe in the 1980s seemed to be on the receiving end of an increased flow of American media products and American media policies. This went alongside American, and then increasingly Japanese, dominance in all of the electronic hardware fields. Europeans found themselves looking at Hollywood images on Japanese screens. This trend was especially marked in the new field of domestic video-cassettes.

But as seen from the United States the global trends looked somewhat different. European, Japanese and Australian companies were buying up core parts of the American industry. True, no foreign companies bought television stations or networks – because this was not allowed by law. Similarly no American companies could, or did, buy even minority shares in any European networks; such foreign ownership as did develop in European TV networks in the 1980s was limited to, for example, an Italian purchase of 25 per cent of one French network.

In this new world of supposedly American-inspired global concentration, the American broadcasting industry was highly fragmented compared with those of Japan or individual western European nations. In Japan in particular the media industry was highly concentrated. In addition to the public service NHK, Japan had four major commercial television networks; these networks were co-owned with Japan's mammoth circulation daily newspapers, as well as with radio networks, recorded music companies, film production, home video interests and sports teams. Alongside a handful of integrated multi-media companies such as Fujisankei and Asahi was a handful of electronics hardware companies, of which Sony was the first to make major foreign media purchases.

Not only was Japan controlled by four or five integrated Press–TV multi-media companies, but to some American eyes Europe was also still a protected territory; in the 1970s European broadcasting was dominated by a single public organization in each nation which used its monopoly strength to buy Hollywood products at low prices. In the 1980s Europe changed – according to this American critique, only from a monopoly to a duopoly; Europe followed the Italian pattern of one state organization and one dominant commercial organization (such as Berlusconi in Italy, TF-1 in France and ITV in Britain).

Certainly the changes of the 1980s did leave the United States relatively open. The New York networks gradually lost their previous degree of dominance; during the 1980s the two already fragmented wings of the industry – the local TV stations and the Hollywood production industry – became more fragmented and also more powerful. Among the local TV stations the non-network 'independent' stations became more salient. Within Hollywood the distinction between 'major', minor and independent companies became less clear. Most important of all, a massive new cable industry came into existence – bringing newspaper companies into the video business and also marking the appearance of completely new all-cable enterprises.

During the 1980s then the American video industry was less dominated by three New York networks, but increasingly was focused upon some thirty or forty companies in which a dozen volatile Hollywood companies had acquired greater market strength. And it was against this background that the Sony–CBS Music–Columbia Pictures and Time–Warner mergers of the late 1980s were so important. These mergers seemed to indicate the end of an era of Hollywood-and-video fragmentation and the arrival of a new era of audio-visual concentration. Sony and Time–Warner also indicated two major forms which this integration and concentration might take.

Firstly Sony's purchase initially of CBS Music and then in 1989 of Columbia Pictures became the outstanding example of hardware-software integration. These purchases clearly had many aspects, not least the switch from the previous marriage of CBS Music and the CBS television network to a new audio-visual marriage of Hollywood production house with a music major. But the dominant goals behind these Sony acquisitions were clearly hardware ones. Sony had strategic hardware goals in such future technologies as mini-videotape, digital audio tape and high definition television; Sony's control of audio and video recorded material would be used in an attempt to 'lock-in' consumers to Sony hardware. In 1990 Sony's lead was followed by Matsushita, which, in acquiring MCA, also obtained movie, TV and recorded music interests.

A variant on this type of hardware driven integration was the General Electric–RCA–NBC merger; General Electric's purchase resulted not only in the merger of two of the largest American electronics companies but the inclusion also of the NBC television network. This merger also clearly had implications for future video technologies and gave some promise of a replay of RCA's leading role in hardware and broadcasting in the early days of both radio and television.

The Sony, Matsushita and General Electric acquisitions, deriving from the already globalized electronics industry, obviously had implications for Europe. These mergers seemed to put software into an 'advance guard' role in relation to hardware – suggesting that future innovations might be hardware driven but software led. This would suggest a more aggressive and perhaps more comprehensive attack on European markets.

A second type of large-scale merger focusing on multi-media integration was exemplified by the Time–Warner merger of 1989. Time was of course a giant in magazines and books. But the merger was most significant in both the US and Europe for its creation of a new leader of America's audio-visual industries. Time–Warner was bigger than, and arguably more powerful than, any of the TV networks. Time–Warner was a leader in four separate audio-visual fields. It was a leader in recorded music (Warner); it controlled the Hollywood Warner studio production of movies and TV series; it included Home Box Office (Time), the dominant force in the profitable business of transmitting new movies and other premium fare into 'pay-cable' services; finally Time–Warner became the second largest operator of local cable systems, spread across some thirty-seven states, and the leading cable force in New York City.

The new Time–Warner colossus had combined sales substantially larger than any New York television network. It controlled its own network in the form of HBO; it was involved in audio-visual production, distribution and local marketing, thus offering many potential synergy (or market power) advantages. Also Time–Warner evaded the regulatory restriction which forbade the networks to own programming and thus largely ruled them out of foreign markets. In terms of foreign sales Time–Warner was a new colossus – bigger not only than a network, but bigger also than the relatively small Hollywood companies which during the television age had always found themselves in a weak position relative to European monopoly state networks. Time–Warner incorporated several major types of established presence in western European markets – not only in selling records, films and TV programming, but also in magazines and books. All of this audio-visual fire-power was also focused at the very point where in 1989 Europe was weakest – namely in television programming. Previous to the Time merger Warner had bought Lorimar, the biggest TV network supplier for the 1989–90 programming season. Warner itself was fourth equal. Time–Warner was producing annually some 300 hours of prime-time US network programming which it could then also offer in Europe.

The Time–Warner merger indicated that anti-trust considerations would not prevent the creation of additional American audio-visual colossi, and probably further Hollywood takeovers. But multi-media integration was clearly also well advanced in Europe as well as Japan. Time and Warner executives in Congressional hearings in 1989 quoted the need for the American media industry to stand tall in confronting the European giants. So also the creation of Time–Warner provided a fresh argument for Europeans seeking to emulate such integrated giants as Berlusconi's Fininvest.

The 1980s several times showed that major media industry developments on one side of the Atlantic can have unanticipated consequences on the other side. In 1989 it was still probably true that most Americans and Europeans had a weak understanding of each others' media industry. Some 1980s European incursions into the US market were perhaps based more on strong lines of credit than on full understanding of why a particular media property was available for sale. American incursions into Europe – despite the substantial sales volumes – were still often a little hesitant and half-hearted.

## TRADE ASSOCIATIONS AND EUROPEAN–AMERICAN ACCOMMODATIONS

Behind the broadcasting policies advocated by European governments in Brussels and Strasbourg there often lay the established arguments of national and Europe-wide trade associations. In addition to the newspapers, advertising and other established Euro-lobbies, a new Association of Commercial Television (ACT) came into existence in 1989; members included Britain's ITVA, TF-1 of France, and Sat-1 of Germany, while the Italian Silvio Berlusconi of Fininvest was ACT's first President.

These European trade associations often negotiated against the positions of their established American equivalents. But not always. Even some public broadcasting organizations – members of the European Broadcasting Union – were against import quotas; one obvious reason is that a cultural channel can easily be short of both audience ratings and cash, a condition which substantial Hollywood imports perhaps of ancient series and movie 'classics' may be best able to remedy.

Of the American media trade associations it was the Motion Picture Association of America (MPAA), in the person of Jack Valenti, which played by far the most vigorous part in US–European negotiations over the Brussels Broadcasting Directive. Mr Valenti made a number of typically flamboyant appearances both in Washington and in Europe in a last-minute attempt in 1989 to remove the import quota provisions from the Directive. The MPAA's interventions were at least partly responsible for the final decision that the quotas, while included, should be voluntary.

But this 1989 compromise was merely the latest of a long series of accommodations beyond Hollywood and Europe. For over half a century the MPAA's export department (MPEA) had been negotiating with European governments, and in the 1930s many of these negotiations had concerned movie import quotas. A broad accommodation continued between Hollywood and Europe, not least because the European cinema circuits and later TV networks needed the attractive entertainment products for their audiences.

Another more recent example of MPEA–Europe accommodation involved video piracy. In the early 1980s pirate copies of American films were widely available in European countries – thus losing Hollywood large amounts of revenue. The MPEA throughout the 1980s conducted a vigorous lobbying campaign across Europe. From the mid-1980s onwards these efforts increasingly proved successful at limiting and then largely eliminating video piracy in western Europe. In these efforts the MPEA found itself working alongside, and sharing commercial interests with, relevant national trade associations. Video piracy threatened

national film industries in Europe as well as imports from Hollywood. By the late 1980s the MPEA's main international anti-piracy
effort had moved on to focus on such nations as Brazil, Saudi
Arabia, Korea and Nigeria. Here also the MPEA's efforts would
benefit both the American and European film industries.

Another campaign of the MPAA was focused on the New
York networks but again had major implications for Europe.
The MPAA was lobbying for the renewal of the Financial Interest
and Syndication or 'Finsyn' regulations which severely limited the
US national networks' rights to own outright the programming they
transmitted; after two network showings the additional rights to
syndicate the TV shows to other markets at home and abroad
reverted to the Hollywood production houses. The networks
argued that their now much reduced market dominance meant
that they should be allowed to own programming outright. In this
'Finsyn' struggle of the TV networks against Hollywood, the right
to sell into the European market was a key item in contention.

But whatever the outcome of the dispute, new forms of trade,
accommodation, partnership, joint-venture and co-production –
between the US and European audio-visual industries – were likely
to result. The trend towards transatlantic integration was likely to
continue and strengthen.

##  THE END OF PUBLIC SERVICE BROADCASTING?

Both 'public service'[15] and 'commercial' broadcasting appear in
many versions and are capable of many definitions. In trying to
chart a continuum from an extreme public service to an extreme
commercial system there are several dimensions. But historically
there seems to be a fairly clear progression in western Europe.

First there is traditional public service broadcasting as illustrated
by BBC Radio and Television up to 1955. A monopoly service;
licence fee finance; educational and other demanding programming
as well as entertainment in peak audience times; limited channels
and programming choice; universal service carried to all corners of
the nation.

Secondly, there is revised model public service broadcasting
– as illustrated by British and German radio and television in
the 1960s and 1970s. Limited competition; licence fee finance
plus some advertising leading to generous funding overall; a
substantial minority of serious programming in peak hours, but

also major amounts of entertainment; continuing universal service. This model was broadly followed throughout western Europe, and it was supported by increasing revenue deriving from growing numbers of colour TV licences and also expanding advertising revenue, with the advertising element being carefully regulated.

Thirdly, after 1980 examples have appeared of commercially led systems, notably in Italy and then France. Here we see competition for audiences between a substantial number of channels; direct inter-channel competition for advertising; aggressively competitive programme scheduling; a sharp decline in serious programming in peak hours; aggressive competition for popular talent, leading to star salary inflation; wholesale resort to imported programming; extension of the broadcast day to include most of the twenty-four hours; aggressive scheduling of repeat programming (including daily 'stripping' of series originally shown weekly).

Many of these latter practices are copied from the United States. But in some respects the *commercially led* system in Europe perhaps more resembles Japan, where a strong public service operator (NHK) competes with four major commercial networks. In both Italy and France by the late 1980s one important phenomenon was the fight-back of the public service networks. This has been especially evident in Italy where the public service RAI retained certain advantages in its three-against-three competition with Berlusconi. The three Berlusconi channels – because not live networks – could not carry live sport, networked news or networked audience participation shows. The RAI channels used their advantages in these areas to compete with Berlusconi's imported series and films and Italian-made entertainment. However in this fight-back RAI-1 and RAI-2 themselves adopted a number of the aggressive commercial practices listed above. If RAI-1's schedules are dominated by a sequence of high audience appeal programming, how much longer can it claim to be a public service broadcaster?

We predict, however, that the European tradition – or rather traditions – of public service broadcasting will not disappear. Deregulation in other fields has been followed by an element of reregulation and the same can be anticipated in broadcasting. The outcome partly depends upon how effective the public service parts of the Euro-broadcasting policy prove to be; and on what happens in the northern European countries which have always taken public service most seriously.

The trend towards a more integrated international audio-visual industry is not necessarily incompatible with public service broadcasting. Some types of public service output (such as news and classical music) are especially suitable for international integration. Another unknown is the role of advertising in the future production of programming; but advertising will not automatically favour low quality programming.

'Europe' itself in its various forms will greatly influence what happens in the specific arena of broadcasting. Even though the 'television without frontiers' policies of the 1980s had few of the intended policy outcomes, this does not mean that 1990s policy will be similarly ineffective. Broadcasting policy in the 1980s moved up both national and European policy agendas; in the 1990s the East–West dimension within Europe is likely to be more salient. European broadcasting policy will need to be more sophisticated and more flexible than in the 1980s.

In various European nation-states, there has been, or will continue to be, a move away from state control to regulation by bodies that keep the state at arm's length. Regulatory bodies, long bedevilled by issues relating to political control and access, take growing cognizance of professional, cultural, economic and technical aspects of broadcasting and also, in some instances, of telecommunications. They oversee channels and stations in which the public service goals and commercial logics may seek some form of accommodation at the level of programme schedules; but these goals and logics seem otherwise at loggerheads when public service channels vie for advertising and sponsorship revenue with commercial channels. It has been argued that in the debate over 'regulation', 'deregulation', and 'reregulation', the situation in the 1990s is one in which regulatory bodies are primarily concerned with 'regularization': corrective rather than prescriptive, 'regularization' would be 'regulation with a lighter touch'. The 'European broadcasting policy' debate reinforces this trend. After much haggling and compromise, with a host of interested parties, the Council of Europe's 'European Convention on Transfrontier Television' (Strasbourg, March 1989), and the European Community's Broadcasting Directive (Brussels, October 1989), indicate how European, as well as national, forces help fashion audio-visual policy and broadcasting regulation.

# Chapter 3

# News agencies and the data business

## REUTERS, MAMMON AND THE SINGLE GLOBAL MARKET

'The single market is a global market': this was one of the comments made by analysts reviewing the circumstances of the US Stock Exchange crash in the week of 19 October 1987. In January 1988, the Brady commission report on the crash noted how many experts had failed fully to appreciate that the US and foreign markets had become a single 24-hour market, served by 300,000 computer terminals. Thus to serve markets across the world and around the clock had long been a central preoccupation of the leading international news agencies.

At the time of the 1987 crash, some 43,000 subscribers paid substantial monthly fees to rent 131,000 Reuters computer screens; these screens would display data from a wide range of financial markets, delivered over what Reuters states is the world's largest private communications network. Its Monitor service (since 1973) has provided subscribers with the most comprehensive real-time database commercially available; the Monitor Dealing service (launched in 1981) enables subscribers to contact each other in seconds and carry out transactions on their Monitor terminals. Monitor has, for a generation now, epitomized Reuters' technological and financial success.

Throughout the 1980s, until the crash of October 1987, Reuters' revenues and profits grew phenomenally, and its sales surpassed those of its main competitors. In 1979, its sales were a third of those of the American financial group, Dow Jones; by 1987, its sales exceeded those of its main competitor by several hundred million dollars. In what at first glance appears a short space of time, Reuters became the indispensable tool of the foreign exchange or currency market: in the first half of 1987, Monitor services for this market accounted for 56 per cent of Reuters' sales. According to *Business Week*, in December: 'traders at more than 1,500 banks now turn to Reuters keyboards and computer screens to handle 600,000 currency and bullion deals per week – which equals about a quarter of all such transactions world wide'.[1]

Reuters has become synonymous with the world's foreign currency market – a market whose growth was stimulated by President Nixon's decision in 1971 to float the US dollar. In 1990, about a third of the world's foreign exchange trade – total value, reportedly about $640 billion *per day* – was tapped out on 11,000 currency monitors, with the company earning revenue in more than 50 different currencies. More generally, Reuters has become the biggest distributor of computer-based information services, with offices in 81 countries and fixed revenue earnings from some 200,000 terminals in 35 countries. For the world's leading electronic publisher, products, technology, markets and systems are interdependent: Reuters deals in real-time information services, transaction products, trading-room systems, historical information and last (as a revenue earner) but not least, media products.[2]

## FROM NEWS TO DATA

Many factors lie behind the success of Reuters, and its transformation over the past quarter century. Some stem from company decisions; others from the growing interdependence of the world economy, and from the integration of commodity, currency, equity and financial markets, around the clock and around the world. Other factors include major investment in Research and Development (R. & D.), allied to commercial acumen; perception of product possibilities due to technological innovation and convergence, and the ability to steal a march on the competition by profiting from (or anticipating) the implications of technology for stock exchanges and other agents of data flows and capital transfers. Reuters successfully made a virtue (and money) of necessity. Its success was encapsulated in the words of André F.H. Villeneuve, president of Reuters North America Inc.: 'We give the client the information, the means to process it, and the means to trade based on it, all on one screen. . . . We're doing something nobody else even comes close to.'

This was a far cry from the situation forty, or indeed only twenty, years earlier. In the early sixties, the prospects for the agency were, if not bleak, at best mediocre. The situation for Reuters was similar, in some respects, to that of Agence France-Presse. For over a century, Paris and London had been the headquarters of Europe's two leading international news agencies – Havas (founded in 1835) and Reuters, founded by Paul Julius Reuter in London in 1851. After the 1939–45 war, American news agencies expanded their international networks and custom, along with the expansion of US influence in liberated Europe, and elsewhere: the international organization of Reuters, and of the main French news agency, suffered from the decline of Britain and France respectively as super or world powers; this was partly – but not solely – the result of their loss of influence when previous colonial possessions acquired their independence.

Reuters, at least, did not suffer the dismemberment experienced by Havas. The British agency was unusual among its peers in not attending to the collection, processing and distribution of British domestic (metropolitan and provincial) news; this task was (and is) discharged by the Press Association (PA), which was founded in 1868. The French agency, by contrast, suffered doubly from war's fortunes; in 1940, the two parts of the Havas organization, advertising and news, were separated. Between July and November 1940, Pierre Laval, vice-premier of Vichy France, bought out the news-agency division and transformed it into the official state news agency, OFI. Havas continued as an advertising agency, under predominantly German influence during 1940–4. Between 1940 and 1944, OFI served the news and propaganda interests of Vichy France.[3]

Reuters had two advantages denied Havas; in its home country Reuters did not supply domestic British news, but it had a commitment from the British provincial and national newspapers. In 1925, the Press Association bought a controlling interest in Reuters (53 per cent); in 1941, the PA and the Newspaper Proprietors' Association (NPA) became joint owners: provincial and national newspaper publishers controlled the major British agency providing them with international news; and, via the Reuters Trust, set up in 1941, the independence of the agency services was enshrined by a declaration stating that the British Press considered the 'new ownership . . . in the nature of a trust rather than as an investment'.[4] Not to be the domestic news agency freed Reuters of one of the causes of possible government interference; in France, during the 1930s, the government influenced the Havas agency's presentation of foreign news for domestic clients and of French news for international clients. Involvement of the Press in the ownership and management of Reuters was a guarantee of pluralism, and of respect for the professional canons of news-reporting.

In continental Europe, and elsewhere, governments have often considered the general news services of agencies as a form of cultural diplomacy. Democratic as well as totalitarian governments have sought (and seek) to influence the news flow so as to reflect the official version of events. There were periods in the history of Reuters and of Havas, when patriotic considerations tainted the news flow. As far back as 1887–9, Bismarck sought to break up existing co-operation between Havas, Reuters and the German agency, the Continental (Wolff's bureau) because of resentment at the 'imbalance' in their exchange of news services; the German agency almost succeeded in persuading Reuters to break with Havas, then considered Europe's leading agency.[5] Reuters, under Sir Roderick Jones (managing director, 1916–41), became identified with the geo-political interests of the colonial power in which it was headquartered. Reuters provided 'supplementary services', reflecting government views (and funded by the government) during World War I, and Jones held a post in the Department (later Ministry) of Information in 1917–18 (with the title Director of Propaganda). In 1941, he left the agency after Reuters' board (of newspaper publishers) discovered the agency had received £64,000 'for propaganda purposes' from the British government since August 1938. More generally, Reuters under Jones became even more identified than before with the Empire; the flow of news and the development of services and custom, reflected British imperial values with the agency serving Britain's geo-political interests; in 1941, Reuters' revenue from India alone was greater than everything it received from British newspapers.[6]

For the French international agency founded in the 1830s, a privileged working relationship with government sources was a journalistic and commercial prerequisite. The agency developed by Charles-Louis Havas in 1835 (from a modest translation bureau, opened in 1832–3) remained under private control until the 'nationalization' of the news agency division in 1940. But, from the outset, Havas established its superiority over the competition by providing services of international and domestic news that were appreciated by a government which accorded it privileges denied the competition. Balzac noted in 1840 (and the historian Gilles Feyel has confirmed) that Havas was entrusted with the management of a government news service for its agents in the provinces, the prefects.[7] In 1845, the electric telegraph was barely four years old in France; Havas was allowed to transmit along the nascent network at a time when only the government and the military could do so. Regardless of the regime in power – France between 1830 and 1870 experienced two revolutions and a *coup d'état*, a monarchy, a republic, a plebiscitary 'empire', and, once again, a republic – Havas, 'the news merchant' (*le marchand des faits*) remained the unloved but indispensable 'semi-official' news agency.

In France and Britain, the national metropolitan-based daily newspapers often resented their dependence on news agencies for the supply of international news. Moreover the supply of political news, because it relied on inter-agency co-operation, tended to give primarily news from official and governmental sources. Most of the agencies supplying news to the agency cartel or alliance which underpinned the international news flow between 1859 and 1940 were official (either in name or deed). But even the London *Times*, respected for its fearless criticism of government, its domination of the daily press, and for the scale and scope of its 'foreign intelligence' needed the news agency services. *The Times*' manager, Moberly Bell (1890–1911), considered agencies objectionable because 'they tended to equalise journalism': to make available to many the hard news-reports that previously *The Times* alone in the British Press had been able to provide.[8] In 1858, at Reuters' third time of asking, *The Times* subscribed to the agency. By 1870, it found the agency service indispensable; agency correspondents operated out of a greater number of news centres, and made greater use of the telegraph, than could the foreign correspondents of *The Times*. But if agencies were first with the news, that news remained suspect to newspapermen. In 1870, during the Franco-Prussian war, *The Times*' correspondent stationed with the French government delegation in Tours told the then Manager of *The Times*, Mowbray Morris:

As regards getting intelligence sometimes earlier than Havas (which supplies Reuter) it is simply *impossible*. . . . The different Continental telegraph agencies are all more or less at the orders of the respective governments, and, in return for making themselves agreeable to the ministers of the day, they get the very earliest information. . . . Havas . . . is entirely at the orders of the government of the day and suppresses or colours what is disagreeable to them. In return they give him facilities which are unfair to other journalists.[9]

During the first century of their existence, therefore, both Havas and Reuters had a number of skeletons in the cupboard. Journalists, agencymen and other pressmen would periodically expose them, or at least point to the contradictions implicit in serving several masters. Havas from the 1830s and Reuters after 1858 numbered government ministries and foreign ambassadors, bankers, businessmen and stockbrokers, as well as the Press among their customers or subscribers. Rapid and accurate coverage of news emanating from as many capitals and centres and from as many diverse sources as was possible – this was an aim shared by journalists, but not always politically possible for the management. The three leading agencies in the cartel had the same commercial strategy; Charles-Louis Havas, Paul Julius Reuter and Bernhard Wolff all believed that, to reinforce their position as the dominant agency serving their domestic market with foreign and imperial/colonial news, it was best to co-operate abroad and so share the costs of international news-operations. The costs of the advanced communications technology at the time – the electric telegraph – proved too expensive for an agency seeking alone to provide comprehensive world coverage. Europe was, at the time, the home of the world's leading powers and agency news services were relatively Euro-centric. The commercial and technical arguments were therefore important in the establishment and maintenance of the agency cartel; the cartel consisted of an increasingly ill-assorted set of political and journalistic bed-fellows, as the number of national official and semi-official or even newspaper-owned agencies proliferated and were admitted to the cartel. The US newspaper co-operative, Associated Press (AP), joined the cartel in 1875.

Reuters enjoyed further advantages denied to Havas. London was Europe's telecommunications headquarters; and the City of

London was the world's most important stock market and financial powerhouse. The cable company networks which straddled the world (Atlantic and Eastern) operated out of London. Paul Julius Reuter's motto was 'follow the cable'. Where the cable went (to the Middle East, India and Australia, for example) so his agents went. Havas noted in 1909: 'Thanks to the English telegraphic cable installations connecting every world centre, London easily dominates all the news agencies.'[10] The situation would change somewhat with the development of short-wave radio, into which, indeed, existing cable companies diversified.

For the first three decades of the century, radio challenged cable in terms of world communications: the development of the short-wave beam system proved a cheaper means of transoceanic communication. By 1927, almost half of the traffic of the cable companies had gone over to the beam. In 1929, Cables[11] and Wireless Ltd was formed; the cable companies had a larger share in a company born of their merger with the Marconi company, which had pioneered the beam system, than did Marconi. Reuters, likewise, ensured that direct competition from the Marconi company did not materialize. In 1919, Marconi announced it would confine itself to carrying messages: 'Wireless would assist the news agencies, not compete with them.'[12] Radio companies had dropped their initial plans – like those developed by electric telegraph cable companies in the 1840s to 1860s – to themselves collect and distribute news. In 1868, the formation of the Press Association arose partly out of dissatisfaction among British provincial newspaper proprietors with the news services purveyed by the electric telegraph companies. In the 1920s, Reuters faced little serious competition from the radio companies; and the BBC, born of the radio manufacturing companies (1926), relied on the news agencies for its main news broadcasts (and made attribution to them: Reuters, PA, Exchange Telegraph, Central News). Furthermore Reuters reached agreement with the British Post Office; it leased the right to transmit news services by radio. By 1941, its broadcast radio systems, via short-wave transmitters, carried over 90 per cent of the news output of Reuters sent overseas.

London as a communications hub contributed to Reuters' success in the 1850s as it did in the 1920s. Paul Reuter himself literally followed the cable; he set up a 'telegraphic office' in London on 14 October 1851, a fortnight before the successful

laying of the Submarine Telegraph Company's cable between
Dover and Calais. (The German engineer Werner Siemens later
stated he advised Reuter in 1850 'to go to London and to start
there a cable agency'.[13]) But equally important in Reuters' success
was the prominence of the City of London, and its need for rapid
and reliable information on share and commodity price movements
and other financial intelligence throughout the world. Thanks to
the Submarine Telegraph cable, the price of securities in Paris
were known to the London Stock Exchange on the same day and
within business hours.[14] London Stock Exchange members – not
the Press – were Reuter's key early clients. He provided brokers
and merchants in London and Paris with twice-daily reports of
the opening and closing prices of the Stock Exchanges of both
capitals.[15] Likewise, Reuter's first (1856) agreements with the
French and German agencies, Havas and Wolff, concerned the
exchange of stock market prices. Thus stock market prices – and
not general news – were the foundation stone of the 'news agency'
cartel.

Nonetheless, luck played a part in Reuter's success in 1850s
London as it had in the success of Havas in 1830s Paris. Both
men began modestly, and both were recovering from failures.
Charles-Louis Havas (1783–1858) had been declared a bankrupt
after the Napoleonic wars; he was already aged 50 when he opened
his newspaper translation bureau in Paris in the early 1830s; his
only surviving private letter portrays a man embarking on a foreign
trip (January 1832) which, as he puts it, would make or break
him.[16] Reuter, in London in 1851, was likewise smarting from
failure; his news-transmission network in the Low Countries and
German states (Aachen, Antwerp, Brussels, Cologne) combined
carrier-pigeons and horses, but was defeated by the construction
in 1850 of the telegraph line from Aachen to Verviers.

Havas and Reuter, however, both established networks of agents
or correspondents, in various news-centres throughout Europe.
These might rely initially mainly on gutting the local press
and sending translated summaries of news-extracts to Paris and
London. But agents were also to use the telegraph to transmit
financial and commercial intelligence, while merchant, banking
and business circles were important sources. However, Reuter,
like Havas, also cultivated relations with 'gentlemen connected
with most of the European governments'.[17]

This underlines a point that Reuters' executives would stress time and again in the 1970s and 1980s. They argued against making false distinctions between on the one hand the general news service, which includes specifically political news-reports, and on the other hand specialist economic, financial, and commercial news or data services. The latter may consist chiefly of market reports and stock exchange quotations, of alphanumeric data, listing share, currency and commodity price movements. These are affected by events, statements and other developments related in the general news service. There was nothing unusual in this. From the days of the late medieval and Renaissance bankers, such as the Fuggers of Augsburg or the Medici of Florence, the *correspondances* and news-letters of bankers' agents related general news that had economic and commercial consequences – the closure of the port of Marseilles in 1347, for instance, following the arrival from the Crimea of a boat with the plague virus. . . . So it was with news agency reports. The house-historian of Reuters, Graham Storey, states that Reuters' telegrams of August 1852 contain short commercial messages, including several from eastern Europe; occasional reports of general news are angled towards their 'bearing on the market': 'a potato disease is reported from Eastern Germany; the concern is only for the effect on prices.'[18] Threats of war – or intimations of peace – have long been the greatest of 'market-movers'. On 7 February 1859, Reuter bought an hour's exclusive use of the Submarine Telegraph cable linking Paris to London; it scooped the British Press with the transcript of a speech by Napoleon III indicating France's potentially hostile intentions towards Austria; in London, as in Paris, the Stock Exchange reacted feverishly. *The Times* published Reuter's scoop.

Periodically in Reuters' history, agency executives, confronted by agency financial difficulties, have 'rediscovered' the causes of Paul Julius's initial success. This success stemmed from the reporting of commercial intelligence, transmitted and processed by the advanced communication technologies of the time. The lesson was relearnt by C. Fleetwood May in the 1920s, as it was by Gerald Long in the 1960s. On both occasions it led to a reorganization and repackaging of news services that once again testified to the specious nature of the distinctions then in operation. After the 1914–18 war, Fleetwood May created Reuters Trade (subsequently rebaptized Commercial) service; he argued that the existing commercial service, confined as it was to market reports and Stock Exchange quotations, failed to tap the market interest in the information of commercial interest contained in the wide range of the general news services. 'Wasted' in the former, it was repackaged and developed in a Trade service aimed at trade publications, businessmen, brokers and bankers worldwide. Thus, in the 1920s a staff of ninety was built up in London to handle messages from overseas special correspondents; wheat prices from Winnipeg reached London within fourteen seconds and were almost instantaneously retransmitted to world commercial centres from Bremen to Shanghai. In the 1920s – as in the 1850s and 1970s – services of commercial intelligence prompted the agency to invest in advanced telecommunications technologies. The development of the Commercial service in the 1920s spurred Fleetwood May to have Reuters lease radio reception and transmission facilities: long-wave, and later short-wave, transmitters were first used to beam Reuters broadcast circular Commercial service (the 'Reuterian').

Advanced telecommunications technology is used for transmission and processing of services appealing to specialist markets; but the content of such services includes general news pertinent to these same markets. In the 1960s and 1970s, these lessons were learnt anew. Gerald Long, appointed General Manager in 1963, subsequently recalled how he meditated in his seventh-floor office on the causes of Paul Julius' success. Reuters Economic Services (RES) again became central to the agency's development and they were baptized as such in 1966. Allied to this was a massive increase in communications capacity and reinforcements in news-processing technologies. The use of the telephonic cable and multiplex lines and, subsequently, of satellite transmission, increased the volume and speed of the flow of data. Beginning in 1963–4, Reuters' entry into computerized services increased the agency's advanced capability in information storage, retrieval and news-processing skills. Electronics and computers – market quotation interrogation and display, storage and retrieval systems – were harnessed to replace the outmoded methods of commercial price reporting, geared, within each Stock Exchange, to the ticker tape and the teleprinter.

Words written in 1987 by the Chief Executive of the Agence France-Presse (AFP) news agency between 1979 and 1986 highlight the turning-point represented by Long's decisions in the mid-sixties. Henri Pigeat, an *énarque* (élite civil servant) and the first non-journalist to be appointed head of AFP (a handicap he never fully overcame), argues that Long's achievements at Reuters served as a model for his own attempts to modernize and diversify AFP.[19] Stark decisions had to be taken in the early sixties in London, as in Paris in the early eighties. The survival of the international news agency tradition of Britain and France depended on the outcome. Pigeat in 1987, and Long earlier, stressed how the survival prospects for the two Europe-based international agencies were declining.

Reuters during the 1960s and 1970s solved its survival problem by becoming a multi-national information and business technology company. The location of its headquarters in London makes commercial and telecommunications sense, but in no way reflects an identification with British interests. AFP, despite notable achievements, failed in the 1980s to resolve problems comparable, in part, to those facing Reuters two decades earlier. Both Long and Pigeat argued that the domestic press could not provide the financial resources needed to ensure the survival of an international agency. Neither France nor Britain constituted a domestic market (media and non-media) comparable to the US domestic market which ensured the bulk of Associated Press revenues. AP's international organization was largely shaped by the news concerns of its US media clientele; the requirements of the AP–Dow Jones economic news services were also important in AP's international operations. Reuters, followed by AP–Dow Jones and other specialist economic news services, moved vigorously into the much heralded new global market for information and data.

## REUTERS' QUARTER CENTURY, 1963–88

How did Reuters succeed, and AFP not succeed? Gerald Long was belligerently opposed to Reuters receiving any government subsidy, even of an indirect kind. The potential revenue which could be earned by general news services was already low and had poor prospects of expansion; prices obtainable for general news were undercut by cheap, or even free, services subsidized by governments. 'The world is full of news services being sold at subsidized rates. There are many reasons for wanting to distribute news which have nothing to do with getting an economic return' argued Long.[20] The Soviet agency TASS distributed some services and receiving/transmission equipment free. The American agencies, AP and United Press International (UPI), were not alone in charging token rates in some (mainly Third World) countries, so as to have market presence. Reuters and AFP had each suffered from their home country's imperial connections and their government's inclination for 'patriotic' considerations to influence news-reporting. The agency's future, argued Long and his close advisers, lay in developing Reuters Economic Services. Reuters began to invest heavily in R. & D. for computerizing its Economic Services for instantaneous distribution via a world telecommunications system now increasingly based on the Intelsat satellite system. Reuters Economic Services – tailored primarily neither for media nor governments – would incidentally finance the general news services.

So it proved. In 1989, the media represented only 7 per cent of Reuters' revenue. The money market provided 55 per cent, securities 19 per cent, commodities 8 per cent and client systems 11 per cent. Twenty-six years earlier, in 1963, two-thirds of the news agency's revenue of £3 million came from media subscribers; the remaining third came from subscribers to Reuters' specialized economic services. The turn-around occurred in the 1970s, and by 1973 economic services already accounted for some 70 per cent of total revenue; non-media clients predominated in terms of numbers as well as of revenue. Massive annual increases in company revenues and profits occurred from 1973 onwards as the 1960s R. & D. investments were handsomely recouped. In 1972, Reuters' profits were £317,191; for 1989, pre-tax profits of Reuters Holdings, 'the international business information group', were £283.1 million. Profits after tax grew from £54.9 million in 1985 to 181.2 million in 1989; overseas revenue represented 82.5 per cent of 1990 revenue of £1,369 million.

Journalists working for the world and media services in the seventies from time to time protested that the specialist economic (RES) tail should not wag the bulldog's head (the world and media services). One response was: better to work for Mammon and international finance than for an impecunious media market or to depend on government subsidy; large R. & D. investment in gaining a competitive advantage via state of the art information and data systems benefited *all* Reuters' services – specialist and general alike. From the pioneering ('primitive') Stockmaster and Ultronic computerized services, aimed at European clients in the mid-sixties, to the Advanced Reuter Terminal (ART) launched in 1986, technologies were developed to serve financial and commercial, equity and bullion markets; this led to a range of increasingly sophisticated Reuter client systems which provide general news (politics, weather, sport, etc.) in addition to specialist services.

The distinction between Reuters World Service and Reuters Economic Services formally ended in 1980 when the reporting networks were merged under a single editor. To demonstrate how artificial was the distinction Gerald Long would quote the classic case: if someone assassinates the American President is that general or market news? We have seen how in the 1850s, as in the 1920s, services were reorganized or developed to take account of the impact of general news on markets in – and specialist data services for – securities, commodities and currencies. In 1980, Reuters argued that the merging of the two networks – to make more effective use of 'the largest international network in the world' – benefited both media and non-media clients; coverage of Iran (where the Shah had fallen the year before and where the war with Iraq began in September) gained in depth and range as specialist economic correspondents were sent to report on what had hitherto been largely a political story.[21]

In short, Reuters' media news services benefited from the revenue and information resources garnered from serving the financial and business community. In 1983, these services, provided to media, governmental and international governmental insti- tutions in 158 countries, represented only 6 per cent of agency revenue. Buttressed by rapidly growing revenue from the financial and business services, the network of Reuters' journalists has also significantly expanded. Moreover Reuters launched (in 1985) a news picture service worldwide – a news sector and market that Reuters had left hitherto to the American and French world agencies. These still photograph services have long been major revenue sources for the US agencies; the new Reuters picture service strongly boosted its 'news' revenues after 1985. In the years 1981–7 the number of Reuters' staff journalists doubled (from 542 to 1,173): in 1990, the company employed 1,154 staff journalists and photographers (out of a total workforce of 10,071) together with 114 editorial employees of Visnews, its television news subsidiary.

In 1985, the agency upped its stake in Visnews, the world's largest international news film agency, and appointed a Reuters executive as managing director. In 1990, it was the majority shareholder

(51 per cent) – the US's National Broadcasting Company (NBC) held 37.75 per cent and the British Broadcasting Corporation (BBC), 11.25 per cent – in a company supplying daily television news material to over 650 networks and individual broadcasting organizations in 80 countries and reportedly reaching 1.5 billion viewers each day. The cost to Reuters of raising its shareholding (from 33 per cent) was £2.6 million. Visnews now shows a profit, helped by the development of television in Europe. Thus, for a relative pittance, Reuters acquired control of an agency that has a film archive, stills library and international satellite facilities. This exemplifies the synergy and diversification strategies underpinning the acquisition policy of Managing Director (1981–91) Glen Renfrew: 'acquisitions help Reuters provide complete information packages'; these give customers the advantages of one-stop shopping and economies of scale.[22]

Some Reuters journalists are troubled by these changes; the collection, processing, storage, retrieval and distribution of data are seen to have ousted news as the agency's *raison d'être*. News priorities were thought to have changed, and stories appealing to single nation markets ('Special Nairobi', 'Attention Lima', etc.) were less likely to be carried; human interest stories would only be covered if they suggested some element of universal or international 'appeal' – such as especially notorious multiple murders.

One key to Reuters' success has been R. & D. expenditure on high-speed electronic communications technology. This aggregated approximately £9.6 million in 1983 and £59.7 million in 1989. Fifteen years earlier, some of the newspaper publishers who sat on the Reuters' board were troubled when Long raised a bank loan of £1 million.[23] Yet this loan more than repaid the interest incurred. It financed the development and installation of equipment for the Reuters Monitor service.

Reuters Monitor was an advance on the existing computerized Stockmaster and Videomaster services. The Videomaster service used computers to assemble and store prices quoted on US and European Stock Exchanges; prices and news were then transmitted over telephone links to screens in the customers' premises. The Monitor service represented a big advance in the sophistication of terminals and software; this was the first computer system conceived and developed by the then small technical department of Reuters. It coincided with what was to prove a goldmine – the advent of the unrestricted international currency market. Reuters' management perceived the commercial gain to be made from linking its R. & D. innovation to the changing nature of the foreign exchange market (forex).

At Bretton Woods in July 1944, international exchange rates were fixed in relation to the US dollar (itself linked to gold). The system of fixed exchange rates operated fully between 1959 and 1971; it ended when President Nixon floated the dollar off the fixed rate and the Smithsonian Agreement of December 1971 left forex rates to world demand and supply. There was no physical trading exchange for money; this was unlike most of the major world commodity data already covered by Reuters.

The Reuters Monitor Dealing system was developed to provide dealers in the international forex market with a faster and more sophisticated service than the cumbersome pursuit of quotations via telex and the telephone. In the breathless but accurate words of recent historians of Reuters: the agency invented 'the electronic market place . . . a delicate composition of microchips and integrated circuits joined together by more than three million kilometres of leased communication circuits'.[24]

Its technical efficiency and commercial superiority over the previously available systems, enabled the Monitor system to transform 'a struggling news agency into a money maker'.[25] Monitor was tailored for the forex market and in 1987 'money' represented 55 per cent of Reuters' revenue. But the Reuters-manufactured terminals could be used to relay price data signals for all types of financial and commercial trade. From 1971 the Monitor system became a centralized information source for what might otherwise have remained fragmented markets dealing in money market instruments, commodities, equities, bonds, shipping, energy, coins and precious metals. Monitor acquired its continuing flows of data from its own terminals located in commodity and financial services houses and banks around the world. Reuters even obtained significant revenue ('client systems') from carrying these price data (11 per cent of total revenue in 1989).

Reuters Monitor system, and its subsequent refinements (Money 2000, etc.), represent the convergence of applied technology, astute management, and changes in the functioning of the world economy. The fluctuations in money rates across the world, like those of commodities, stimulated the volume of trading; the 1973 OPEC oil embargo made trading even more volatile. The depreciation of the dollar after 1985, the stock market crash of October 1987 (and subsequent market trends) represented additional stimuli to what, since the launch of Money Monitor on 4 June 1973, has become the 'largest, most comprehensive data-base that is commercially available'.[26]

The commercial element transformed the traditional *modus operandi* of the agency business. By 1990 Reuters had three main sources or feeds of information and news: first over 1,300 full-time journalists, photographers and cameramen; secondly, 164 securities and commodities exchanges and over-the-counter markets; and thirdly 'contributed data' – information provided by some 3,800 dealers about the markets in which they operated.[27] Dealers pay to input data into the Monitor system; they do this because, as market makers, they want their prices to be among those offered to customers on their office screens. The Reuters Monitor provides, in real-time on-line communication, the most comprehensive batteries of data. Marshall McLuhan's global village has arrived, but the village houses are financial houses, and the villagers are dealers.

The willingness of banks and market makers to pay for access to the system reflects the superiority of the Reuters system over that of its competitors, be they news agencies or, indeed, Stock Exchanges. Reuters sees it as normal that contributors pay; they thereby gain access to the electronic market-place and the requisite publicity in the centralized information source.[28] Banks, dealers and producers of raw materials receive exposure as data contributors; data contributed by one subscriber to a Monitor service is available to all fellow subscribers except those which the contributor directs should be precluded from such access. And contributors also pay, along with non-contributors, as *subscribers* to Monitor services. In 1990 some 2,060 organizations in 80 countries fed in money rates. Market makers pay to see their own data and those of competitors on their Reuters terminal; non-contributors pay so as to follow market movements.

Another major qualitative change occurred in 1981; progress in real-time technology enabled Reuters to add another function to its traditional role as purveyor of information. From 1974, it had run news with quotes flashed on the screens to give subscribers not only numerical data, but also relevant background news stories; this represented a further step in the provision of an integrated specialist and general news service. The Monitor Dealing service, introduced in February 1981, enables dealers not only to display prices and offers to each other but also to buy and sell through their Reuters video terminal, to negotiate and conclude trades within seconds; hard-copy print-outs (confidential to the two parties), from a terminal attachment, confirm the transaction. This represented the final stage in the passage from the provision of 'general and financial' news services to Reuters' confirmation as a leading 'information technology group'; Henri Pigeat of AFP would subsequently call Reuters 'the IBM of financial and economic information'.[29]

The full implications of the electronic market-place became apparent; dealers buy and sell through Reuters screens, via Reuters-designed terminals and software, and via advanced satellite and cable transmission technologies leased from telecommunications authorities. The convergence and evolution of advanced information technologies on the one hand and the deregulation of financial markets and, indeed, of telecommunications on the other, enabled Reuters to gain the competitive edge. By late 1981, subscribers in New York, Moscow and Beijing could contact and trade with their foreign trading partners in just four seconds, a critical eleven seconds faster than by telephone.[30] Automated forex trading via Monitor terminals spearheaded Reuters' expansion in real-time services; in 1987, the two currency market systems (the Money Monitor and Monitor Dealing service) accounted for over half of the group's turnover. But Reuters battled, notably with telecommunications and Stock Exchange authorities, to enable its subscribers to use its Monitor network to interact and trade not just in currencies but in stocks and commodities. Glen Renfrew, the Australian who succeeded Long as managing director in 1981, put it thus:

> It's become increasingly difficult to divorce the concept of information from the concept of telecommunications. . . . The faster and further you move information, the more valuable it becomes.[31]

> Services providing information and dealing facilities to the money and foreign exchange markets in the main European, Asian and North American financial markets . . . generate most of Reuters growth. Revenue from equities grew sharply as liberalization encouraged market activity.[32]

In December 1981 (the year the Monitor Dealing service was

launched) the average daily contacts were 20,000; in 1986, the network experienced peaks of 89,300 contacts per day. As noted earlier, by late 1987 traders at over 1,500 banks handled 600,000 currency and bullion deals per week via the Monitor network – almost a quarter of all such transactions worldwide.[33] During the exceptionally heavy volume of trading in the week of 19 October 1987, the International Stock Exchange of London alone recorded over 100,000 trades on the Wednesday and Thursday (compared to 40,000 per day the preceeding week); in Singapore, the leading futures market in the East Asian time zone, trades on Tuesday 20 October soared to 49,900.[34]

Reuters profited from the blurring of the distinction between information and telecommunications, and between information and dealing systems. 'When' – asked the *Financial Times*, rhetorically, in October 1985 – 'does an electronic information network become a stock market?'[35] The question troubled the City of London Stock Exchange. Throughout the world, indeed, as the deregulation of Bourses proceeds, Exchange regulators fear that round-the-clock electronic trading (dear to such as Reuters) will weaken or end the time-honoured face-to-face, over-the-counter, open outcry system. By 1985, Reuters' ambitions for the Monitor dealing system exacerbated this fear; it had effectively created the international foreign exchange market in the 1970s and a forex transaction network in 1981. In May 1985, Reuters revealed its plans to launch in the UK an international share, or equity, dealing network; it was to market outside the US the automated share-dealing network of Instinet (a US company which, two years later, it acquired outright).[36] Technology developed for forex could be applied to other markets. Instinet, initially limited to information on US equities and American Depository Receipts, could be expanded to include other international equities, if overseas Stock Exchanges were willing. The London Stock Exchange saw this as a threat to Topic, its existing information network (3,000 terminals around the City), and to its planned Stock Exchange Automated Quotation System (SEAQ). SEAQ was to be an essential element in the 'Big Bang' of October 1986, the electronic off-the-floor trading system that would replace jobbers and allow market makers to disclose prices and volumes to each other; these would include Stock Exchange member firms, and possibly others. The Council of the Stock Exchange, in devising SEAQ, were favourably impressed by the US Automated Quotation System (NASDAQ): members of

NASDAQ, acting either as market makers or agents rely *inter alia* on the Reuters Money Line service in deciding on the price at which they are prepared to buy or sell a given company's stock.

In the age of electronic and global markets, Reuters and Instinet appeared to hold the trump card. George Hayter, director of Stock Exchange information services, declared: 'It will be a Stock Exchange system even if we buy in the software. We are more than a match for the Reuters of this world.'[37] Reuters and Instinet sounded more accommodating – 'we want to work closely with stock exchanges in every country'.[38]

But the competition from its US-based rivals – Quotron, in the field of share prices, and Telerate, in international money markets – reinforced Reuters' determination to use its network for internationally traded stocks, including British ones.[39] In September 1985, Reuters launched a series of composite pages listing quotations for international equities from various competing market makers; this was part of the screen-based price data and dealing system to serve global investors in equities. The Stock Exchange refused member firms permission to contribute to these composite pages, arguing that they should not mix with non-member firms. Such an attitude appeared unrealistic in view of the international market in financial services. London firms would be disadvantaged, and business would continue to move to the New York Stock Exchange – to which Quotron and Reuters–Instinet gave London investors easy access, and which advanced its opening time to 9.30 a.m. (2.30 p.m. in London) to encourage international business.

In short, Reuters, in the forefront of technological development, ran up against the regulatory authorities of the London Stock Exchange (LSE); in anticipation of 'Big Bang' the LSE sought to ensure that Reuters and other international data transmission networks did not take business away from the Stock Exchanges by venturing into their central activity – the trading of securities. The difficulty was compounded by some markets, Eurobonds for instance, being much more lightly regulated than others. Anyone with the right telecommunications equipment could join and on the Reuters screens used for Eurobonds, each market-maker listed all the bonds it traded, with 'indicative' prices; trades were completed by telephone and telex. On SEAQ, by contrast, shares were accompanied by the names of all firms making a market in them, and their prices; these prices were firm, except for large trades. Stock Exchanges argued that the development of screen technology required new, not less, regulation.

'Big Bang' would usher in the era of true 24-hour trading. As the 27 October 1986 deadline grew ever closer – and as the LSE's development of SEAQ, SEAQ International and Topic advanced – compromises with Reuters were reached. In February 1986, they announced agreement on combining their competing electronic systems for displaying the share prices of leading international companies. But it was only a month before the Big Bang of 27 October 1986 that agreement was reached concerning Reuters' introduction into London of Instinet; Instinet UK became a member of the LSE. The LSE had feared dealers in equities, who would otherwise use its own SEAQ, would be diverted to the Reuters' dealing facility.

The performance, during the first weeks after the Big Bang, of the Stock Exchange's computerized and screen-based price quotation system, did not impress; in October, SEAQ was out of action for 2.5 per cent of the time. Topic, which disseminates the price information on SEAQ and displays it on viewdata screens throughout the City, was out of action for 2.7 per cent of the time. A year later, during the crash of October 1987, Topic experienced further failures: 'teething problems' argued the chairman of the Stock Exchange, Nicholas Goodison;[40] the Stock Exchange was designing a market-place of computer integrated trading, where everything from the initial order to final settlement would be managed and controlled automatically; London was to be the centre of a web of information networks taking in stock market information (from not just London) and distributing it widely.[41] This inevitably made for a prickly relationship with international independent information services like Reuters.

Reuters' goal remains the extension of the dealing system, developed for the Money Monitor, to everything from government securities to futures. It has broadened its range of news, information and databases, and acquired hardware and software systems ($265 million worth between 1985 and 1987) that were integrated with the company's client systems developed by its own R. & D. division. In mid-1987, through the ubiquitous Monitor service, it was the dominant provider of forex rates, providing real-time information on over a hundred of the world's currencies. In March 1987, the LSE agreed to provide Reuters with the British domestic share price quotations it gathers from market-makers via the

Topic screen network. In May Reuters launched Equities 2000 – followed, weeks later, by Commodities 2000. It stated that it would provide quotations for every instrument traded on every significant stock, commodity, option and futures exchange in the world. The dealing function was not emphasized. Rather, Equities 2000 ('after five years dedicated research and development') was promoted as supplying information for traders in the international equities markets; these had boomed with the deregulation of key stock markets. Reuters stressed the universality, pertinence, speed and manageability of its newest data services. Reuters had long stayed out of the US equities market, where Telerate and AP–Dow Jones were market-leaders. But with Equities 2000 it marketed data not only on North American issues but also on 40,000 foreign stocks, bonds and other securities. Carrying quotes from more than 110 exchanges (1987), Equities and Commodities 2000 were the first services to be delivered over the Integrated Data Network (IDN): intended, eventually, to carry all Reuter data, IDN is the Reuters delivery network using the latest technology to handle information and it is gradually replacing Monitor.

In the quarter-century since the development of the first computerized news and data services, Reuters developed a range of increasingly sophisticated information systems; selection, packaging and processing of data are as important to the end-user as the range of real-time and historical databases, and the high-speed communications network. Reuters is in the 'added-value' business; extra value is added to the basic information by giving the customer the capability further to 'manipulate' the data to suit his needs. In forex technology, for instance, Reuters moved from the simple electronic distribution of prices via video or screen technology to the provision of refinements which add further value to the basic services; the Monitor Abacus provides instant cross-rates and broken data and arbitrageur calculations based on real-time process. Internal rate calculations enable customers to keep ahead of the market by inserting their own specialist rates. 'Added value' gives the user the possibility of securing competitive advantage rather than simply cutting costs. The ART was developed to this end; launched in mid-1986, the Advanced Reuter Terminal bridges the gap between video-based information systems and the digital systems. ART is now Reuters' standard keystation.

In the 1970s the video technology of Reuters Monitor was limited in the ways information could be modified on screen. The ART –

and digital technology – resolved many of these difficulties, and problems experienced by dealers who may havc to watch several video screens simultaneously; the colour terminal displays prices, graphs and news simultaneously on a single screen. The screen can be divided into 'windows' of varying sizes; price information can be converted into graphs, and a facility alerts dealers when a predetermined price level has been reached. The ART allows dealers to put together their own personal pages of real-time information drawn from the different pages of the Monitor system. It was integrated with other Reuters systems and services – the Monitor dealing service and the Composite Information key station, combining video and digital data. R. & D. and the acquisition of pertinent business technology companies aim at flexibility and integration within the range of client systems developed either by Reuters or by companies in which it buys a controlling interest.

For instance, the ART is in effect a personal computer for the dealer, linked to an interface of Reuter/Rich systems. In 1985, Reuters acquired Rich Inc. of Chicago, a world leader in designing video and digital trading room systems; in 1986, it acquired Wyatts, the British-based supplier of voice communication products, so that Reuters could integrate dealer boards and other voice services with the video and digital systems available to the dealer. In 1988, Rich reached agreement with Sun Microsystems of California and gained access to its powerful desk-top computing technology. Reuters, through its R. & D. and client systems, sought to keep the market edge in a range of equipment extending to dealer workstations of 'unprecedented sophistication, power and flexibility'. Triarch 2000, for example, is an advanced digital information delivery network, enabling clients to combine a wide selection of market information with data from their own computer systems, thus aiding decision-making. Under Glen Renfrew, Reuters' $55 million purchase of Rich Inc., and the $111 million takeover of Instinet Corp., exemplify a strategy of owning the systems, as well as the services, serving the agency's subscribers worldwide.

Two events in 1987 indicated the potential and pitfalls of Reuters' osmosis with Mammon. Glen Renfrew pursued the goal of round-the-clock and round-the-world trading in everything from forex to equities, from government securities to futures. The dealing capacity, via automated trading systems, disturbs Stock Exchanges worldwide. Problems that appeared in 1985, when the LSE cavilled at the Reuter–Instinet pretensions, surfaced again in

September 1987. The Chicago Mercantile Exchange (CME) signed an agreement with Reuters to launch in 1989 the Post (Pre) Market Trade system. This screen-based trading system would function during the hours when CME futures pits were closed; after the frenetic daytime action in the pits, Reuters' computers at night would match up the trades. Stock Exchanges across the world feared that this could presage round-the-clock electronic trading, and the end of the face-to-face open cry system.

Links between Exchanges seeking to capture the global market had met with little success, partly because of the incompatibility of regulatory mechanisms. CME had formed such a link with the Singapore International Monetary Exchange (SIMEX), the most important futures market in the East Asian time zone, which it helped set up. SIMEX and CME operated the world's first international offset system; contracts or trades opened in Singapore could be closed in Chicago during the Singapore night, and vice versa. The Reuters–CME agreement would enable traders to deal via their Reuters screens during the sixteen hours when CME was closed; SIMEX feared that the users of 120,000 Reuters Dealer Trading System terminals would suck all the liquidity out of Singapore. 'It could mean the end of follow-the-sun trading in which trading books are passed around the globe daily to different exchanges.'[42] Reuters and others argued that these fears were illusory; the Reuters system was complementary and forex money brokers continued to thrive even though Reuters provided a direct dealing facility in foreign exchange. Yet the very technological advance of Reuters disturbs Stock Exchanges whose members both appreciate the new services rendered, and fear that they could signify the end of open cry trading, their original *raison d'être*.[43] Some Stock Exchanges eschew such fears; they see the writing on the wall. In June 1990 Reuters and three US Stock and Options Exchanges undertook to develop a joint trading system to facilitate worldwide after-hours trading.

The Stock Exchange crash of October 1987 stemmed in part from a malfunction, caused by computer trading, between Chicago futures markets and the New York Stock Exchange: 'Just before noon on Tuesday October 20, the two markets came close to destroying each other.'[44] For level-headed Reuters journalists in New York, Black Monday (19 October) signified a record number of stories and a sense of excitement rather than of panic. In its post-mortem on the crash the Brady commission pointed out that regulatory bodies had not adjusted to the fact of one global electronic market fed by 300,000 computer terminals working round the clock. News agencies, of course, bear no responsibility for the computer program trading that contributed to the malfunctions of 19 October. Yet some of the facilities provided on Reuters' terminals are tools to help dealers play the market. Index arbitrage – how to exploit the price inconsistencies between markets – presupposes the real-time monitoring of markets which is of the essence of Reuters' worldwide operations; the ART offers an arbitrage package to help 'enhance a dealer's tactical skills in the minute by minute interplay of trends'.[45]

## FLOATING REUTERS HOLDINGS

Nemesis or not, Reuters' own financial fate is bound up with Stock Exchanges worldwide. In 1984, the agency went public, as shares in the new company, Reuters Holdings plc, were sold on the London and New York Stock Exchanges; according to a London Stock Exchange estimate based on a survey carried out in the second half of 1984, 50 per cent of total buying and selling in Reuters' stock was in the US.[46] In 1987, Reuters announced plans to be quoted on the Tokyo Stock Exchange. With the Stock Exchange crash of October 1987, Reuters' own stock fell by over 50 per cent before the end of the year, only to recover substantially subsequently: in volatile financial markets, the need for global information and trading services becomes ever more critical.

The discussion of the flotation of Reuters began in 1982, when it became apparent to agency executives and to its British and Commonwealth newspaper owners that, following the R. & D. investments of the 1970s and the success of the Monitor services and dealing system, the agency was embarked on a phase of 'substantial rising profits' (Glen Renfrew). A system of share ownership was devised that enabled the objectives of the Reuters Trust Agreement, guaranteeing the agency's 'independence and integrity', to be preserved, while allowing the existing shareholders to retain voting control and (along with agency senior executives) to cash in on Reuters' commercial success. Since the formation of Reuters Holdings plc in 1984, the British NPA and PA, the Australian Associated Press and New Zealand Associated Press control the 'A' class of shares, which have a quarter of the equity but over half the voting rights.[47] 'B' class shares, offered to the public, are worth only one vote per share compared to four per 'A' share. NPA members – publishers of national and/or London daily and/or Sunday newspapers – owned 'B' as well as 'A' shares; several of them cashed in on their 'B' shares in the months and years following the flotation of the company on 5 June 1984.

During the long-drawn-out flotation negotiations, Glen Renfrew and his deputy, Michael Nelson, penned a memorandum on the interdependence of the general and economic and financial news services of the agency. They recalled with distaste previous 'arcane discussions on cost allocations between the two divisions',[48] such as existed between 1966 and 1973, when Reuters Economic Services functioned alongside, but distinct from, the World (and Media) Service. Since 1973, management worked to integrate the News Division and the Economic Services: as Gerald Long had argued, general and economic news were virtually indistinguishable.[49] The reporting networks of the World Service and the Economic Services were merged in 1980, as we have seen. Information is a broader concept than news. Similarly, the R. & D. and acquisition policy has made Reuters into an information group and not a mere news agency. In 1991, when Peter Job succeeded Glen Renfrew as Chief Executive, Reuters even argued that this policy would continue to bear fruit in times of rationalization in the main financial markets of New York, Tokyo and London: cutbacks in manpower mean greater demand for its automated services; each terminal gains added value with new products and innovations.

## AFP: TRYING TO MAKE ENDS MEET WITH GENERAL NEWS

Agence France-Presse is more centralized than Reuters and France provides three quarters of its revenue; some two thirds of its (under) 2,000 full-time employees are located in France. During the 1980s AFP tried to reduce its dependence on the French market; and, in 1986, management sought to decentralize news/editorial operations by transferring journalists from Paris to world regional news centres.

The headquarters of AFP face le palais Brogniart, the seat of the French Stock Exchange. In 1987, the Chirac government reformed the Stock Exchange (notably by ending the monopoly of the stock-brokers' corporation) with the avowed aim of making Paris the leading Stock Exchange of continental Europe, by overtaking

Frankfurt and Zurich. Paris is less important an Exchange than London; and AFP (like its predecessor Havas) has done considerably less well than Reuters in serving the information-needs of the stock market, banks and other financial institutions.

After 1973 there were several attempts to modernize the AFP's news-transmission and processing technologies, to diversify its clientele at home and abroad, and to reorganize the structure and workings of the agency. The real achievements failed to quieten management anxieties as to AFP's competitive decline. AFP did not have the resources for R. & D. to develop economic and financial services such as the Monitor range introduced by Reuters in the 1970s. AFP remains a strong world competitor for general news services. But revenue for general news does not cover production, transmission and processing costs. Arguing thus, Henri Pigeat, the 'p.-d.g.' (*président-directeur général*; the chairman and managing director) announced in July 1986 a plan to reorganize the agency, which involved the elimination of 300 jobs (from a full-time work-force of 2,000) and the aforementioned decentralization; this meant the transfer of the German-language desk to Bonn, of the Latin-American desk to Washington, and the reinforcement of the Arabic-language service, based in Nicosia (Cyprus). Opposition to his plan contributed to a strike which in December 1986 led to Pigeat's leaving the agency; but several aspects of the plan were subsequently implemented. Management (under the following 'p.-d.g.', Jean-Louis Guillaud), presented the plan as the 'last chance' for AFP to survive as a world agency.

## AFP SINCE 1944

From its creation in August 1944, AFP attempted to square the circle: how to maintain a world agency headquartered in France, with an international news-collection and distribution network, without depending overly on revenue from the French tax-payer. De Gaulle, in 1944, wanted France to have a quality prestige daily newspaper with an international reputation and his support was instrumental in the creation of *Le Monde*.[50] He was less committed to the need for a French international news agency. His attitude to the nascent AFP – like that of most governments of the Fourth Republic (1946–58) and of some under the Fifth (1958– ) was: 'qui paie commande' – 'he who pays the piper calls the tune'.[51]

'AFP', wrote its first Director-General, Claude Martial-

Bourgeon, in October 1944, 'lives off public charity.'[52] From 1944 to 1957 AFP was a public body (*établissement public*), its chief executive appointed by government decree. Every year, then as now, when Parliament debates the budget, payment for AFP news services appears among the 'funds for information' listed in the finance bill. Particularly (but not only) before 1957, the competing US agencies and Reuters eagerly pointed out to prospective news agency subscribers that AFP was government-controlled and editorially suspect. French newspapers themselves wanted AFP to be a news-agency co-operative, like the PA in Britain. But most were neither willing nor able to finance the expensive international news organization built up by AFP in the post-war years. Some French regional newspaper publishers only required AFP coverage from correspondents based in a handful of mainly western capital cities and news centres. Some were content to subscribe to Reuters or an American agency for coverage of world news. But most AFP journalists have always regarded a comprehensive and independent world news service as essential.

A law voted in 1957 appeared to succeed in squaring the circle. The state, which continued to provide over 60 per cent of the agency's revenue, was held at arm's length; the editorial independence of the agency was guaranteed by the appointment of a Director-General accountable to a board of directors on which the representatives of publishers of daily newspapers had a majority. A High Commission (*conseil supérieur*) was established with the task of guaranteeing that the independence, accuracy and impartiality of agency services, and the international character of the organization, were maintained. The rate of a subscription to the AFP general news service by a French newspaper was fixed with reference to its daily circulation. Government ministries, official bodies and other 'public administrations' together paid the equivalent of 383 subscriptions taken out by a daily newspaper with a print-run of 180,000 copies. In 1987–8 such a daily paid a million francs a year; the French state provided 50 per cent of total AFP income. Thus, the 'subsidy' voted annually by Parliament was transformed into a commercial contract akin to those between AFP and its media clients.

Under Jean Marin, who ran AFP from 1954 to 1975, and thanks to the *modus operandi* of its journalists, the application of the 1957 statute effectively guaranteed the news and editorial independence of the agency, whilst its international ambitions were maintained.

On Marin's departure in 1975, at the age of 66, his successors feared for the latter. Claude Roussel had been AFP deputy manager (*secrétaire général*) in 1944–51 and 1954–75; as 'p.-d.g.' or chief executive (1975–8), he invited Henri Pigeat to be his deputy, and to review the organization and management of AFP. Pigeat was a young *énarque* with ten years experience of civil service posts in government ministries and organizations dealing with information issues. As deputy between 1976 and 1979, Pigeat addressed the issue of whether AFP was still a world agency. As 'p.-d.g.' (1979–86), he developed strategies, and sought funding, to enable it to remain one. But diagnosis and prognosis were not reassuring: AFP was losing out internationally as Reuters and AP (with Dow Jones) reinforced their grip on the most lucrative markets. Both AP and Reuters computerized their services five to ten years earlier than AFP; they both profited – Reuters more in Europe, AP more in the US – from the explosion in the demand for economic information and on-line data services. AFP's strength lay in general news; but general news does not pay – or at least it does not cover the high costs of maintaining an international organization to collect, process and distribute news.[53]

AFP depended primarily on the French domestic market for general news and on French public (national, regional and local) authorities rather than on the media. In 1968, 1978, and 1982 revenue from public administrations (*services publics*) represented 55 per cent, 61 per cent and 59 per cent of AFP income. In his annual report on the finance bill, the senator Jean Cluzel reckoned that state subscriptions to AFP represented 56 per cent of total AFP income in 1986 and 55 per cent in 1987.[54] Pigeat sought to reduce the figure to below 50 per cent: by developing other categories of revenue, AFP cut its dependence on such subscriptions from 63 per cent to 53 per cent during the ten years of his association with AFP (1976–86).[55] The corollary – argued Pigeat – was to increase revenue from foreign markets, which represented only 12–13 per cent of total revenue in the early 1970s. When he left the agency in December 1986, foreign revenue had risen to between 17 and 18 per cent – still short of the target figure of 25 per cent, which Pigeat believed to be indispensable to the survival of AFP as a world agency.[56] Neither the French press nor French broadcasting media were capable (nor, in some cases, desirous) of the financial sacrifice needed to help the agency in its international ambitions. Since representatives of the Press have a majority on the board of directors, they are able to block the increases in the rates of subscription to agency services – which, in times of inflation, they have not hesitated to do. The French daily Press thus gets its international news on the cheap: Pigeat (with caution) and others (more vehemently),[57] pointed out that, during the previous quarter-century AFP subscription rates rose by less than the sale-price of newspapers, while the range and extent of services had greatly increased.[58]

These arguments surfaced during the crisis which AFP experienced in December 1986, when, after the second strike in five months, the journalists forced Pigeat to resign. But such arguments were not new; in June 1950, an MP described the subsidy paid to the agency as an indirect aid to the French newspapers 'which pay a ridiculously low price for their news'.[59] In 1988, state aid still represented 13 per cent of total French press industry turnover; after the statute of 1957, if not before, the Press was inclined to treat AFP as a form of indirect state aid.[60]

## FRANÇOIS MITTERRAND: A HELPING HAND

Government ministers have sometimes proved more supportive of the international role of AFP than publishers of regional daily newspapers. François Mitterrand was one such politician. In 1949, he was Secretary of State for Information in the Queuille government, which backed a bill for the payment of a 'news tax' that would help finance AFP. Nothing came of this. But, during the Fourth Republic, while other politicians when in office showed themselves more concerned with resolving the issue of the status of the state broadcasting network, Mitterrand proved 'a good friend' to a news agency in search of a status.[61] In June 1954, Mitterrand became Minister of the Interior, with responsibility for information in the (Socialist) Mendès-France government. In September 1954, he appointed Jean Marin as AFP Director-General – a post subsequently transformed into that of 'p.-d.g.' or president and chief executive by the statute of 1957. Marin, who ran AFP for twenty-one years, was a journalist but also a politician, belonging to a parliamentary group with both Gaullist and Socialist connections. Mitterrand, for his part, in 1957 was Minister of Justice in the Socialist government of Guy Mollet which enacted the law giving AFP its subsequent legal status.

A quarter of a century later, Mitterrand – as President of the Republic – provided decisive support for a plan, canvassed for over four years by Henri Pigeat, to preserve AFP as an international agency. Among Mitterrand's journalist and Socialist associates were men with long experience of AFP; Marc Paillet, Mitterrand's campaign manager in the 1965 presidential election, and a noted essayist, rose during a thirty-year career in AFP to head the agency's (modest) economic news service. When Pigeat became 'p.-d.g.', Paillet joined his staff as 'special adviser' and produced a new version of the agency style-book.[62] Other prominent Socialist politicians who, after the Resistance, had worked for AFP in the 1940s included Gilles Martinet (whom Mitterrand appointed ambassador to Rome in 1981). The point should not be laboured: during the past fifteen years or so, professional journalistic and managerial criteria counted for more than political connections, or rather, AFP editors-in-chief have long reflected a diversity of political views. This very diversity has underpinned the agency's journalistic independence. As has – some would argue – the relatively high union militancy of its Paris-based journalists.

The development and diversification plan devised by Henri Pigeat aimed to reduce the competitive gap between AFP and the two leading UK and US international news agencies; to strengthen the business and commercial organization of an agency where Gallo-centric journalistic reasoning, attitudes and corporatisms appeared excessive. Pigeat also wanted to broaden the agency's product-line – 90 per cent of AFP revenue came from subscriptions to its (press oriented) general news service. AFP's economic services, such as they were, were more macro-economic analyses and commentaries than price data, and represented, in terms of revenue, the crumbs from Reuters' table.[63] AFP's news-photo service was distributed only in France. In view of these AFP weaknesses, Pigeat's plan was to provide services for business and companies, just as Reuters and others had done.[64]

The main lines of the plan were devised in 1980. Its implementation would require funding beyond the resources and powers of AFP; as a result of the 1957 statute, the agency was not a company and had no shareholders or the possibility of raising capital (other than through bank loans). The two major previous investments by AFP (the reconstruction of its headquarters on the existing site and the computerization and modernization of its telecommunications networks) had been financed primarily through bank loans, guaranteed by the state. An agency with a turnover of 800 million francs (and which did not even have a R. & D. budget) could not finance the 200–250 million francs needed for the development plan.[65] The representatives of the Press and broadcasting media who, with those of the 'public services', sat on the AFP board, received no dividends;[66] they showed little enthusiasm when the 'p.-d.g.' made his annual request for increases in subscription rates, and were even less likely – or able – to help finance the development plan.

It took four years for the plan to be approved. The final decision in favour of the funding of the plan was taken by François Mitterrand as President of the Republic, in 1984. Yet already, in 1980–1, the then Prime Minister, the conservative Raymond Barre, indicated to Pigeat his support for the mode of funding envisaged: a mix of AFP funds and of state funding; the latter would come partly from the state investment body, FDES, and partly from an advance on the subscriptions from public service administrations. Initially, the investment programme was costed at 595 million francs over twelve years; this was equivalent to about half the state aid to the metallurgy industry, one of the hardest hit of French traditional industries. Pigeat subsequently argued that, in seeking state aid, his plan would not increase the danger of state influence over the agency – all state funds would be repaid.[67] Barre, he believes, approved a mode of funding that combined the respect of the independence of the agency with the necessary R. & D. effort that only the state would finance. The Socialist victory in the 1981 presidential and parliamentary elections delayed matters.

At 8 p.m. on 10 May 1981, AFP journalists watching the TV election coverage burst into applause on hearing the news that Mitterrand had been elected President of the Republic. Many AFP journalists were left of centre (to say the least), and politically active; the degree of unionization was high among AFP journalists; in the weeks, months and years that followed – until the crisis of 1986, the strikes of July and November–December and the departure of Pigeat – the growth of union influence compromised 'management's right to manage'. As an *énarque*, and not a journalist, elected 'p.-d.g.' during the Giscard d'Estaing presidency, Pigeat appeared to lack the necessary contacts with (and support of) the new politicians in power.

Pigeat had never met Georges Fillioud, the new Secretary of State for Communication Techniques.[68] The new President of the Republic, however, was a 'friend' of AFP of over thirty years' standing; in 1948, as Information Minister, he had pressed for what would subsequently become a modified version of the statute of 1957. As already noted, Mitterrand had signed the parliamentary bill of 1957, whence originated the agency's status – as had Gaston Defferre, who was Minister of the Interior in the Mauroy government appointed by Mitterrand in May 1981.[69] The statute had proved itself as the guarantor of the agency's independence. Despite alarmist rumours to the contrary, Pigeat did not succumb to what its detractors termed the 'media witchhunt' – the expulsion of journalists and executives (too closely identified with the preceding Giscard d'Estaing presidency) from public service broadcasting: during the (first) Mitterrand presidency (1981–8) he was re-elected for additional three-year terms as 'p.-d.g.'(in 1982 and 1985).[70] Pigeat's long-term objective remained the pursuit of the development and diversification strategy – by raising the necessary funding from the state and by developing increasing agency services, market penetration and revenue.

Reuters' profits for 1981 were £16 million; AFP operated at a loss in 1981 and 1982. AFP broke even in 1983 but, thereafter, it operated at a loss for three consecutive years, with a deficit in 1986 alone of 150 million francs. Salaries rose to 70 per cent of costs. As Pigeat battled to obtain state-funding for the development plan, he encountered resistance from top civil servants from various ministries. He was not without allies; the former 'p.-d.g.' of the agency, Claude Roussel, sat as General Inspector for Communication on one of the two inter-ministerial commissions of enquiry that analysed agency finance and projects. But the Ministry of Finance attached strings to the November 1982 decision to award 250 million francs over five years for the first phase of the development plan: these included a reduction in the rise of labour costs.[71] This sum was greater than any state aid previously accorded to the agency; but it was insufficient to finance the development plan. In July 1986, Pigeat proposed what was euphemistically termed 'a restructuring plan'; this included the abolition of 300 posts and a further step in the decentralization of the agency, with the transfer of some foreign desks from Paris to the country or region they were to serve. Representatives of the Finance Ministry considered that the proposed economies were too little, too late. Pigeat had to appeal to Matignon (the Prime Minister's office) to obtain the minimal funds necessary to implement this restructuring plan, intended to complement the development and diversification plan.[72] Union (and indeed non-union) opposition among agency journalists to restructuring led to a four-day strike in July, followed by an eight-day strike in November–December, and Pigeat's departure. But his successor, Jean-Louis Guillaud, later implemented its main policies.[73]

As to the services offered by AFP, Pigeat's diagnosis of market demand differed little from that of Gerald Long of Reuters – the more general a news service, the more it costs to collect and the less the client is willing to pay; specialist news, on the other hand, costs less to process, yet the client is more willing to pay.[74] The difficulty for AFP was that others – led by Reuters – had preceded it in the most lucrative markets for specialist news – financial services.

AFP began the computerization of its services in 1973; between 1975 and 1985 the number of items processed and transmitted on its French wire services doubled, chiefly because of improved telecommunications and computerization facilities. In January 1988, the 'France' desk transmitted an average of 150,000 words per day. Agency clients protest that there is too much copy, just as easily as that there is too little.[75] Computerization makes, in principle, for increased interaction with subscribers, for greater flexibility in news-processing and formatting, and for greater ease in responding to specific demands within the context of the general service. For over a century, French newspapers have demanded that their specific needs be met within a general service. Computerization should facilitate this: but, as Pigeat admits, there is always the danger that the agencyman, in his role of gate-keeper, of selector of copy, will transmit too much rather than too little.[76]

Pigeat sought to end the mono-product nature of AFP copy – in the mid-1970s, the general news service (in its various forms and languages) represented over 90 per cent of AFP revenues. AFP coverage of sports news (results, data and reports and features) was one of its strengths worldwide. But AFP attempts to develop other product lines met with varied success. Three reasons, of varying importance, can be adduced for this.

As a general news agency, AFP sought to develop services that would appeal to the media and, especially, to the Press in France and abroad. In many developed countries, however, daily newspapers were a contracting market. In France itself, the situation was particularly severe. In 1984, France ranked thirty-first among the 160 UNESCO member states for the number of copies sold daily per 1,000 inhabitants – 184 copies;[77] in 1947 there were 175 provincial dailies and 28 Parisian dailies – 40 years later, their ranks had dwindled to 70 and 12 respectively. Between 1970 and 1987, circulations of national titles fell by 9.5 per cent, those of regional titles by 8.5 per cent. The difficulties of daily 'general interest' newspapers contributed to the reluctance of the Press representatives on the AFP board of directors to increase subscription rates. According to AFP, an average daily newspaper spent under 0.5 per cent of its cover price on the purchase of the AFP service; for the daily with a circulation of 180,000 copies, the 1 million francs spent on an AFP annual subscription represented the total cost of employing just three journalists.

Two strategies towards the Press were possible: either to develop services for growth sectors or to reinforce AFP services for the daily Press, so that AFP was preferred to the competition. The first strategy involved the development of feature material (as opposed to spot news). In many countries, news magazines were an expanding market; and in daily newspapers, feature pages were developed – which attracted advertisers, and cost less than hard news coverage. With a worldwide news collection and distribution network, AFP developed this approach and range of services. But the more costly task concerned the second strategy, more directly related to AFP's vocation as a hard news agency, centred on speed and universality.

Under Pigeat, AFP elected to make a major R. & D. commitment to photo-technologies in order to enhance its penetration of world markets for news, and to interactive information technologies for videotext services – the AGORA historical database of AFP despatches. Many subsequently criticized this choice. The investments needed for the R. & D. costs of digital processing, transmission and reception of still photos appeared excessive given available resources and the nature of the market. One counter-argument was that, in the past, prospective clients of AFP news (text) services – in Latin America, notably – had stated they could not abandon US-based agencies, AP and UPI, which provided them with both text and photo services, for an agency that failed to provide the latter. Furthermore, in 1980, when Pigeat conceived the development plan, the situation was different from that in 1984–5, when the state funds became available: the two US agencies then dominated the market for international news agency photos. Pigeat and the executive chiefs of other western European agencies sought to co-operate by creating a European Press Photo Agency (EPA, 1984) aimed at reducing this dependence, and at encouraging co-operation between European national agencies. With the disappearance of the international distribution organization of UPI photos, some European agencies turned to AFP's International Telephoto service. Unfortunately for AFP, it did not launch this service until late 1984. In January 1985, Reuters – for the first time ever – launched an international news picture service (outside the US); Reuters had rights to UPI photos of the US. AFP pledged a substantial part of its R. & D. resources to being competitive in the 'news pix' market, at a time of costly technologies and intensifying competition (with Reuters, AP and specialist news-photo agencies). And, in October 1985, as noted, Reuters became the majority shareholder in Visnews, the world's largest international television news agency.

In developing the AGORA historical databank of AFP despatches, the agency claimed to be the first news media database in France. For the agency sought to accompany – or precede – the development of 'new media' markets in France. The development of local radio stations was a case in point. In the two years prior to November 1986, 98 French local radio stations subscribed to AFP; it provided a total of 7,000 news flashes. In 1988, it went a step further in providing, via satellite, a 24-hour service for what are predominantly 'music'n'news' stations; it acquired the distribution rights of a company providing the music programming while it furnished news on the hour. The modernization of the agency's telecommunications network was part of the 1984–8 development and diversification plan; as a result, AFP joined with a subsidiary of the DGT (France–Câble et Radio) to create a company, Polycom, to develop the transmission of its news and photo services via the satellite Télécom 1 A. By June 1987, AFP distributed thus to its Parisian and provincial subscribers its audio, telephoto and teleprinter services. It negotiated with telecommunications authorities outside France to use this combination of satellite beam and earth reception dish to distribute these services elsewhere.

In 1986, the longest strike in the agency's history and the departure of Henri Pigeat stemmed from the restructuring plan. Pigeat had not obtained, in 1984, all the funds for the modernization plans that he had first asked for in 1980–1. In 1986, Pigeat had to go cap-in-hand to the AFP board and to the Ministry of Finance for additional funding; the agency's deficit had increased, and the returns on the investments following the adoption of the plan had not, as yet, borne (much) fruit.[78] The transfer of desks from Paris to countries situated in or close to the (language) areas they were to serve[79] and the abolition of 300 posts, led to the November–December 1986 crisis.

AFP's late 1986 drama was a chastening experience for both management and unions, for French newspaper publishers (with their majority on the board), for journalists and for the French government, confronted at the same time by student unrest. AFP subscribers world-wide threatened to desert an agency embroiled in what the French Press presented as 'the longest strike in the history of news agencies'. The circumstances of Pigeat's departure were hardly becoming; nor, indeed, were those in which, in January 1987, the name of his successor was announced. The board of directors were entitled to choose a new 'p.-d.g.' but Prime Minister Chirac, after a meeting with Jean-Louis Guillaud, announced on January 12 that Guillaud was to be the new 'p.-d.g.' – a situation that did not endear Guillaud to the eight Press representatives on an AFP board of fifteen members. The board did not elect him until 22 January. AFP unions and the journalists' association, for their part, were apprehensive of the reputation of Guillaud as a tough negotiator; during the events of May–June 1968, he had led the non-striking journalists of the state broadcasting organisation ORTF (Office de la Radio-Télédiffusion Française) when tough management had been at a premium.

At no time – argues Pigeat – during the heated atmosphere of December 1986, was there a considered analysis in France of the situation of AFP.[80] Such analyses, in Parliament or the public prints, are rare. In times of crisis, such as 1975, when Jean Marin retired after twenty-one years as chief executive, or in December 1986, government politicians examined the 'AFP file' as an exercise in crisis-management, rather than with a considered understanding of AFP's complex national and international operations and standing. Franco-French considerations regrettably distort the vision of government politicians – which does not help the inter-national reputation of AFP, and undoes the painstakingly acquired reputation for credibility. Thus, in 1975, Giscard d'Estaing report-edly favoured the appointment of a French ambassador, a diplomat, as chairman and chief executive: American journalists in France (Pierre Salinger among others) pointed out the harm this would do AFP as an international news organization. In January 1986, Chirac's precipitate announcement of Guillaud's 'appointment' provoked the ire of the representatives of newspaper publishers on the board, and made Guillaud appear 'the government candidate'.

Guillaud's career had been primarily in broadcasting: under de Gaulle and Pompidou in ORTF management (and production); as head of TF-1 between 1978 and 1981 under Giscard d'Estaing, and, subsequently, as head of the television department of the Hachette group. Some commentators did not hesitate to represent him as 'one of a kind' – a member of 'Chirac's band' of media appointees, journalists and managers who had run ORTF under de Gaulle and Pompidou and who were given top positions by the Chirac government after March 1986. 'A severe Norman' ('Normand strict'): perhaps one of the least remarked features of Guillaud was that he renewed a tradition – many previous chief executives of France's leading international news agency (beginning with Charles-Louis Havas) hailed from Normandy, a region with a reputation for the financial acumen of its inhabitants. On assuming the post of 'p.-d.g.', he spoke of the need for 'authority and dialogue' as a way of ending 'the crisis of confidence' that marked all levels of the agency's operations. Under Guillaud (1987–90), management was reorganized, the development plan partially applied and labour unrest (journalist and non-journalist personnel) subsided. But the fact remained that, in 1986, the agency had escaped from bankruptcy by a hairbreadth, while the maintenance of the agency as a world news organization depended on continued state funding. Senator Cluzel, in his annual report on state funds for culture and communication, rejected all talk of the privatization of the agency (as 'utopian') and stated baldly: 'the existence of a press agency with an international stature is one of the missions of the state, in terms of both its cultural and foreign policies.'[81]

In January 1990, the three representatives of the government and the two representatives of public service broadcasting who sit on the fifteen-member board of directors of AFP failed to vote for a new term for Guillaud, a 'p.-d.g.' allegedly 'imposed' by a government of a different political complexion in 1987. Many commentators claimed that, once again, the chief executive of the agency could not operate without at least the tacit support of the state. Claude Moisy, the new 'p.-d.g.' and AFP-man of thirty-three years standing, continued, like Pigeat and Guillaud before him, to 'dream of doing a Reuters' – to build up the clientele of non-media subscribers, attracted by specialist services, such as an English-language European economic news service. Despite the success of some of its diversification strategies, and new product lines, AFP cut back on its personnel: the number of staff journalists fell from 748 in 1986 to 675 in 1989, when the wage packet still accounted for 80 per cent of turnover. The deficit in 1990 was twice that of 1989. The dream remains distant.

## CONCLUSION

AFP is a journalistic success: its services (in French, English, Spanish, German, Arabic and Portuguese) reportedly reach, directly or indirectly, two billion people; it claims to have 12,500 direct or indirect subscribers; these include 637 print media, 400 broadcasting media and 96 national Press agencies. Through the latter, AFP reaches 7,000 newspapers, 2,500 radio stations, and 400 television channels. AFP has some 1,500 non-media subscribers (administrations and public services, private and public companies). But diversification, substantial R. & D., new products and a reinforced sales team have not as yet reduced the overall importance of the media clientele and of the indirect state subsidy.

AFP turnover in 1989 totalled 849.6 million francs; it rose 40 per cent between 1983 and 1988. Its deficit was in the order of 30 million francs. In 1989, Reuters revenue totalled £1,186.9 million and had more than doubled since 1985. Reuters turnover is about twelve times that of AFP; the turnover of the joint AP–Dow Jones service (economic, financial and commercial data from the leading US agencies) was in the order of 40 per cent that of Reuters in 1989. These figures give some measure of Reuters' advance.[82]

When Harold Macmillan assumed power in Britain (1957) and Charles de Gaulle in France (1958), Europe's two leading news agencies were still marked by an imperial and world legacy, but as news organizations operating internationally they were in danger of losing out to US news agencies: the merger of UP (United Press) and INS (International News Service) in 1958 promised to turn UPI into the second leading world agency, alongside AP. Yet, despite the importance of the US – much the richest single news market in the world – UPI failed to generate sufficient revenue to maintain an international news organization. Reuters bought UPI's non-US pictures division in 1984, thereby heralding a series of investments in news photography – a sector from which, unlike the other world agencies, it had been absent hitherto.[83] News pictures and Visnews make Reuters more competitive in the media field.

But media services, for an organization with the telecommunications, computing and other news and data transmission and processing technologies of a worldwide agency, do not generate sufficient revenue of themselves. Because of its early investments in R. & D. – more than recouped, in particular by the Monitor Dealing services – Reuters could buttress its media services. Furthermore, following the flotation of 1984, Reuters 'bought companies like most people bought shirts'.[84] It acquired ten companies between 1985 and 1987 which deal in what it terms 'trading tools' and 'intelligence'. Each acquisition contributes to the aim of offering deeper databases – information that can be shaped into whatever form the customers want – and systems that handle transactions and automatically record details. Information, once enriched and refined, becomes 'intelligence'.

Thus 'intelligence', the eighteenth-century term for 'news' has become synonymous with the late twentieth-century emphasis on 'value added' services. AFP tries, with varying degrees of success, to diversify away from the general news service, its 'mono-product'; it rings the changes on its range of services for the media and on developing videotex databases. But as a world organization with services in six languages it could not survive without state (tax-payers') funding.[85]

Following the crash in global financial markets of October 1987, Reuters' shares fell by over half. Yet such doubts proved short-term. In post-crash months, securities firms sacked people but could not do without their screens; some 10,000 video terminals were installed between 19 October and 31 December, taking the (then) total to 141,000. The US Brady Commission, as noted earlier, spoke of 300,000 terminals working round the clock to service the single global market. In volatile financial markets, the need for global real-time information is ever more critical. This is Reuters' strength. Thus, in 1990, it introduced Money 2000, the successor to the Reuters Monitor in international forex and money markets, the company's most important source of revenue.

Mammon finances Mercury: or rather Mercury, for the Romans, was the god of travellers as well as that of commerce (and thieves). Reporters, those winged messengers, have increased as Reuters has expanded. In December 1990, Reuters' staff totalled 10,810. This included 1,300 staff journalists, photographers and cameramen based in offices located in 115 cities in 74 countries. It served business clients in 127 countries (via 200,000 video terminals) and the media in 158. The collection, processing, packaging and distribution of news and data (in five languages)[86] for specific targeted customers is a fine art, transcending the traditional discussion of specialist, as opposed to general, news. All staff journalists and photographers (and a legion of part-time reporters, photographers and cameramen) file into a world news database, serving media and business subscribers. Media services remain the most prestigious of the agency's products: the major editing centres are in London, New York and Hong Kong, with the German and French services based respectively in Bonn and Paris, and the Middle East desk in Nicosia. The news/editorial stress is on accuracy, clarity and speed. Elsewhere, the emphasis is also laid on Reuters' products as an aid to informed decision-making. Consider, for instance, the Country Reports service, available via the Monitor screen, and covering 190 countries (updated economic indicators, economic developments and power-structures, biographies of leading figures, investment requirements, etc.). Promotional material stresses how a Report is 'organised to ensure executives can go directly to the information they need'. The information package even lists local taboos – such as 'touching another person's head or showing the bottom of one's foot', 'what to tip and whether it is proper to conduct business over lunch'. Thus 'raw data', 'through objective analysis and careful organisation' is transformed from 'information into intelligence'.[87]

# Chapter 4

# European media lobbying

This chapter looks at the lobbying activities of European print media and advertising industry companies and, in particular, of their trade associations during the 1980s. It centres initially on the Press and on newspaper publishers associations (NPAs). The Press has a long history of lobbying, at the national level, and also internationally: in the mid-nineteenth century, newspaper publishers obtained preferential rates or tariffs for the electric telegraph. In an age of television and of burgeoning communications technologies, and of growing European integration, NPAs lobby hard, on issues old and new. The first case study analyses publishers' attempts to preserve access to duty-free raw materials, and their battle to import newsprint into the Community without paying tax.

During the 1980s, the advertising industry became one of the best organized media lobbies in Europe – in Brussels, Strasbourg and elsewhere: the second case study examines how the various advertising industry interests (advertisers, agencies, the media and media buyers) effectively put their case in the European debate over 'television without frontiers'.

## TRADE ASSOCIATIONS AS LOBBYISTS

'Hitherto protected territory is under threat': this is the fear of newspaper publishing companies, big and small, from Bergen, Norway to Catania, Sicily. Already in the inter-war years, the response of British and French publishers to the advent of sound broadcasting reflected a similar fear; newspapers worried that their supremacy as a news, entertainment and advertising medium was coming to an end. Likewise, in the 1980s, 'new media', such as videotex, were perceived as likely to 'satisfy information needs which were up to now *protected territory* for newspapers'.[1] In terms of the discussion – and influencing – of media policy, however, the relative importance of national, European and international fora has changed substantially over the past fifty years. In the inter-war, and immediate post-war, years, media policy was largely formulated and implemented within the framework of the nation-state. Today in western Europe, national policies take greater cognizance of European and international actors. How do the representative trade associations of newspaper publishers and of other media and advertising interests respond to this situation?

The Communauté des Associations des Editeurs de Journaux (CAEJ) groups the national (and regional or provincial) NPAs of EC member states. It was founded in 1961; in 1983, NPAs represented in CAEJ published titles totalling sixty-six million copies and employing 250,000 people. CAEJ itself has to be studied in the context of the International Newspaper Publishers Association (FIEJ), a body founded in 1948 which represents the interests of twenty-six NPAs of the western world – including those of the twelve EC member states. Launched in 1961, IFRA – the INCA–FIEJ Research Association – was initially the R. & D. unit of the FIEJ: it advises over 600 newspaper publishers on technologies and equipment of relevance to the modernization of the industry.[2] Finally, CAEJ is one of the member-organizations of the European Advertising Tripartite (EAT), a lobby representing the common interests of advertisers, agencies, the media and other advertising outlets – of which more later.

### 'BETWEEN THE DEVIL AND THE DEEP BLUE SEA'

However simplistic and antithetical, this proverbial phrase expresses the traditional fears of newspaper publishers in parliamentary democracies. Their suspicion of the state goes back centuries and, in recent decades, they have fought a rearguard battle against the advance of advertising in television. For some thirty years after 1945 – despite the advent of commercial TV earlier in some countries than in others – there was a certain stability in the battlelines of the various belligerents shaping media policy. Primarily concerned with developing their company's individual strategy, newspaper publishers jointly attended, within their associations, to the defence of common interests (low postal tariffs for newspapers in discussion with state controlled PTTs (post, telegraph and telephone administrations); or the introduction of new production technologies in discussions with the unions). The contours, the topography, of the battlefield were relatively clearly defined. On the one hand, the defence of the freedom of expression, of opinion, and of information, against threats from the executive, legislative and judicial powers: 'the freedom of the press is the freedom of the citizen,' proclaims a (1978) FIEJ declaration.[3] On the other, the defence of the traditional sources of revenue held to be indispensable to the maintenance of a pluralist press: advertising and sales revenue, under threat from state fiscal policy, and from the development of other advertising-based media, including television.

From about 1975 the contours of democratic media policy-making and lobbying promised to change. In most European nation-states, television came of age as a mass medium, achieving saturation household penetration.[4] European governments trad-itionally regarded television as a limited resource, imposed a high degree of state regulation and allowed advertising (if at all) primarily to help finance state or public service broadcasting. Partly because of resistance from NPAs, television's share of advertising budgets in Europe in 1980 remained low (13 per cent), compared to other major world regions – Latin America (36 per cent), Asia (33 per cent), Australasia (26 per cent), North America (21 per cent), the Middle East and Africa (10 per cent).[5] But the writing was on the wall. In the early 1980s, governments in countries which had long refused advertising on television – Belgium, Denmark, Norway, Sweden – gingerly inched towards its introduction. Other governments – irrespective of their political complexion – eased restrictions on the volume and nature of advertising on terrestrial television. NPAs in France and Italy – and they were not alone – cried 'wolf!': in Italy, largely because of the success of the private TV networks broadcasting *de facto* nationwide (primarily those of Silvio Berlusconi), total TV advertising revenue in 1981 exceeded print media ad revenues for the first time. Furthermore, the much-heralded (but long-delayed) impact of cable and satellite TV channels promised further to destabilize newspaper advertising revenues. Newspaper publishers were, in many respects, a house divided: should they diversify, or not, into commercial broadcasting? Should companies publishing paid-for titles themselves launch or acquire free newspapers?

In such a period of flux, newspaper companies studying the implications of new communications technologies and their commercial potential, attributed increased importance to European bodies such as CAEJ, FIEJ and IFRA, and to the fora of European communication policy-making in Brussels, Strasbourg and elsewhere.

## CASE STUDY ONE: THE EUROPEAN 'NEWSPRINT SCANDAL'

In March 1982, the CAEJ held its seventy-fifth meeting. The venue was Brussels, an appropriate choice. The chairman of the CAEJ, Ernst Klaebel, managing director of the Copenhagen daily, *Politiken*, recalled how, from the outset, one of the most vexed issues affecting NPAs was the EC's policy towards the import of newsprint from outside the Community. CAEJ policy was simple: newspaper publishers wanted to be able to import all the newsprint they needed duty-free from wherever they wanted. A brief review of the situation in 1982–3 – when the newsprint issue caused divisions between member states, and was personally discussed by the British and Canadian Prime Ministers, Margaret Thatcher and Pierre Trudeau – highlights the role of the CAEJ.[6]

The CAEJ has considerable political and economic muscle. The 'newsprint scandal' of 1983 led the CAEJ to flex this muscle. On December 16, Ernst Klaebel sent a letter to the EC Commission Vice-president, Viscount Davignon: 'On behalf of the EC newspaper publishers, I protest in the strongest terms against the totally unacceptable conditions imposed on the newspapers by the Commission and Council (of Ministers) as a result of their lack of resolution and continuing vacillation.'

The EC is pledged to support the European newsprint industry. This affects its attitudes towards the import of newsprint and towards the duties charged to non-EC countries; the latter involve Canada, but also members of the European Free Trade Association (EFTA), including Finland. In 1982–3 (and the situation has changed little since) the CAEJ represented the consumers of newsprint who wanted the lowest purchase-price possible and a diversity of suppliers, while the EC commission supported the Community newsprint industry. The governments of member states sought both to encourage domestic newsprint manufacturers and to respond positively to the increasingly vociferous protests of national NPAs.

'1982 was an awful year for the worldwide newsprint industry': capacity increased, demand shrunk, output fell.[7] The situation was worst in the EC: output decreased by 7.6 per cent to 1.3 million tonnes, less than one-third of EC consumption, while demand fell for the second successive year, by 5.3 per cent to 4.1 million tonnes. With the EC paper industry producing 1.3 million, 2.8 million tonnes were imported, primarily from Scandinavian countries, headed by Sweden, but also from Canada.

Here lay the problem that subsequently prompted the CAEJ letter of protest. Because of the substantial rate of imports, the domestic EC paper industry, led by the Italians and the French, sought protection from the Commission: the basic duty on non-EC newsprint was some 10.5 per cent. But complications arose. Some Nordic countries supplying newsprint were better placed than Canada; in 1973 Denmark, Ireland and the UK joined the EC. Special agreements were concluded with the remaining EFTA countries whereby the Community imposed neither customs duties nor quota limits on these countries – which included Finland, Norway and Sweden, but not of course Canada – as of 1 January 1984. At the same time, the GATT regulations required that the EC offer compensation to countries which traditionally supplied newsprint to Denmark, Ireland and the UK – i.e. including Canada.

The EC–GATT arrangement went back many years. The 'GATT-bound quota' originated in 1974 as an offer from the Community, designed to compensate Canada for the damage done to its trading position on the accession of the three new members (1973) to the Community; the negotiations were lengthy, ended in 1974, and resulted in an offer accepted by Canada in 1975: the Community opened a duty-free newsprint quota of 1.5 million tonnes each year; open to all supplying countries, the agreement would primarily benefit Canada, among non-EC countries who belonged to GATT. However, following the EC–EFTA agreement (June 1972), from 1 January 1984, producers of newsprint in Sweden, Norway and Finland would be able to ship their newsprint into the Community on a duty-free basis without any quantitative limit.

The EC–GATT arrangements provided that, when demand exceeded the 1.5 million tonne 'GATT-bound quota', additional quotas might be allowed by the EC Council of Ministers. From 1975, negotiations within the Council for additional quotas were increasingly heated as ministers defended their national interests.

Such decisions had to be taken unanimously. Some countries including Italy appeared more concerned with selling the output of their domestic newsprint manufacturers than with securing the best possible supply in terms of price and quality for its newspaper publishers: Italy was the EC country nearest to newsprint self-sufficiency (69 per cent of 1982 needs).

In 1983, matters came to a head. The Italians had long sought, within the Council of Ministers, to keep the duty-free quota as low as possible. They now twice vetoed a CAEJ request for an increase in the quota originally demanded for 1983; while the CAEJ sought a supplementary quota for duty-free imports, primarily from Canada and Finland, the Italians replied that they had 20,000 surplus tonnes in Sardinia and that EC goods should have preference over outside supplies. The UK – where demand for newsprint was the largest in the EC (1.28 million tonnes in 1982) – counted among its major import sources Canada, Finland, Sweden and Norway; with domestic output falling from 375,000 tonnes in 1979 to 86,000 tonnes in 1982, British NPA officials were prominent in CAEJ measures to counteract Italian arguments. H.M. Stephen, the then Managing Director of the *Daily Telegraph* and Chairman of the Newsprint Raw Materials Committee was also a member of the CAEJ newsprint committee. The NPA argued that Britain was the hardest hit of countries by the Italian 'blockade'.

For CAEJ, the crisis over the supplementary quota was exacerbated by the EC's failure to resolve the issue of imports from Canada; as noted above, after 1 January 1984, producers in Nordic countries belonging to EFTA would have duty-free access to EC markets. CAEJ supported the Canadian suppliers who, in recent years, had exported 6–700,000 tonnes to the EC; CAEJ members did not want to be left without room for price manoeuvre with the Scandinavians.

In November 1983, after five years' efforts, the issue was still unresolved. In 1982 and 1983 – estimated Wilhelm Haferkamp for the EC Commission – Scandinavian countries accounted for 75 per cent and Canada for 25 per cent of EC newsprint imports (of 2.8 million tonnes). After 1 January 1984 would not this imbalance increase further? Canada argued that this would be contrary to GATT. And even CEPAC, the EC pulp and papermakers' association, which represents *inter alia* the European newsprint manufacturing industry, was fearful at the expansionism of Nordic newsprint manufacturers, when the transitional period of the

EC–EFTA treaty ended: 'The ambitions expressed by the Scandin-avian paper-makers are no secret. Some aspects of this danger lie in excessive investments, creating strategic over-capacity (already existing and being planned), and the financial aid our competitors get from their governments and financing bodies.' So argued the outgoing president of CEPAC, Jacques Calloud, in a speech to the association in November. Meanwhile, a report by the Brussels correspondent of the *Frankfurter Allgemeine Zeitung*, which found favour with the German NPA, the BDZV, argued that the interests of EC newspaper publishers were being sacrificed; the EC Commission was primarily concerned to support the Community's newsprint industry; the interests of member countries diverged; and the Council of Ministers failed to provide the necessary leadership. Many similarly reasoned articles appeared in the trade and quality Press in late 1983.[8]

Newsprint was traditionally one of the most important issues on the agenda of CAEJ meetings. With the approach of the 1 January 1984 deadline, and with the backlog of problems relating to the 1983 quota (10 per cent below that for 1982), CAEJ officials multiplied their contacts and meetings. At the CAEJ meeting of 19 September (Munich), Ernst Klaebel reported on the unsuccessful outcome of a CAEJ–EC meeting on 7 June. In Munich, the CAEJ prepared a memorandum for Viscount Davignon, the EC Vice-president, with whom a meeting was to be held on 7 October (Brussels). It was following the failure of the meeting that Klaebel sent Viscount Davignon the strongly worded CAEJ protest of 16 December, quoted above. CAEJ members could recall at least three occasions when Scandinavian producers sought to push up prices when they felt that had control of the market.

From March 1983 (when the CAEJ met in London) to March 1984 (when it met in Strasbourg), NPAs consulted with officials of the governments of EC member states (foreign, trade and industry ministries), with newsprint manufacturers both within and outside the Community, with GATT and other bodies involved in determining quotas and customs tariffs. Within the EC, the CAEJ policy of 'having access to supplies of newsprint at the lowest possible prices' was recognized by Vice-president Davignon, in his reply (in February) to Ernst Klaebel's letter of December. Within each member state, the national NPA sought, with varying degrees of success, the ear of the relevant minister. In Britain, Trade and Industry Minister Paul Channon proved responsive to

NPA arguments; he, in turn, advised Prime Minister Thatcher on newsprint policy discussed in the Council of Ministers and in the European Council (of heads of state and government). The CAEJ monitored, and sought to influence, the deliberations of the Committee of Permanent Representatives (COREPER), which (composed of the ambassadors of the member states appointed to the Community) considers all Commission proposals in detail before they are passed to the Ministers. It is sometimes said 'the Commission proposes, COREPER haggles and the Ministers decide'. CAEJ officials were not particularly impressed with the technical expertise informing the discussion of newsprint issues within COREPER.

CAEJ argued for the continued observance of arrangements for Community newsprint imports that in some respects dated back to 1967: a GATT-bound quota complemented by an autonomous quota. According to the Italian NPA, FIEG, Italy opposed these arrangements for the following reasons. Alone of the EC countries, Italy had a domestic production capacity that exceeded domestic demand. Until 1982, the government required newspaper publishers to purchase domestically produced newsprint if they wanted to benefit from state aid to the press. Under the 1981 press law, Italian newspapers seeking such aid were required to purchase Italian or EC-produced newsprint. Italian newspaper purchase of EC (non-Italian) newsprint rose to 38,000 tonnes in 1982. This aggravated the difficulties of Italian manufacturers who needed to sell 40 per cent of their production outside Italy. Hence the Italian government veto on EC countries seeking supplementary quotas from countries outside the EC.

At an EC Council of Ministers meeting of 21 November, the Italian minister wished to discuss neither the duty-free quotas for the rest of 1983 nor those for 1984. It appeared that if no decision was reached by 29 November, publishers of daily newspapers would have to pay duty on the newsprint needed for the rest of the year.

The British and German NPAs, which had already used up their 1983 quotas, were particularly indignant. It would be the first time since World War II that newspapers would have paid duty on newsprint. In London the NPA held a press conference; German and Belgian newspapers carried reports similar in tone to the *Guardian*'s 'Antiquated Italians could hit Fleet Street'.[9] Italy maintained its veto concerning the 1983 (supplementary) and 1984 quotas at the EC Council meeting of Ministers of Foreign Affairs, in Brussels on 29 November. Canada threatened EC Commission officials that it would bring an action before GATT. CAEJ members – notably the Belgian, British, Danish, German and Italian NPAs – continued to lobby hard. On 7 December, the Italian government apparently agreed to abandon its veto concerning the supplementary 1983 quotas; Ernst Klaebel stated that this 'victory' was due in part to the joint efforts of CAEJ member associations.

In short, after a lengthy campaign in the Press and in the lobby the CAEJ achieved many of its newsprint objectives for 1983. The duty-free newsprint quota was 2.5 million tonnes. At the end of the year, the quota was raised by 180,000 tonnes, when Italy finally withdrew its veto. The newspaper publishers had requested a supplementary quota of 250,000 tonnes. The total of 2,680,000 tonnes accorded was not – it subsequently transpired – sufficient to cover the needs of all countries during the closing months of 1983; Germany and Benelux had to pay duty for about 12,000 and 200 tonnes of newsprint respectively.[10] Thus, for the first time in years, daily newspapers had to pay duty on newsprint. As to 1984 – and subsequent quotas – CAEJ officers periodically recalled that CAEJ sought to import newsprint 'at the lowest possible prices' but did not wish to destroy newsprint production in Europe; of course, it should be recalled that, whereas the EC newsprint industry (CEPAC) employed some 5,000 people, the total CAEJ newspaper industry workforce was 250,000 people.

## CASE STUDY TWO: THE ADVERTISING INDUSTRY EURO-LOBBY

Established media interests – certain newspaper publishers or public service broadcasters, for example – often appear on the defensive when all about them is in a state of flux. The advertising industries, by contrast – during the past decade and in most of Europe – have often appeared those best placed to profit from the flux. The advertisers, agencies, media buyers and vendors often have different (even opposing) interests. But all have benefited from the growth of advertising expenditure during the past decade and, indeed, from the blurring of boundaries between advertising in particular and marketing in general.

It is generally recognized that total European advertising spend

– in a market of some 17–18 nation-states – increased during the 1980s and will continue to increase. Reputable industry estimates claim that western European advertising spend increased by 103 per cent in real terms between 1980 and 1987; TV advertising spend, during this period, accounted for the biggest single growth.[11] Furthermore, advertising represents something like 1 per cent of Gross Domestic Product in many countries – ranging, say, from 1.54 per cent in Spain to 0.62 per cent in Portugal.[12]

Industry sources claim that the EC now considers advertising is a 'vital component in the creation of the Single European Market'.[13]

Here, we shall briefly suggest how the advertising interest lobbied hard and successfully to influence the texts that now 'govern' broadcasting across Europe – the EC (twelve member states) Directive on 'television without frontiers', and the Council of Europe (twenty-four member states) Convention on 'cross-border television'.[14] To anticipate the most obvious conclusion: the advertising industries in Europe have developed efficient lobbying tactics that have seen off what, in the early 1970s, appeared potentially dangerous 'consumerist' pressures. Much water has passed under the bridge since the time when lobbying by consumerist associations was partly instrumental in the EC initiating proposals that culminated in a Directive on 'misleading advertising' (1984).

## 'EATING SPROUTING BRUSSELS . . .'

The story is complex and the actors involved are numerous. In 1972, the EC began consideration of a text on misleading advertising: the final version of the Directive, adopted twelve years later, was less favourable to the views of European consumer associations than initially appeared probable.[15] During the 1970s, various trade associations representing different advertising interests, and generally led by advertising agencies (the European Association of Advertising Agencies, EAAA), gradually learned to co-operate so as to better argue their common case in Brussels. In 1980, the European Advertising Tripartite (EAT) – 'a veritable alliance for action' – was set up to represent, at the European level, all the actors of the advertising industry. In 1990, the EAT had four types of member or associate member:

1  advertisers (the World Federation of Advertisers (WFA));
2  advertising agencies (EAAA);
3  trade associations of various advertising media or outlets, such
   as EC newspaper publishers associations (CAEJ);[16]
4  various national tripartites (such as Britain's Advertising Association) and informal advertising interest groupings.[17]

It is useful to distinguish two phases in the debate over Europe-wide
broadcasting – a debate in which advertising was an important but
not the sole issue. In June 1984, the EC Commission published
a green book (or discussion document) on 'television without
frontiers'.[18] In 1986 the EC Commission issued its draft Directive,
partly as a result of the debate that followed the publication of the
green book; and the same year the Council of Europe began to draft
the transfrontier broadcasting convention.

   In the pre-1986, as in the 1986–9 phase, the advertising
industries proved skilled not only in presentation and lobbying, but
also in the provision of the data central to an 'informed' debate. For
instance: the green paper contains seventeen appendices, intended
to provide a statistical overview of the funding, organization,
technologies and availability of broadcasting in Europe. Six of
these appendices came from a study conducted by Alastair Tempest
of the EAAA, 'New Communication Developments' (November
1983). At least two others were taken from studies compiled for
advertising groups (including J. Walter Thompson).

   The EC Commission lawyers (within Directorate-General III)
who drafted the green book[19] and those who drew up the 1986
draft Directive,[20] sought both to prove that broadcasting policy fell
within the remit of the EC Commission, and to show that freedom
to advertise should be guaranteed throughout the Community
(irrespective of national laws or self-regulatory practices and
variations). They used industry-supplied data to document their
case.[21] In a separate, but not unrelated, development, advertising
industry spokesmen argued that constitutional guarantees (at
national or European levels) of freedom of speech applied also
to the freedom of commercial speech, i.e. advertising.

   As the EC draft Directive and Council of Europe draft Convention went through various stages of textual modification in
1986–9 (with governments and various interested parties alter-
nately blowing hot and cold for the different proposals), the British
AA and the European EAT and EAAA proved some of the most

active lobbyists in ensuring that 'European advertising interests are taken into consideration'.[22]

By early 1988, concern centred on the 'blocks and breaks' issue. Trade lobbies pointed out that 'the original intention at least in the EC was to have a single framework of a liberalising nature';[23] 'commercial advertising has positive contributions to make and it is able and entitled to be carried out under the Treaty [of Rome]'.[24] By 1988, the lobbies mobilized their resources to oppose at least two of the measures that figured in both drafts: the fixing of specific maximum percentage of time per day and per hour for advertising; provisions for advertising to be mainly 'in blocks', and only to a limited extent in 'natural breaks'.

When it became apparent that the fixing of specific percentages was inevitable, the advertising interest helped ensure that the limits chosen were very liberal.[25] On 'blocks and breaks', the article (no. 7) in the EC Commission's amended draft Directive was reckoned, by mid-1988, to be 'broadly acceptable' to member states employing the natural break system; but the advertising lobby fought tooth and nail the equivalent article – initially no. 14, then no. 13 – in the draft COE Convention.

In June 1988, there appeared what purported to be the final draft of the Convention that European Communication Ministers were to examine in Stockholm the following November. Article 14 appalled commercial broadcasters practising the natural breaks system in general, and British advertising interests in particular: feature films could be interrupted only once by ads;[26] films made for TV, which included documentaries and series and serials which were longer than forty-five minutes, could contain one break for each complete period of forty-five minutes.[27]

British commercial TV was generally considered the most mature (and lucrative) in Europe and stood to lose most from article 14. It did not, however, appear judicious for the UK – either the government or the advertising trade associations – to appear to lead the opposition, both because of the deep-seated distrust of British motives within Europe and of latent anti-Americanism; in the past, European broadcasters tended to perceive UK commercial TV as heavily influenced by its US counterpart.[28] European advertising interests considered action imperative; while a COE Convention is not binding on individual countries, unless they choose to adopt it, it was proposed that the same wording concerning advertising breaks should also figure in the EC Directive. This would be binding on all

Community member states: 'these television restrictions therefore set severe limitations upon advertising opportunities represented by 1992'.[29]

The trade associations stepped up their lobbying and commissioned 'research' in their support. The British AA and Institute of Practitioners in Advertising (IPA) lobbied the Home Office, which accordingly pressed for the adoption of a text comparable to existing UK legislation.[30] In July 1988, this 'general formulation' was backed by the UK, Ireland, Luxembourg, Spain, the European Parliament and the EC Commission.[31] But the 'restrictive formulation', with the limits outlined above, still figured in the COE draft Convention.[32]

The EC Commission (D.G. III) requested Alastair Tempest (EAT) to prepare 'an assessment of the likely commercial damage which would result from the proposed regulations'.[33] The EAT worked with other European and other international trade lobbies and, in particular, the British AA and ITVA (the association of ITV broadcasters); it appears that the London bureau of an American advertising agency Young and Rubicam did much of the actual research.

Arguing for 'breaks' rather than 'blocks', the resulting EAT memorandum estimated that 'the convention's restrictions would cost commercial channels more than 15 per cent of their total revenue':[34] Britain's ITV and Channel 4 would lose 17.4 per cent, France's TF-1 22.4 per cent, etc.

The memorandum identified two categories of COE member state: (a) thirteen countries whose broadcasters operate the natural break system of broadcast advertising, of some two-and-a-half to three minutes, occurring during, as well as between programmes; and (b) countries, such as Germany, given to much rarer, but longer 'blocks' of advertising (of up to, say, ten to twelve minutes).[35] 'The long block system is not so cost effective or popular', argued the EAT memorandum organizations: 'organizations in those Member States are losing the opportunity of making their advertising facilities more competitive' and, accordingly, of generating 'more money for the widely desired European productions and co-productions of good quality'.[36]

The EAT memorandum was despatched to advertising industry lobbyists throughout Europe; the US-based International Advertising Association was also mobilized.[37] The explicit aim was to convince the government representatives of COE member states to

support the British government 'general formulation' as opposed to
the German-backed 'restrictive formulation', at the November 1988
Stockholm meeting that was to finalize the COE Convention.

British ministers were briefed and lobbied, as was the British
ambassador to the European assembly in Strasbourg. The EAT
and AA even compiled lists of the voting intentions of COE member
states. Countries were listed as:

**in favour** of the restrictive formulation (Austria, Belgium,
Germany, Liechtenstein, the Netherlands and Switzerland);
**possibly willing to compromise** (Cyprus, France, Portugal and
Turkey);
**hostile** (Ireland, Luxembourg, Malta and the UK).


## SUBSTANTIAL MODIFICATION

The end result of the co-operative lobbying by national, regional
and international advertising trade associations both dramatized
the importance of advertising in an economy (and in the funding
of broadcasting) and 'produced favourable "compromises"'.[38]

At the COE ministerial conference at Stockholm in November
1988, article 14 of the draft Convention was substantially modified
– in a sense favourable to the advertising interests – allowing up to
three breaks for advertising during transmission of feature films of
at least 110 minutes and of films made for television, whereas the
earlier draft allowed for only one break in feature films and one
for each forty-five minutes of broadcasting time for films made for
TV.

Series, light entertainment, etc. would be allowed a break every
twenty minutes. The old-established UK practice of breaking in
the middle of a half-hour programme, such as a situation comedy,
would end, except during the most lucrative programme, ITN's
News at Ten, the networked ITV news.[39]

The 'Stockholm compromise', concluded principally between
the UK and Germany, covered issues other than just advertising
(programme quotas, for instance). The advertising interest was
broadly satisfied – especially as the 'liberal' provisions in the
Convention also figured in the EC Directive.[40] Alastair Tempest
observed that 'a number of important issues have been resolved
in the ad industry's favour' – even if he added that there remained
many potential sources of aggravation.[41]

The issue of the advertising of tobacco products has for years seen the industry on the defensive, and in April 1989 the EC department dealing with the anti-cancer programme produced a draft Directive on tobacco advertising which led to yet further EAT lobbying.[42] Yet the advertising interest has won the main argument within the EC; this was by no means self-evident when one recalls consumerist influence on the EC Commission in the 1960s. As the EC prepares for the 'integrated' market of January 1993:

> advertising is considered as a vital component in the creation of the Single European market. Once the barriers are pulled down and goods and services can circulate freely, the EC recognises that producers must be able to promote their products in order to conquer new markets, or defend their present brand-shares against new competition.

This was the concept behind the advertising rules in the TV Directive – the creation of a broad framework of rules which member states must apply if they wish to see their products (in this case TV) crossing frontiers. Member states, according to the TV Directive, have the right to apply stricter rules *to their own broadcasts*, or less strict rules if they can guarantee that their broadcasting will not cross into other EC states (e.g. for local TV channels), but the central tenet is that 'the originating country retains the right (and obligation) to control the advertising which appears on broadcasts originating with its territory'.[43]

## CONCLUSION

Lobbying is an integral part of the functioning of western parliamentary democracies. This is true at the national level.[44] It is developing apace in the various fora and policy-making (and policy-influencing) centres of the European Community – of which the Council of Ministers, the Commission and the Assembly are merely the most visible. The media and advertising industries, therefore, do not act very differently from other sectorial interests in intensifying their lobbying activities. But the inter-relation of accelerated European integration, on the one hand, and the growth of advertising and of its importance to burgeoning communication outlets – including media 'old' and 'new' – on the other, strengthens the hand of communications industry lobbyists, and justifies their increased activities.

At the national level, newspaper publishers and advertising interests have a long and successful track-record as established lobbyists – Britain's Newspaper Publishers Association, the Newspaper Society and Advertising Association have many victories to their credit.[45] In the European debate on 'television without frontiers', several factors contributed to the success – by and large – of the advertising industry.

Whether discussed in the more economically-minded European Community, or in the Council of Europe (more concerned with human rights and cultural issues), the 'European' media concept,[46] in the age of 'television without frontiers', led to a reduction in the importance of public service broadcasters (and of their chief European association, the EBU) and to a preoccupation with new advertising-and-sponsorship-funded channels, several of which were transnational.

The press and advertising lobbies worked together and not in opposition – newspaper companies often support the development of commercial television, provided they can be involved. The arguments and joint interests of both industries were simple, cogent and commanded the support of most member organizations – less taxation and more advertising. The chief officers of the various trade associations enjoyed good access to politicians and Commission officials.

The media enjoy certain tactical advantages: politicians, of course, are attentive to their influence and public relations role (and perhaps grant their lobbyists more ready access than other lobbyists?); the media are used to moving quickly and to deploying their resources over a long campaign.

The legalistic and economic character of the EC, and the legalistic and cultural nature of the COE, played into the hands of the press and advertising lobbies. It was only in the early 1980s that the EC Commission first argued that broadcasting – as a service industry – fell within its remit. By contrast there have been advertising and media trade associations active internationally since at least the 1920s. Furthermore, these have often been heavily marked by American influence and expertise.

The FIEJ, CAEJ, and the American Newspaper Publishers Association (ANPA) have long deployed their lobbying skills in the name of the defence of press freedom: 'commercial speech is free speech' was a concept that first gained acceptance in the US. In the 1920s and even earlier, US advertising agencies – in response to the demands and expansion of US advertisers – set up shop in major European capitals; they have a long experience in seeing Europe as a totality. During the past ten to fifteen years, advertising agency trade associations have been prominent in persuading the advertising industry to get its European act together. The European Association of Advertising Agencies (EAAA) was the spur to the creation of the EATripartite. Likewise, British nationals – the AA's Roger Underhill and Mike Waterson, the EAAA's Ronald Beatson and EAT's Alastair Tempest – have been in the forefront of European advertising industry lobbying – marshalling arguments, masterminding tactics and presentational skills, and providing statistics. The latter is particularly noteworthy: EAT, EAAA and media trade associations provide the data informing EC policy debates; the industry actors help set the agenda.

In 1990 the twelve CAEJ member associations published 1,800 newspaper titles totalling 75 million copies daily, and 33,000 magazines. This was higher than Japan (68 million copies daily) and the US (63 million). But newspaper publishing in Europe was still marked by distinctive national traits – VAT rates on daily titles, for example, varied from 10 per cent in Ireland to a zero rate in Britain. Publishers feared European Commission regulatory and harmonization proclivities. 'Hands off our newspapers' was their rallying cry at the European assizes on the press in July 1991. Although their own house is divided, newspaper publishers lobby as one against 'Brussels'. Groups such as Prisa, Burda, Mondadori, Rothermere, News Corporation and Elsevier are leading members of such lobbies.

In the 1970s, lobbying by consumerist associations was partly instrumental in the EC Commission initiating proposals, which ultimately led to a text on 'misleading advertising'. By 1990, the boot was definitely on the other foot: advertising and media industry lobbyists appear more skilful, and certainly have more resources, than bodies representing other views in the debate over the future of the media in Europe.

# Part II

# Media moguls in western Europe

# Chapter 5

# Euro-media moguls

A 'media mogul' we define as a person who owns and operates major media companies, who takes entrepreneurial risks, and who conducts these media businesses in a personal or eccentric style.

Given this last characteristic – personal or eccentric style – any two media moguls must differ from each other. We have in mind such prototypes as Hearst, Murdoch and Berlusconi; but even these rather extreme examples do not possess all of the media mogul characteristics in full.

Our use of the term media mogul indicates a person who largely built up his own media empire; this entrepreneurial element can include the launching of new media enterprises, but in practice often consists largely of buying up, and taking over, existing media companies. This entrepreneurial and growth aspect distinguishes the mogul from the 'crown prince'. The crown prince is the second-generation media entrepreneur, who typically inherits major media properties from his pioneering father. The inheritor in some cases is not a son, but a widow, nephew, or other relative.

Thus the initial media mogul is distinguished from his heir, typically a crown prince. Separate, also, by our definition, is the 'baron'. The mogul may be supported by several barons, who normally manage divisions or companies within the mogul's larger interests. The baron can be a chief executive, he may also take entrepreneurial risks, but he is not the ultimate owner or controller of the overall enterprises.

The pure or classic example of the media mogul confines his business activities largely to the media. Most media moguls, of course, own some non-media businesses. There are also examples of entrepreneurs who are primarily captains in some other industrial field, but in addition own and operate major media interests. The captain of industry who also had major media interests became a common pattern in 1980s Italy.[1] We are interested in this latter model – the industrialist/media mogul – although our main concern is with the 'pure' media mogul.

Another basic problem – for definition and analysis – is the media mogul's unusual relationship to publicity. As the owner-and-operator of media enterprises, the mogul can command personal publicity on a massive scale; he is also of special interest to his fellow and rival media moguls and managers. The mogul exercises a special fascination for all journalists and publicists – for whom he may be a past, or potentially future, employer. Moreover the mogul's distinctive personal style often involves a highly distinctive personal publicity stance.

Some media moguls are self-publicists on a grand scale, but other moguls seek to minimize publicity, seldom give interviews and avoid photographers. Most moguls, it seems, pursue some combination of high and low publicity profile – for example carefully limiting their public appearances while talking profusely and 'not for attribution' to selected journalists.

Great public concern and major controversy focus on media moguls in general and certain individuals in particular. We must remember, however, that relatively few people both read and understand the media mogul's annual report – indeed some moguls operate private companies or control public companies through private trusts. Few people – even academic content analysts – attempt to inspect or assess the full range of media output from even a single mogul's media enterprises. Public debate and controversy inevitably relies quite heavily on the media coverage of relevant moguls. Thus the mogul's media image – contrived both by himself and his employees as well as by rival moguls and their employees – is a formidable barrier to objective understanding.

In 1980s France, for example, media moguls such as Robert Hersant were commonly referred to with the prefix 'citizen' – imagery which derives from the French love affair with *Citizen Kane* and Orson Welles. Yet this movie itself involves layer upon layer of myth and fiction. Leaving aside the question of how much Orson Welles contributed to the script, *Citizen Kane* told a story which departed in numerous major and minor respects from the reality of William Randolph Hearst's career as a media mogul. Hearst's influence outside the US was minimal. Even within the US in 1935 – at the height of Hearst's political and media importance – his twenty-six daily newspapers had only 13.6 per cent of the national daily circulation.[2] Hearst certainly conducted his aggressive tabloid papers in a highly dictatorial manner but his well documented personal and social life, and his relationship with Marion Davies, bore little resemblance to the startling images of *Citizen Kane*.

With television, of course, the whole business of constructing media images has changed. In recent times Silvio Berlusconi, who has produced perhaps the most remarkable of all media mogul business careers, has also proved himself the most astute and the most *bravura* personal image builder.

But it is the media moguls' political connections and electoral support which lead to the greatest public controversy, the greatest anxiety among politicians and the greatest disputation as to the relevant facts. Hearst's newspapers were concentrated in large cities (such as New York, Chicago, San Francisco, Pittsburgh and Boston); Hearst's belligerent opposition to President Roosevelt and other Democrats had little electoral success but he was accused of delaying US entry into the World War II. In Australia Keith Murdoch and his son Rupert Murdoch played an actively involved, sometimes leading, role in nearly every national election between 1931 and 1987.[3] Rupert Murdoch's newspapers were also highly partisan and belligerent in British national elections of the 1970s and 1980s; and Murdoch was no less partisan in city, state and national elections in the US. Axel Springer in West Germany and Robert Hersant in France were also belligerent right-wing partisans of the mass circulation Press in a succession of elections.

In addition to delivering partisan support at national elections, media moguls may actively influence the evolving national political agenda through their ownership of prestige newspapers. Axel Springer (*Die Welt*), Robert Hersant (*Le Figaro*) and Rupert Murdoch (*The Times* of London) all by the 1980s controlled prestige dailies; and all of the leading Italian dailies came to be controlled either by industrialist media moguls or by Berlusconi. Such prestige dailies have a tendency to lapse into financial loss which makes them vulnerable to mogul takeover.

Media moguls also tend to be politically involved in yet another way. The moguls seek favours from their political friends – in return for electoral and agenda-setting support. There is also the implied threat that if a business favour is not granted, then a less friendly editorial stance could result. In their business activities, and

Can be seen with Murdoch + Thatcher.

especially in their attempts to buy new properties and to enter new media fields, media moguls come into political conflict with media law and regulation on several fronts. Most obviously in entering new fields, media moguls tread on uncertain legal ground; this typically leads to court cases. Moguls come into conflict with independent, or quasi-autonomous, regulatory agencies; but moguls may also face regulatory decisions which lie within the direct power of politicians in office. Finally moguls face the threat or promise of friendly or damaging new legislation.

In Italy this political–business bargaining and deal-making is especially prevalent, especially potent in terms of its business consequences. Silvio Berlusconi in the 1980s became the only individual in any nation outside Latin America to acquire effective personal control over three national television channels; but he did not achieve this without political opposition – or support. Indeed in all the areas just mentioned Berlusconi and his Fininvest company had a cliff-hanger existence, well worthy of serial fiction tradition. Berlusconi faced a long succession of court, regulatory, administrative and legislative threats. Berlusconi's dubious legal position was partially regularized by (1985) national legislation introduced by the then Prime Minister Bettino Craxi who was also Berlusconi's long-time personal friend and political ally. Berlusconi was also friendly with other Italian Prime Ministers, such as the Christian Democrat Giulio Andreotti.

There are other examples of regulatory/political decisions which are not merely helpful to the media mogul but which largely determine his business success or failure. Robert Hersant's 1975 purchase of *Le Figaro*, which established him as a major French media mogul, depended heavily on his own political influence in general and upon acceptance by the then President Giscard d'Estaing and Prime Minister Chirac in particular. The crucial event in the massive growth of the Thomson interests was Roy Thomson's move into North Sea Oil – a move facilitated by his friendly political connections. Murdoch's purchase of *The Times*, the *Sunday Times* and *Today* in Britain all depended on favourable Thatcher interpretations of ambiguously worded monopoly law. Successive Australian governments were even more indulgent of Murdoch (and his belligerently partisan Australian papers) in a series of decisions, which ultimately allowed Murdoch – despite acquiring US citizenship – to control some two thirds of all Australian daily newspaper circulation.

These regulatory and legislative favours, in return for partisan mogul support, are especially transparent in two areas. One is in the body of law and regulation which governs press diversification into commercial television; the second area is monopoly law and regulation within the press itself. Even the United States has monopoly legislation which provides certain special exemptions and favours to newspaper owners. All of the four largest population countries of western Europe have since 1945 evolved bodies of specific press monopoly legislation. In Italy such legislation limits one owner to a maximum 20 per cent of press sales. In both West Germany and France lengthy press monopoly debates have focused on Axel Springer and Robert Hersant. The legislative results in both cases were deliberately weak and full of loopholes; similar weaknesses were evident in Britain.

Are moguls, then, party political loyalists? The answer seems to be no. While usually favouring the political right, mogul political allegiance tends to be opportunistic. Rupert Murdoch has on occasions in Australia, Britain and the US supported the more leftward party. Berlusconi in Italy has inclined to the left. And even the low-profile and balance-seeking Bertelsmann in West Germany has found itself more friendly with the Social Democrats. But moguls are not always loyal and certainly not to a party. Mogul political alliances tend to be with individual leading politicians, not with parties. Berlusconi in the 1980s was a Craxi-ite, not a Socialist; Murdoch's outspoken loyalty was to Thatcher, not to the British Conservatives.

This personal approach to politics is in line with the highly personal style, typical of the classical media mogul. As an own-and-operate entrepreneur the mogul is a risk-taker who, to a greater or lesser extent, follows his personal inclinations. We, of course, are primarily concerned with successful media moguls. Too much eccentricity in personal business style may have contributed to many individual inabilities to make a success of the media mogul role. But looking at broadly successful moguls, we are dealing with people who have not only indulged their personal hunches and played to their individual strengths, but have done so with considerable commercial success. They have themselves put together a group of media companies, which they now run, often out of quite a small central office. There may be relatives and long-time friends in senior positions. The mogul's working life tends to spill into his private life and vice versa. Business strategy and personal characteristics tend to merge into a single business–personal image. This merging seems to appeal to both show business and financial journalists; it makes for volatility, not least in terms of image and reputation, but also in terms of business reality and financial performance. The mogul, keenly aware of his larger-than-life image and his previous spectacular record of successful risk-taking, may be inclined to plunge into yet larger risks; business associates and bankers – also dazzled by image and track record – may encourage yet further leaps into the financial unknown.

Media moguls with track records of successful profit-making are of considerable interest to the financial services and banking industry. The media in the 1970s and 1980s were seen as a growth industry; advertising expenditure increased, while new technologies led to new markets for media outputs – cable, VCR and audio. The New York and London stock markets each have a lengthy list of media companies. This led not only to an active market in media company shares but also to an active market making loans to media companies. Media moguls such as Murdoch and Hersant, moreover, had a strong interest in bank-borrowing, which enabled them to avoid issuing new shares and thus reducing their own control. Hence media moguls became significant figures also in the financial world, beyond the scale warranted by the size and strength of their companies. The large bank loans fuelled additional growth and purchases, additional regulatory decisions, additional celebrity and notoriety. Under radically changed financial conditions in 1989–91, heavy bank debt found Rupert Murdoch and several prominent media moguls in severe business difficulty.[4]

## DIFFERING NATIONAL STYLES OF MEDIA MOGULS

In the 1980s one media industry trend was the attempt of major companies to bestride the Atlantic. The goal of the transatlantic company was pursued by media moguls in general and by Rupert Murdoch in particular. But the US and Europe have quite different media mogul histories.

The American press grew explosively in the late nineteenth century and produced, in men like Pulitzer and Hearst, the first wave of media moguls. When the American film industry appeared, it quickly produced its founding father owner-operators. The same occurred also in radio and television; and similar figures appeared in advertising.

In Europe the emergence of media moguls took a different form. Various conceptions of state or 'public' broadcasting predominated in Europe; funding was largely by licence fee. European broadcasting quickly produced 'baronial' radio executives (such as Reith in Britain and Bredow in Germany) who operated, but did not own, the public system. Broadcasting moguls only arose in Europe with the much later emergence of commercial television.

Compared to the US, the Press in Europe has remained more closely linked to party politics. If newspapers are owned by parties, trade unions or prominent politicians, there is little room for the emergence of a separate breed of media-based mogul. Just as media have been owned for political reasons, a parallel phenomenon has been ownership by big business. Phrases such as the 'perfume press' (Coty) were proverbial around Europe.[5] In inter-war Germany, Alfred Hugenberg's interests spread from the Ruhr Steel industry into newspapers, magazines, news agencies and advertising, as well as into dominance of the film industry.

In the United States for much of the twentieth century the development of giant multi-media empires was restricted by anti-trust legislation and action. This lengthy anti-trust tradition has meant that the USA has retained – compared with Europe – a relatively wide spread and large number of significant media companies. In 1987 the ten largest US newspaper companies had only 43 per cent of the market, the five largest book companies 34 per cent and even in feature film production the five largest companies had only 50 per cent.[6]

One consequence is that the leading European media companies are quite large, even by world and American standards. In the mid and late 1980s especially this facilitated a number of takeovers of American media companies by European companies and media moguls.

Europe, of course, has a very long media history. The Albert Bonnier who presided over the Bonnier company, controlling Sweden's two largest daily papers and many other publications until he died in 1989, was the great grandson of the Bonnier who founded the company in 1837. But Sweden is atypical – in the length and strength of its free press tradition and in its (related) resistance to television advertising.

More typical of much of western Europe is France where in 1944–5 everything (in theory at least) began afresh. Broadcasting across Europe was re-established under some combination of state and/or political sponsorship with sheltered financing. In the brave new post-1945 world the media had supposedly been re-established as small-scale, correctly democratic, and protected against any media Napoleons of the future.

In retrospect, however, the post-1945 conditions merely made probable the arrival of a new wave of media moguls. In Germany regional press arrangements left a vacuum at the national level which was partly filled by Axel Springer. In France, also, a very different restoration led to a somewhat similar result – a very strong regional press, with one national press mogul (Robert Hersant) in a dominant position.

In 1980 television advertising was still severely restricted across most of western Europe. Typically it was used to supplement licence fee income from public broadcasting systems. In 1980 the UK had much the largest television advertising expenditure level. Britain, therefore it might seem, had the best opportunity in Europe to produce some TV moguls. But while the years 1955–80 did see Britain outspend the rest of Europe on TV advertising, its ITV system was still too regulated and fragmented to allow much opportunity for full mogul expression.

Sidney Bernstein, Lew Grade and Roy Thomson were all successful TV entrepreneurs at the British regional level. All three of these cases also illustrate the tendency of television success to generate more profits than regulators will allow to be reinvested in television; thus the profits are forced into diversification. Independent Television regulations, designed to prevent single company – or single mogul – dominance within TV, thus directly contributed to the spreading of such influence across the media.

After these British ITV moguls – who had their most dramatic advances in a few years around 1960 – there was a distinct pause. It was some two decades until the next great European television mogul emergence. Within a few years before and after 1980 Silvio Berlusconi emerged as a television mogul of much greater proportions than any seen previously in Europe. Television's share of Italian advertising nearly doubled in 1980–5. In terms of ECU millions this TV expenditure rose from 269 in 1980 to 1,259 in 1985. Berlusconi achieved direct personal control of some 45 per cent of all Italian TV viewing, with additional indirect influence on other channels. This was only possible because of a combination of unique features in the Italian case. These included the complete lack in Italy of any effective general anti-monopoly law. Italy also had a special political balance which in turn led to reluctance or inability to legislate effectively for broadcasting. Italian courts have repeatedly been in conflict with each other on broadcasting issues. The Berlusconi phenomenon also played some part in drawing Italy's leading industrialists into media ownership.

Thus in the 1980s Italian media developed within a distinctive national political economy and this, in turn, encouraged a distinctive Italian school of media moguls. Britain also continued in the 1980s to develop its own distinctive patterns of media and media moguls. In Britain the legal and regulatory framework altered little; but there were further developments in the integration of British media with those of the United States. Britain's distinctive national style included a number of transatlantic media moguls.

Both Germany and France entered the 1980s with their media still constrained within an established framework of legislation, including a strongly regulated broadcasting system. Germany and France each had only one major example of a (press) mogul – Springer and Hersant. But in the 1980s both France and Germany moved decisively towards a much more deregulated and commercial pattern of broadcasting. Both countries retained a highly distinctive national media culture which powerfully shaped the national school of media moguls.

In Germany the regional state control of public broadcasting was very slowly and gradually undermined by Conservative politicians, using federal Post Office initiatives in cable television. But the German style remained highly cautious, step-by-step, and legalistic. In keeping with this cautious and legally correct national style, German media moguls mainly adopted low-profile publicity stances.

In France the emerging national mogul style of the 1980s was rather different. France in 1986–8 took a sudden leap into deregulation, more channels and commercial broadcasting. But the media mogul pattern, like the French media pattern itself, remained confused, if not chaotic. The French style was European both in combining elements of the Italian, German and British patterns and also involving new elements of trans-European and international media and media moguls.

# Chapter 6

# Media moguls in Britain

British media history has had few dates marking revolutionary changes; a history of gradual and step-by-step change has produced a particular pattern not only of media, but of media moguls. The year 1945 in Britain brought neither a reborn Press nor a newly minted newspaper mogul. British-style commercial television arrived in 1955 wrapped in compromise and regulation. There was no sudden explosion of several new commercial channels; Britain's ITV, born in 1955, remained the sole advertising-financed channel for the next twenty-seven years and it produced no British Berlusconi.

This national tradition of step-by-step media change was established in the 1855 removal of the taxes on newspapers; more precisely this removal was in fact spread over three dates.

The emergence of the British media and media moguls in the twentieth century has gone through several phases. The first of these phases occurred around 1900 and involved Britain's first modern media mogul, Lord Northcliffe; he launched the *Daily Mail* (1896), which ninety-five years later still sold 1.8 million copies daily. From humble beginnings with children's publications, Northcliffe crossed over into evening and then morning newspapers. By 1910 he owned three London morning papers (*Daily Mail*, *Daily Mirror*, *The Times*) with 39 per cent of all national morning sales and his *Evening News* had 31 per cent of London evening sales. He also owned Sunday papers, the *Observer* and the *Weekly Dispatch*; these London papers in 1910 sold 11 million copies per week.[1]

Northcliffe had all the mogul characteristics; he took risks, he built his holdings by launching new titles as well as rescuing old ones. He personally was the dominant operator and owner, although he also pioneered the stock market flotation of his enterprise as a public company. He was highly controversial (attacking the war leadership in 1916), politically interventionist, and idiosyncratic to the point of ultimate insanity.

Northcliffe also was the first of the British 'Press lords'. The latter term neatly encapsulates a British tradition which continued for the first fifty years of the twentieth century. Broadcasting existed (until 1955) only in the form of the BBC. From 1900 to 1955 media owners were Press lords; throughout this period six or eight companies between them owned most of Britain's national and provincial circulation. These companies and their press lords (or lords-to-be) constituted a loose cartel. There was a balance between competition and semi-monopoly or duopoly in particular sub-markets (such as provincial cities).

In this era of press lords and a loose press cartel, innovation tended to come from outside. A prime example was the Canadian, Max Aitken, who purchased the small *Daily Express*. Aitken joined the cartel as Lord Beaverbrook, and became a genuine own-and-operate mogul; his combination of the *Daily Express*, *Sunday Express* and *Evening Standard* became a formidable media force. Beaverbrook also fully satisfied the eccentricity canon; he was a vigorous propounder of his own eccentric pro-Empire views.

Beaverbrook illustrated another major theme of British media and media moguls in the twentieth century. Not only have most important changes in the British media been imported from North America (if possible in muted form) but often the chief individual innovators have been North American moguls. An element of truly British media compromise has led also to United States ideas being introduced into the British media by Canadian moguls. Beaverbrook was followed in the 1950s by Roy Thomson and in the 1980s by Conrad Black (all three from eastern Canada).

In addition, of course, Rupert Murdoch came to Britain from Australia and moved on from London to New York. This Murdoch progression illustrates two other relevant points. Australia obviously shares with the US and Canada the English language and other Anglo-American media traditions. But Australia and Canada were also countries in which aggressive commercial competition continued in the media, largely unabated in the 1940s and 1950s; this was in contrast to Britain where even the pre-1939 level of competition was largely suspended for many years. Roy Thomson had experienced commercial broadcasting in provincial Ontario. When Rupert Murdoch inherited a daily and Sunday newspaper in

Adelaide, he entered (at age 22) a bruising circulation war with the competition; this was in 1952, when newsprint rationing and muted competition still prevailed in Britain.

The Thomson and Murdoch stories also combine the theme of London as entrepôt – a place of passage not just for media products, but also for media moguls. Thomson (Roy) and Murdoch exercised their media mogul skills in London; Thomson's son (Kenneth) and Murdoch both subsequently went west to New York and Toronto. The magnetic appeal of 'going west' for British media moguls took yet another form in the 1980s – massive purchases of US media properties making for companies British in name, but heavily American in terms of revenue.

The quickening appeal of American media acquisitions in the 1980s had 'push' as well as 'pull' aspects. The pull, of course, was the size and openness of the US media market and the possibility of making purchases during a weak dollar era. But the push out of London derived from the newly configured loose British media cartel of the 1980s. Media ownership was still dominated by a very small club of well established owners, few – if any – of whom were willing to sell.

## 1955: THE CONSTRAINTS OF ITV OWNERSHIP

When commercial television began (initially in London only) in 1955, media entrepreneurs emerged into prominence who were quite different from either BBC managers or the established entrepreneurs of the Press. We will look briefly at three of these – Bernstein, Grade and Thomson.

The 1947–9 Royal Commission on the Press reported on a scene which changed little between 1939 and 1955 (paper rationing largely froze circulation level). The *Daily Mail* and *Daily Express* groups had dominant owners – Lord Rothermere (nephew of Northcliffe) and Lord Beaverbrook; Lord Kemsley and Lord Camrose, with their families, owned two other major groups. Lord Astor owned *The Times*. Of the seven major enterprises only two (those owning the *Daily Mirror* and the *Daily Herald*) were not controlled by the press lords and their families.[2] The press lords in 1954–5 saw commercial television as an enemy to be resisted; and the new Independent Television Authority (ITA) initially had great difficulty in attracting even a modest level of press investment in the new television franchises.

Consequently the ITA had no choice but to award franchises to those who were willing to take the risks and accept the inevitable early losses. The ITV system, from 1955 to 1968, was dominated by four companies, three of which had their origins in the cinema and show business. Initially the key company was Associated–Rediffusion (London weekday) but it and ABC were forced into a merger in 1968.

This left Associated Television (ATV), initially in London and the Midlands and later the Midlands only, as the leading company of the first twenty-six years (1955–81) of ITV. And the dominant figure within ATV was Lew (later Lord) Grade. Grade was a show business agent and variety show impresario; his favourite product was *Sunday Night at the London Palladium*. Lew Grade was born in Tsarist Russia in 1906, of Jewish parents who emigrated to London. He was the eldest of three brothers, all of whom became theatrical talent agents. By the 1960s the three Grade brothers had established a remarkable citadel of show business talent and performance. A celebrated investigation by the *Sunday Times* in 1966 revealed that the three Grade brothers – Lew, Bernard and Leslie – via a large number of linked companies, ran an interlocking cartel of agent-contracted talent, live performance venues, and televised variety entertainment. The Grades were agents for nearly all the leading actors and entertainers; they dominated the major London theatres and also the main provincial theatre circuits as well as the impresario, show-creating, function. Finally Lew Grade at ATV was the leading force in televised entertainment which was networked throughout Britain and sold abroad.[3]

The cartel was built on several versions of 'packaging' and cross-over between media which enabled the Grades to extract multiple fees, and to generate massive free promotion for their own interests. Contracted talent would appear at Grade-controlled theatres, which would then be televised by Lew Grade at ATV. Networking on ITV would enhance the performers' fame, leading – for example – to film roles and additional agent's fees.

Lew Grade and his brothers ran a cartel within a cartel. The larger cartel was the ITV, commercial television system itself; Lew Grade became the operator – not the owner – of one major company within the ITV cartel. As such he was one of a club of barons who ran ITV.

In the field of talent, however, Lew Grade was more than one baron. He was in the classic mould (and supported by the familiar mogul family back-up) – the own-and-operate mogul of the rights to handle the cream of British theatrical and entertainment talent. Clear conflicts of interest (such as being both talent agent and theatre owner) were allowed to persist, not only during and after the war but also into the risky early days of ITV. There was no prohibition on *brothers* who ran formally separate companies but in fact acted as an informal cartel. Another negative was the initial lack of objection from other ITV companies, who were all members of the ITV network system and extracted profits from the right to screen Grade entertainment in their own regions. A final negative was the relative lack of public concern about a cartel in mere show business and non-political entertainment.

Lew Grade exported his TV series (*Danger Man*, *The Saint*) to US TV syndication and won Queen's Awards for exporting achievement. He increasingly developed a mogul style – although he lacked the full ownership substance at ATV. The breadth of the show business cartel, and the constraints of ITV, muted major risk-taking. The extent to which Lew Grade had been a protected monopolist was suggested by his end-of-career efforts at feature-film making, which were commercially disastrous (*Raise the Titanic*).

A second ITV mogul was Sidney (later Lord) Bernstein of Granada, an ITV company in the Manchester region since 1956. Granada was a somewhat unusual ITV company in being dominated by one man (and his brother) from the outset. Sidney Bernstein also was Jewish but he was a more sophisticated and intellectual figure than Lew Grade. He was a genuine own-and-operate mogul. He was unique among leading ITV founding figures in being loosely identified with the Labour Party; this probably assisted Granada in being the only ITV opening major company to survive into the 1990s still with a major contract – the ITA/IBA would not want to defranchise the only left-of-centre major company. Bernstein was also adept at cultivating Granada's northern and quality image. Granada in practice was increasingly run from Golden Square in London and engaged in a policy of systematic diversification. The early massive profits were used to diversify into television set rentals and sales. By 1989 rental and retail (mainly TV sets, VCRs and computers) accounted for half of turnover and the television franchise only for 17 per cent. Alex Bernstein (nephew of Sidney) was the dominant shareholder (and trustee) – the presiding crown prince.

Perhaps the most widely influential of the early ITV moguls was Roy (later Lord) Thomson; he struck gold twice – once in Scottish Television and secondly in North Sea oil. Thomson came from small-town Ontario; his major achievements occurred in Britain, *After I Was Sixty* – as he reported in a book.[4] Thomson was a true own-and-operate mogul. He was, on the British scene, idiosyncratic mainly as a major media proprietor who remained obsessed with the apolitical pursuit of money. A hallmark of the Thomson interests under the succeeding crown prince, Kenneth Thomson, was a concern with eliminating losses – hence the sale of Times Newspapers to Murdoch in 1981; Thomson also was unusual in demanding 20 per cent profits on all operations.

Thomson's early years were spent in a dour slogging struggle in the small towns of rural Ontario. The basic skills were keeping costs low and selling advertising; Thomson also became a specialist in buying out small radio stations and newspapers, and ultimately television stations. His first success was the acquisition and control of Scottish Television in 1956 – his famous 'licence to print money'. What others saw as a risk, he knew – from his Canadian experience – was a safe bet. He was lucky in his previous knowledge combined with his instant Scottish identity as recent purchaser of *The Scotsman* newspaper. He was lucky also in the timing; he was applying for the franchise while ITV in London was still losing heavily, but when Scottish Television began – 31 August 1956 – the worst unprofitable months were already past. The Scottish Television profits were used to buy more newspapers, notably in 1959 the Kemsley group, which included the *Sunday Times*; eight years later *The Times* (daily) was also acquired.

Thomson was already diversifying out of media-based advertising dependence, notably into the travel business. Thomson evidently was also looking for other diversifications. In 1964 he became a Lord – Thomson probably saw this as a way of getting back at the city slickers in Toronto. Meanwhile with his generous rescue of *The Times* in 1967, Thomson became a respected exhibit of the London establishment. He was doubtless well aware that this respect (and condescension) could have business benefits; it did in 1971 when three American oil companies wanted a respectable British partner for their entry to North Sea oil exploration. Occidental, Getty and Allied Chemical were so eager to have Thomson in the consortium that they offered to lend him the money for his 20 per cent share. The Occidental-led consortium quickly struck oil on a grand scale

(Piper and Claymore fields); Thomson's connections – based on newspaper ownership – had led to a cash gusher. Thomson himself died five years later, aged 82.

Kenneth Thomson (the crown prince) based himself in Toronto and presided over a slow migration of the Thomson interests and cash to Toronto. Thomson in 1989 decided to sell its remaining oil interests and to move International Thomson from London back across the Atlantic. Thomson is the dominant owner of newspapers and department stores in Canada; it is also a leading owner (with Gannett) of *small* US daily newspapers. Thomson is an extreme example of a highly fragmented structure of subsidiaries (and a high number of separate titles) combined with demanding central financial guidelines. Kenneth Thomson has retained his father's obsession with 'market dominance' (i.e. monopoly) and high profit margins. Thomson successfully focused on two media areas where this is achievable – one being the traditional Thomson business of small-town (monopoly) daily newspapers. Secondly, Thomson discovered how to make 20 per cent plus profits out of books – a target which Thomson's British publishing activities long failed to achieve. The answer was to acquire dominance in specialist business and professional areas where high prices can be charged because the customer is often a company or business. The other key to profits is that – after many years of trial and error – successful synergy was increasingly achieved in the 1980s between print publishing and data-on-screens.[5] Thomson became in the 1980s the largest medical publisher in the world, and then also targeted legal publishing; in May 1989, Thomson bought The Lawyers Publishing Company (a US law publisher) for $810 million. As the disparate elements were assembled into 'The Thomson Corporation', Kenneth Thomson was revealed as a low-profile media billionaire – he and his family owned two thirds of a company with annual sales of over $5 billion.[6]

## MAXWELL – MOGUL OF PRINT

Maxwell and Murdoch have been the two most remarkable moguls of British media history. Each began life far away from Britain, each focused initially on print media. Both have been largely financiers – buyers (and sellers) of media properties. Both have been own-and-operate entrepreneurs. Both have been politically partisan – Maxwell was a Labour MP, while Murdoch was a populist conservative and Thatcherite. Both men's careers have gone through a number of distinct phases.

The differences, however, are equally remarkable. Maxwell's career has been mercurial – with many zig-zags and ups and downs; Murdoch's career has been more directed and controlled. While both men were poker players and business risk-takers on a grand scale, their styles of acquisition were quite different. Maxwell has been more like a conjuror, performing a succession of startling tricks but also sometimes dropping his cards on the floor; he has seemed to enjoy selling companies even more than he enjoyed buying them. Murdoch's style has been more relentless – a combination of long-term strategy with short-term opportunism and quick response; at any time he has relied on a few main profit centres, while he has nursed one or two current losers and pursued one or two major current targets. Murdoch has evolved a broad strategy, moving ever westward from Adelaide newspapers to American television. Maxwell's more mercurial style, and repeated changes of direction, seem to have taken him from book and journal publishing via much else back to book, journal and data publishing.

For Murdoch Britain has been a stopping point between Australia and New York; Murdoch's identity has changed only from American-Aussie to Aussie-American. Maxwell loves and understands the United States; he is a true western European; and he is a genuine British patriot whose finances are based in Liechtenstein.

It is in their relationships with the financial world that Maxwell and Murdoch have most differed. Maxwell has won admiration for his skills in publishing, printing and trade union negotiation; but the financial world has had little confidence in his balance sheets or his financial stamina. Murdoch is admired as the most complete own-and-operate media mogul; he is seen as having a unique combination of skills in finance and journalism, in print and television, and in his three chosen locations. Murdoch's massive borrowing is seen against strong underlying assets and his financial track record.

Robert Maxwell was the son of a poor Czech Jewish labourer who was murdered by the Gestapo; in 1989 he was described in a rival publication as the eleventh wealthiest Briton, worth about $1 billion.[7] His career, however, has been far from a steady climb; through most of the 1970s he was an ex-mogul, an apparently spent force. During World War II Maxwell had several nationalities, several different names, and several different fighting units; he won the Military Cross for reckless bravery and was promoted to the rank of Captain. He lost several relatives in German concentration camps. Shortly after the war, however, he was in business with Germans – he had seen the possibilities of publishing war-time German scientific research for the outside world.

Maxwell is typically engaged at any one time in both buying and selling a number of companies. He relishes conducting negotiations in several adjacent rooms simultaneously; he is a linguist of exceptional ability; he has an insatiable appetite for self-publicity. His high publicity profile and his extravagant behaviour as a newspaper owner in the late 1980s antagonized many journalists. Consequently Maxwell has not been adequately recognized as a pioneer; he has pioneered a number of British innovations which other moguls – notably Rupert Murdoch – have happily adopted.

Maxwell's initial great entrepreneurial success was in scientific publishing. His first step was a 1947 deal with Ferdinand Springer to distribute Springer Verlag scientific journals in the outside world.[8] Starting in 1948 Maxwell built up Pergamon Press in Britain, Europe and the US as a major publisher of academic and specialist journals and books. In 1969 Maxwell suddenly decided to sell out to the American Saul Steinberg and his Leasco company. This was the great disaster of Maxwell's career – an impetuous, ill-conceived deal – leading to a government inspectors' 1971 report which denounced Maxwell as 'unfit to run a public company'.

A decade later, Maxwell returned to centre stage by beginning the long-delayed reform of the London printing trade unions. In July 1980 Maxwell commenced his takeover of the British Printing Company (BPC). Its disastrous commercial record enabled Maxwell to buy BPC for £10 million – a small fraction of the asset value; within two years Maxwell closed five printing plants, radically reduced the labour force and returned BPC to sizeable profits. Maxwell also purchased another major magazine printing company, Odham's, with similar profitable results. Maxwell's technique involved confronting the printing trade unions; this in turn depended partly on his personal negotiating belligerence and experience, as well as partly on Thatcher's trade union legislation from 1981 onwards. Meanwhile, Maxwell, the printing mogul, was generating large profits.

Maxwell's third phase of innovation finally led him to newspapers – the 1984 purchase of the *Daily Mirror*, *Sunday Mirror* and *People* from the disillusioned Reed Group. His success in cutting back on manning and out-negotiating the print unions continued; he was less successful in other aspects of newspaper management. Maxwell at first shamelessly used the *Daily Mirror* as a pulpit, and sales fell. He mismanaged the launch in 1987 of a new London evening newspaper which was quickly closed. Maxwell had pioneered major manning cuts in the super-competitive daily tabloid field and he was also well ahead of Murdoch in the successful use of colour in a three million sale daily. But after about four years his interest in newspapers seemed to recede. Maxwell bought up much of the (largely inactive) British cable industry and dabbled in cable channels; at one stage he owned three professional football teams.

By now Maxwell was adopting entirely new corporate strategies on an almost annual basis. His 1987 annual report recorded massive purchases of US printing companies; Maxwell seemed destined to become the second largest commercial printer in the United States.

But by the next year the strategy had changed again. Maxwell had decided to become a major book publisher and data supplier instead. His latest change of direction involved purchasing one of the world's largest book publishers, Macmillan of New York, for over $2 billion. Maxwell also purchased the Official Airline Guides – an acquisition intended to give him a dominant position in supplying airline schedule data. This new strategy had coherence – an extension of Maxwell's original specialist publishing strategy into the US market and into data-on-screens.

Maxwell's latest moves meant that the bulk of his corporate revenue now came not from Britain, but from the United States. The publishing acquisitions also led Maxwell quickly to sell his recent massive printing purchases. In 1988 Maxwell's acquisitions cost $3.8 billion, but his huge debt was on a short-term basis only. Unwilling or unable to raise long-term finance, and unwilling to lose control to shareholders, Maxwell found himself selling the printing half of what for a few months had been one of the few largest communications companies in the United States.[9] After other disposals, in 1991 the mercurial Robert Maxwell made yet further changes of direction. He sold his first love, Pergamon Press, and decided to buy and personally rescue the sinking *New York Daily News*.

## RUPERT MURDOCH – THE MOST COMPLETE MOGUL

Murdoch, like Maxwell, is an own-and-operate mogul of considerable wealth. Like Maxwell, Murdoch has been willing to change both his strategy and his location. But the evolution of Murdoch has a much clearer pattern. Unlike Maxwell, Murdoch had a running start. From his father he inherited one daily newspaper, in Adelaide (South Australia); he went to Australia's most exclusive school and to Oxford University. He also had privileged early access to experience as a journalist at the London *Daily Express*.

Murdoch started by building an Australian and then a British newspaper empire before moving to New York; there he began with newspapers before switching to magazines, a Hollywood production studio and a chain of TV stations. Only after more than a decade of New York residence did he become a citizen.

Murdoch has striven for large market shares in a limited number of markets within three main territories. In 1990 he was the leading newspaper owner in both Britain and Australia; the only person to own both a major group of US TV stations and a major Hollywood studio; owner of a massive circulation US weekly magazine (*TV Guide*) and five other major magazines; owner of book publishing interests (the US Harper & Row and the UK Collins) of truly world significance.

Other Murdoch properties mainly belonged to the category of disposals (US newspapers) or new projects (Sky television). The Murdoch empire consists basically of a small number of large properties; Murdoch resides in New York but patrols his other main locations (London, Sydney, Los Angeles) at frequent intervals. There is a steady trend to larger and larger purchases; the 1988 purchase of Triangle (*TV Guide*) for $2.85 billion was the 'largest deal in publishing history'.

Murdoch's empire has always been heavily dependent on advertising. His entire career can be summarized as a long sequence of acquisitions, increasingly financed by bank debt. After the purchase has been achieved Murdoch typically makes major changes in the top management; within a year of the purchase, up to half the commercial and advertising managers, editors and senior journalists have been fired or left. In most, but not all, cases the commercial results improve, the new management digs in, and Murdoch's personal visits become less frequent.

As the owner of an Adelaide daily and Sunday newspaper, Murdoch in 1958 successfully applied for the Channel 9 television franchise in Adelaide. At age 27 some of the main strands of Murdoch's acquisition career were already established. He had used his commercial strength and political weight in the press to cross over into television; he also became a dominant force in the single market of Adelaide, and he quickly placed his TV station under a trusted manager. He used the profits of the Adelaide station to acquire his first major market publication – the *Daily Mirror*, then one of Sydney's two evening newspapers.[10] Other acquisitions followed and during the 1960s Murdoch became a major Australian media owner.

For just four years (1969–73) Murdoch resided in London. In 1969 he acquired first the Sunday *News of the World*, then the daily *Sun*; the latter by 1973 had risen from one to three million circulation and was generating enough profits to fuel Murdoch's next move.

The decade 1973–83 was Murdoch's New York based American newspaper phase. His first purchase (1973), the San Antonio (Texas) dailies, was a monopoly and a commercial success; subsequent purchases, however, were of problem publications in competitive metropolitan cities – New York (1976), Boston (1982) and Chicago (1983). The loss-making major dailies were paid for by some successful magazines, including a dominant position in New York City magazines. Murdoch was not only studying the American media scene, he was also applying its lessons to Australia and Britain. By late 1981 he had acquired *The Times* and *Sunday Times* of London and performed his usual shuffling and firing of managers and editors.[11]

From 1983 Murdoch commenced his second American phase. This involved using his newspaper base to move into audio-visual media. In April 1983 he bought a majority holding in an abortive American direct broadcasting by satellite venture, which he renamed Skyband Inc. Also in 1983 Murdoch pursued Warner Communications and temporarily became its largest shareholder. In 1985 Murdoch completed the purchase of Twentieth Century Fox for $575 million; this was a huge increase on his previously most expensive US purchase – the *Chicago Sun-Times* for $100 million. After a hasty and quickly aborted bid for CBS, Murdoch then purchased Metromedia, the leading US group of independent (non-network) television stations. Both Fox and Metromedia were high-priced and high-risk purchases; trying to link the two via a 'Fox Network' was another daunting task which Murdoch set himself. In order to own the television stations Murdoch also became a US citizen.

The years 1986–7 saw a new wave of Murdoch activity in the newspaper properties. In 1986 Murdoch achieved a high-risk out-manoeuvering of the London printing unions, in moving to a new plant at Wapping; this move added some £60 million to Murdoch's annual profits. In Australia – as the result of legislation basically restricting ownership to either Press or TV – Murdoch acquired the *Herald* and *Weekly Times* group. He thus in 1987 came to own well over half of all Australian daily circulation, while selling off his TV stations for an inflated price – and evading the problems of his now being a US citizen.

Also in 1987 Murdoch bought Harper & Row, which he followed up in 1988 by completing his purchase of Collins; for a total expenditure of nearly $1 billion he became a globally important book publisher. There was in 1988 the $2.85 billion purchase of Triangle; its major magazines – *TV Guide*, *Seventeen* and *Daily Racing Form* – were all dominant in their particular sectors.

Critics might say that Murdoch has benefited from the buoyancy of advertising in his three main locations since the 1950s; he also benefited from the buoyant market in media properties. The deregulated financial services industry of the 1980s saw the media as a growth sector and happily backed Murdoch and his exemplary track record of profit. Through the year 1988, for example, Murdoch's bank debt averaged around $7 billion. Murdoch's bank borrowings, of course, derived from his desire to retain ownership control of News Corporation (the Australian company) and its US and UK subsidiaries.[12] During 1989–91 the risks of this huge bank borrowing were fully revealed by a rise in interest rates and a general economic downturn in all three of his key territories.

Unlike Maxwell, Rupert Murdoch has been a good delegator. Indeed he has always relied heavily on a few barons to manage his properties and territories. K.E. Cowley has run the Australian operations since 1980; Barry Diller is Murdoch's Hollywood man in charge of Fox. Richard Searby is Murdoch's lawyer, chairman of the master company and corporate trouble-shooter. In 1990 Andrew Knight took executive charge of all Murdoch's activities in Britain.

Murdoch seems to focus mainly at two levels – finance and acquisitions – although he dabbles in many other areas including editorial. In 1988 (speaking to financial analysts in New York) Murdoch described his financial control system as follows:

> Every day I receive print outs from each country on each operation item by item. Every newspaper, every magazine, every issue, a profit and loss covering the operation up to, and including, the previous Sunday. On Fridays those sheets are followed by thick books with itemised details of profit and loss figures on every single operation whether it be from Perth in Western Australia or in London or San Antonio.
>
> These figures are what keep us up to date. We compare them with previous years and compare it with our budget and take whatever management action is called for.
>
> We do it very simply, very low overheads, very small head office here in New York. What we do it with is management information and for that we spare nothing. We operate the company with weekly information. We can do this because of modern communications which we use not just for our customers but for our internal information.[13]

Murdoch also sees his role as stepping in to tackle situations of continuing loss; he is always willing to change managers, including major barons.

Murdoch finally matches the mogul canon of idiosyncrasy and controversy through his high political profile in all three major locations. Starting with vaguely left-of-centre views, Murdoch soon switched to the political right. To some extent Murdoch seems to have followed his instincts in matching his own views to his media empire; to some extent his support of conservative politicians is simply an exercise of newspaper mogul seigneurial privileges. There are also his obvious interests in attracting advertisers and repelling trade unions. But there is more than an element of business calculation in attacking Labour politicians in both Australia and Britain. Murdoch has been the grateful recipient of a long list of political and regulatory favours. In Australia successive governments have been remarkably tolerant of Murdoch's absentee landlord status. In Britain the Thatcher government twice waved through major Murdoch newspaper purchases, although the law appeared to require a reference to the Monopolies and Mergers Commission. The element of business calculation seems most obvious in New York, where the pro-Israel Murdoch's most sustained political alliance was with a Democrat – Ed Koch, mayor of New York City. Murdoch has also received very friendly treatment from the Federal Communications Commission, not least in his purchase of Metromedia while still not a US citizen.

Murdoch's personal and business styles overlap neatly in his search for acquisitions. In both London and New York he has been contemptuous of most media inheritors. But he has still successfully cultivated personal relationships with selected media moguls – because these are the people who own the prime media properties which he wants to buy. Murdoch, of course, also cultivates media barons – such as Gordon Brunton who effectively chose him as the purchaser of Times Newspapers.[14] Murdoch's New York breakthrough resulted from his ability to persuade Dorothy Schiff to sell him the *New York Post*. Murdoch's friendly relationship with the oil magnate Marvin Davis enabled him to buy Fox. Murdoch has then used his New York location to pursue socially the owners of desirable media properties. When 80-year-old Walter Annenberg, announced his decision to sell Triangle Publications, he had already decided to sell to 'his friend Rupert Murdoch'.[15]

## NEW MOGULS OF THE BUOYANT 1980s

The 1980s was a financially buoyant decade for the British media. Costs were cut (notably in newspaper publishing) while advertising revenue grew faster than the British economy as a whole. The political climate favoured 'deregulation' without, as yet, flooding the market with enough new video channels to drive down media profits. The bankers and financiers of the City of London 'discovered' the media; some one hundred media (broadly defined) companies were quoted on the London stock market by 1990. City perceptions of the media industry, as one of the more dynamic growth areas of the British economy, in practice encouraged growth via takeover. The City supported budding media entrepreneurs with both equity and loan finance.

City involvement in financial deregulation and the internationalization of the financial services industry coincided with fashionable media industry rhetoric about global brands and television without frontiers. City of London sentiment also favoured the domestic media industry of the United States as an investment area. Major beneficiaries of these financially buoyant media times were both Maxwell and Murdoch.

The City of London financial community had always been geographically close to the Fleet Street newspaper community. The Pearson company, for example, included not only the *Financial Times*, but also a merchant bank (Lazards). Such ties grew closer; a city accountant and investment manager was transformed into Lord Stevens, presiding baron (not mogul) at United Newspapers.

The 1980s saw the rise of other new media executives who were operators but not controlling owners. Of the ITV franchise companies of the 1980s the most dramatic rise was achieved by TVS; its chief executive, James Gatward, was not an authentic owning mogul, but he developed the company in a vigorous baronial style. Supposedly not one of the networking Big Five, TVS – based in Southampton – was the fourth largest ITV regional company by 1990. After small excursions into Superchannel, and MIDEM (the television sales fair), Gatward purchased MTM – the Hollywood independent production house – for £190 million in 1988. It was a disastrous decision, leading to James Gatward's demise as a TV baron.

This hazardous combination – of baronial management rather than mogul control and of expensive involvement in the United States – had its most celebrated expression in the advertising agency field. In the 1980s Britain produced a new high-risk strain of advertising baron – the brothers Charles and Maurice Saatchi and their former finance man, Martin Sorrell. These three youngish men during the 1980s came to operate (but not to own) four of the world's ten largest advertising agencies. In 1988 Saatchi and Saatchi swallowed Ted Bates; in 1987 Martin Sorrell's Wire and Plastic Products (WPP) acquired J. Walter Thompson and in 1989 the Ogilvy Group. The constituent parts of the two resulting global mega-agencies placed some $30 billion worth of advertising in 1990. But also in 1990 the onerous financial obligations acquired in the construction of these agency-combines put both Saatchi and Saatchi and WPP onto the corporate sick-list.

These were not own-and-operate moguls in anything like the Murdoch or Maxwell moulds. They were neither dominant owners, nor controllers in the common media mogul style. The Saatchi brothers who began in London in 1970 became the top British agency in 1979. Previously American advertising agencies and their European subsidiaries operated on the basis of 'professional' rules suitable for an Ivy League gentlemen's club. These rules – 15 per cent commission, no unsolicited approaches to new clients – the Saatchis deliberately rejected.

From the outset the Saatchi brothers saw their role, not as running the day-to-day operations of the agency and not even as talking to major clients. Initially Maurice Saatchi used to solicit (on the telephone) twenty-five possible advertising clients per day; but very soon he and his brother were also writing to other larger agencies politely offering to buy them. The Saatchi brothers concentrated on new business, finance, and buying other agencies. Ted Bates was their thirty-eighth takeover. All takeovers were friendly and depended on a high-risk financial formula, dubbed the 'earn-out'. Under this buy-now pay-later system, the existing management was contracted to stay in place and the ultimate payment was related to agency profit. Several cases were David-swallows-Goliath acquisitions of agencies larger than Saatchi and Saatchi at the time. The US agency, Compton, had twice Saatchi's billings when they bought it in 1982. 1984–5 saw nineteen Saatchi takeovers; they were increasingly focusing on sizeable American agencies leading up to the purchase of Ted Bates.

The purchase of Bates was especially risky: How would US advertisers react to Bates being bought by the two reclusive Britons? And how would they react to the two agency networks handling competing accounts under single corporate ownership? Another Saatchi insight had been, *de facto*, that major advertising accounts moved less frequently than was commonly supposed. The Saatchis also assumed that size was compatible with creativity; large consumer companies preferred large agencies, which got better discounts from the media.

Nor did the Saatchis *operate* the advertising agencies in the usual sense. Their style was to continue at the corporate/financial/ acquisitions level, while employing others to run the agencies. During much of the period of most rapid growth in the late 1970s and early 1980s, the agency was run by Tim Bell; he met the major clients – including the Conservative Party at the 1979 and 1983 elections, British Airways and many others. Even after the massive 1986 Bates takeover, the Saatchis delegated the executive role of sorting out the acquisitions and reducing client defections.

One of the Saatchis' key lieutenants was Martin Sorrell, their finance man for a decade. Martin Sorrell's own subsequent rise and rise was even more meteoric. In 1985 he purchased WPP. By 1988

Sorrell had made fifteen takeovers; his sixteenth was the J. Walter Thompson takeover, which again looked to be an exceptionally hazardous deal. It was the first ever contested (hostile) takeover of a major advertising agency; Sorrell's WPP became the world's fourth largest agency company. Within two years Sorrell had reorganized JWT and brought it back to a significant profit; he had fought a New York court battle with the principals of a JWT subsidiary agency; and he had launched his second mammoth bid – for Ogilvy Group (then the world number five).

Martin Sorrell was, like the Saatchis, not a classic own-and-operate mogul. His directly owned slice of WPP was extremely small. However he has not cultivated the idiosyncratic reclusiveness of the Saatchis. Nor does he, as yet, get involved in election advertising campaigns. Sorrell was financed by backers who were impressed by his track financial record at Saatchi and Saatchi; his early handling of WPP had been spectacular, and hence the primacy of financial track record was further underlined.

Saatchi and Saatchi's own financial performance finally hit trouble in the late 1980s. Several underlying problems surfaced simultaneously. Their attempt to buy a major bank (Midland) was so amateurish as to annoy the City and to throw doubt on their competence generally. Similar doubts were raised by their ineffective attempts to become a world leader in management consultancy. More seriously the late 1980s revealed advertising agency management problems[16] – notably a loss of several top managers in quick succession. Martin Sorrell's style of management at WPP seemed to exhibit a surer touch, and avoided some of the worst Saatchi mistakes.[17] But both of these mega-agencies were inherently unstable. It is not easy to run a predominantly American business from London. And having financed their mammoth purchases with both share issues and heavy debt, their vulnerability to further takeover assaults was obvious.

We turn now to three new media moguls of the 1980s, Michael Green, Richard Branson and Conrad Black. Each of these three reached 1990 with his own-and-operate status intact. Michael Green in 1990 was still almost entirely confined to video hardware and services. In 1988 he consolidated his London video facilities business by buying Technicolor for £459 million. This was Green's fourteenth significant takeover; Carlton was already the largest UK video facilities house. The Technicolor purchase left Green with a claimed 40 per cent share of two world markets – video duplication and feature film processing; the spread of VCRs, video purchasing, and multi-screen cinemas made both into growth fields. Green operates his company with a familiar combination – he largely leaves managers to go on running the acquired companies but at the centre he operates 'almost an obsessive financial control'.[18] Green already owns 20 per cent of Central (one of the ITV companies) and in 1985 he came near to acquiring Thames, the London weekday ITV company. The IBA would only allow Green to buy 49 per cent; his reluctance to accept a 49 per cent share indicated his obsessive concern with complete control.

Another new mogul is Richard Branson, who launched the Virgin record label in 1973. Branson pursued a high-risk business strategy with frequent changes of direction including several related to his Virgin retail stores and to Superchannel, the English-language satellite service which reached cable systems across Europe but also made large losses. Branson's turnover was running at about £400 million a year when in 1988 a decision was made to 'go private' again – evidence of both own-and-control and some idiosyncrasy. Branson was also a favourite of Margaret Thatcher; political connections did not harm the steady rise of the Virgin airline business.

Gradually Branson devolved responsibility for running the separate divisions into the hands of a small group of barons. Branson was unusual as a media mogul in lacking any facility with finance; he seems instead to have focused on 'the deal' as the key. He also apparently has little feeling for popular music.[19] Branson's other forte appears to be publicity for himself and Virgin in general, the Virgin airline and record label in particular. He has resolutely pursued a semi-bohemian image – photographed in a floppy sweater, but carefully surrounded by fellow directors wearing baronial dark suits. For years Branson used a houseboat on a North London canal as his office. In 1985, in order to promote his airline, Branson began a series of outlandish record attempts – fastest across the Atlantic by boat, and then by hot-air balloon. Having lost confidence in the City of London, he invited the Japanese media giant Fujisankei to buy 20 per cent of his Virgin music company;[20] to consummate this deal and to achieve trans-Pacific publicity he conceived the next bravura publicity attempt – by hot air balloon across the Pacific. Following these show-business activities, Virgin airline acquired additional routes to the US and Japan.

A further 1980s media mogul is Conrad Black, a Canadian, who in 1985 acquired the *Daily* and *Sunday Telegraph*. Black, not unlike his fellow Canadian Lord Beaverbrook, had made a huge fortune at an early age.

Black was thus a financier–mogul, although since age 24 he had owned some small newspapers in Quebec. His acquisition of the Telegraph newspapers was only made possible because in 1985 the papers were in dire need of new finance and new management. The now 74-year-old Lord Hartwell was still in charge; the advertising management was weak, the print over-manning spectacular, and the introduction of new printing technology badly handled. Because of these manifest problems – and the shrinking and ageing readership, the banks were reluctant rescuers of the Telegraph company. Asked at the eleventh hour to buy a slice of the company, Conrad Black set 'unrealistic' terms – including an option to purchase all of Lord Harwell's shares. The terms were accepted, the financial picture worsened and six months later Conrad Black had a controlling interest.[21] Four years later Black and his designated baron, Andrew Knight, had brought the Telegraph papers back into good financial and editorial health. By 1990 Black had taken over operational as well as ownership control at the Telegraph; he also owned the *Spectator* and the *Jerusalem Post* and was looking for other purchases.

## BRITISH MEDIA MOGULS: COMING OR GOING?

It is easy to caricature the new British media moguls and barons of the 1980s – Richard Branson, the charismatic but inarticulate communicator, with his huge hot air balloons and moderately priced condoms; the super-secretive Saatchi brothers trying to buy the Midland Bank; James Gatward and his imperfect understanding of American television syndication; Martin Sorrell equipped with not much more than a supermarket trolley, setting out to land two of Madison Avenue's finest, and then censoring his name from his own annual report; Conrad Black, the newspaper mogul with his neanderthal views about journalists.

But such caricatures cannot hide the fact that the moguls and barons of the 1980s were all hard-working, competent, and rather conventional people. They were conservative in more ways than one. Their success depended on much optimism and good luck as well as on sound judgement. Nevertheless their businesses are highly volatile and uncertain for two major reasons. Firstly these businesses are mainly not in the securer sectors of the media with the best cash flow prospects over time. Secondly these are highly international businesses where the competition is strong and getting stronger. Most of these 'British' businesses in fact earn most of their revenue in the United States and the rest of the world.

The basic cash-flow areas of the British media – newspapers and television – will be more competitive in the 1990s; and the tendency for British media moguls and their properties to end up in the American field is likely to remain strong.

# Chapter 7

# Media moguls in France

'Mogul' and 'tycoon' are terms of Asian origin. French media lore long favoured a term that came likewise from Asia – from the Indian subcontinent where, in the eighteenth century, France and Britain vied for influence. *Un nabab* (from the Urdu *nawwab*) was someone who had acquired a fortune abroad in mysterious circumstances, for instance, Europeans returning from India. Under the title of *Le Nabab*, Alphonse Daudet published a novel set in the Paris of the second Empire (1852–70). For many a late nineteenth-century novelist – Emile Zola (*L'Argent*), Guy de Maupassant (*Bel-Ami*), Maurice Barrès (*Les Déracinés*) – the press entrepreneur has something of the shady origins and self-made fortune of the *nabab*.

During the past century, French terminology often differed from that in use in Britain and America to describe 'press barons' or 'media magnates'. Hollywood, however, is the great leveller. The 'movie moguls' of yesteryear are the forebears of the multi-media moguls of today. French journalists now refer to *les moguls* (*des médias*) – a nice touch, as the term *nabab* used to be the title of Moslem officials acting as governors of provinces of the Mogul Empire. Perceptions of French moguls, marked as much by the history of the Press as by Hollywood, have in Robert Hersant, the quintessential mogul of the old school, both in the *papivore*, the ogre devouring individual newspaper titles, and the French 'Citizen Kane'.[1] Both epitomize fears concerning concentration of ownership.

The idiosyncrasies of the French media tradition colour perceptions of media moguls in contemporary France.[2] We shall focus here on the individual who appears to best span the transition from press baron to media mogul – Robert Hersant. But we shall look also at moguls of more recent vintage. Some are apparently as brash and overweening as Hersant and his predecessors. Others appear more the corporate manager, bestriding a multi-media group (often with interests outside the communications sector), with the corporate good highlighted more than the individual ego. Hachette is the one French group that generally figures in lists of the top ten world communications empires; Jean-Luc Lagardère, its president, appears sometimes more 'corporation man' than, say, his flamboyant associate, Daniel Filipacchi; the reality, however, we shall see is more complex.

One of the gains of the French Revolution of 1789 was the affirmation of the right to freedom of expression. But the struggle, against an overweening state, to establish the political freedom of the Press in France, was only won 'finally' in 1881; except for brief periods during wartime and civil unrest, this freedom has not been curtailed. Public service broadcasters, by contrast, only acquired effective protection of their independence in the 1980s: regulatory authorities hold the state, and party politicians, at arm's length.[3] The same is largely true of private sector broadcasting; the first authorized private TV channels only began transmission in 1986. But, while the issue of the political independence of the media appeared of central importance from the 1780s to the 1980s, mogulry, and its related traits, have been a major sub-plot. Beginning at least in the 1830s, press entrepreneurs and shady financiers – influenced in part by the creation of news and/or advertising combines or brokerages by Charles-Louis Havas (1783–1858) and Emile de Girardin (1806–81) – appeared an economic threat to pluralism. Even today, France has little anti-trust legislation. And the methods by which moguls build, extend and preserve their media empires were held to favour what a Russian diplomat once called 'the abominable venality of the French press'.[4]

Reviewing developments in the communications sector during the first Mitterrand presidency (1981–8), J.-F. Lacan of Le Monde observed that perhaps no other sphere had seen the advent of so many new entrants. Major banks, finance houses and industrial groups – Bouygues, La Compagnie Générale des Eaux (CGE), Générale occidentale (GO), La Lyonnaise des Eaux, Paribas and Suez – now fund operations as diverse as laying down cable networks and audio-visual production to owner-operating print media combines; all of these groups were entirely absent from the sphere in 1980.[5] Likewise, international moguls and groups such as Silvio Berlusconi, Rupert Murdoch (peripherally), Robert Maxwell (loudly), Germany's Bertelsmann, America's Dow Jones, Britain's Pearson–Longman, and the Belgian Bruxelles–Lambert group now strut the French media stage where formerly the major foreign player had been the Luxembourg-based CLT.[6] There are new players: and there are established actors in new roles – these include the 71-year-old Robert Hersant, and the Havas and Hachette groups (whose origins date from the mid-nineteenth century). But – to pursue the theatrical analogy a step further – France is more a stage for others than the world is a stage for the French. See Figures 7.1 and 7.2.

French governments, while they no longer seek overtly to influence the content of broadcasting media, still use discretionary (and other) powers to assist French media combines, sometimes in association with fellow European groups, against American interests. François Mitterrand argued thus on 21 November 1985, when justifying the award for the franchise for the (first ever) private channel, la Cinq, to a consortium involving Silvio Berlusconi: better an Italian mogul, however much decried, operating with a French group new to television, than Rupert Murdoch, 'one of the major audio-visual magnates from across the Atlantic', in tandem with the Luxembourg-based CLT run by the Belgian Bruxelles–Lambert group.[7] François Léotard – Mitterrand's Culture and Communication Minister, albeit of a different political persuasion – argued no differently in 1986–7 when justifying the need for large multi-media groups in France. 'I must help Hachette, Bouygues or other (French) groups to become major players on the European stage . . . prior to 1992. French communication groups are weak compared to the Murdochs, Maxwells and Bertelsmanns of the world.'[8]

## 'CITOYEN KANE'

Periodically re-elected one of the ten best films ever made, *Citizen Kane* is a loadstone for French studies of media moguls.[9] Britain has had its press barons. Republican France, at the turn of the century, referred to 'Her Majesty the Press'; it had in Maurice Bunau-Varilla (co-director (1895) and subsequently sole master (1903–44) of the daily newspaper *Le Matin* for half a century) a megalomaniac, given to observing 'my empire is worth three

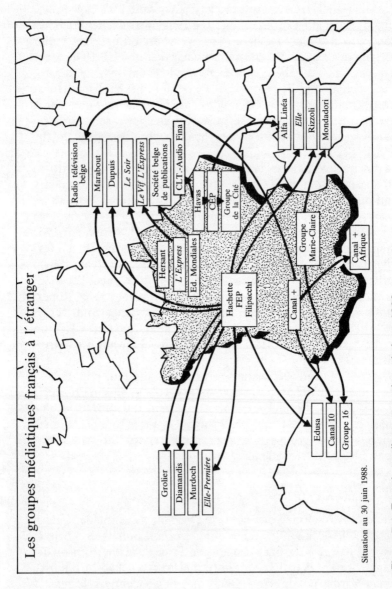

Figure 7.1 French media groups abroad, June 1988
Source: *Communication and Business* no. 70

Les groupes médiatiques français à l'étranger

Radio télévision belge
Marabout
Dupuis
*Le Soir*
*Le Vif L'Express*
Société belge de publications
CLT.-Audio Fina

Havas
CEP
Groupe de la Cité

Hersant
*L'Express*
Ed. Mondiales

Hachette
FEP
Filipacchi

Canal +

Groupe Marie-Claire

Canal + Afrique

Alfa Linéa
*Elle*
Rizzoli
Mondadori

Grolier
Diamandis
Murdoch
*Elle-Première*

Edusa
Canal 10
Groupe 16

Situation au 30 juin 1988.

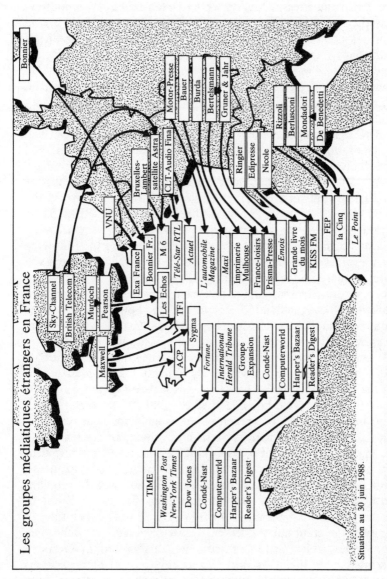

Les groupes médiatiques étrangers en France

Situation au 30 juin 1988.

Figure 7.2  Foreign media groups in France, June 1988
Source: Communication and Business no. 70

thrones'. The effrontery of Bunau-Varilla (or what legend has preserved) was no less great than that of William Randolph Hearst, the American Press mogul on whom Orson Welles (very loosely) based *Citizen Kane*. Bunau-Varilla used to observe: 'There are no journalists on *Le Matin*, merely employees'; he had a blacklist of politicians whose names were never to be cited in *Le Matin*; the newspaper whose slogan was 'we see all, know all, say all', at times excluded from its columns the name of Georges Clemenceau, Prime Minister during 1906–9 and a major twentieth-century statesman.

The right-wing *Le Matin* of the 1930s became a pro-German collaborationist propaganda sheet during the Occupation, and the bullying and nefarious Bunau-Varilla should not perhaps have sullied the reputation of all French press barons, just as in Britain, the final 'insanity' of Northcliffe did not tarnish the reputation as a newspaperman of Alfred Harmsworth.[10] But, partly through the survival of his private papers and company archives, Harmsworth-Northcliffe can be studied in detail as the prototype of the press tycoon: he, like Beaverbrook later, and others still later, planned and worked for the ultimate 'combine' or what would now be termed 'horizontal and vertical integration'; ownership of forests in Newfoundland to provide the wood pulp needed for the countless publications of a group controlling its own news and features services, and distribution organization; Northcliffe (in 1901) foresaw the day of the 'simultaneous newspaper', of multiple editions distributed worldwide.[11] By contrast, French press barons of the past often remain shadowy figures: their reputations owe as much to rumour and polemic as to corroborated evidence. Well-documented studies of French media moguls are relatively rare, partly because of the paucity of qualitatively significant material.

This partly results, of course, from the chequered and turbulent course of French politics from 1789 to 1945: archives have been lost, and published studies sometimes highlight the mogul's relations with politicians and the establishment more than their operations as media owner-operators. In 1944–5, on the Liberation of France, the state impounded the assets of newspaper publishing companies which had operated and collaborated in German-occupied and Vichy France; it also revoked all authorizations to broadcast previously accorded to private radio stations. On paper, and indeed often in practice, the French press began anew. In the provinces even more than in the capital, new press barons subsequently emerged, sometimes establishing fiefs reminiscent of the dismantled empires of before the war. In broadcasting, the state quasi-monopoly of production and programming – and its total control of the airwaves – only began to weaken significantly in the 1970s.

Not all French press owners were flamboyant, controversial figures à la Bunau-Varilla. Indeed, heading an empire based on the mass circulation daily, *Le Petit Parisien*, Jean Dupuy (1844–1919) and his sons Pierre and Paul, belong more to the mould of 'media managers' than to that of media moguls.[12] New dynasties replaced, acrimoniously, the old.[13] In French provincial newspaper publishing today, there are many *fils à papa* – sons of men who founded or acquired control of regional titles in the late 1940s; to these we may add the sons-in-law – newspaper executives who married into the controlling family. Mogulry – the building and running of empire by controversial figures – often generates wars of succession, with dynastic rivalries. The battle within the Delaroche family for control of the *Progrès* press group of France's second city and attendant region, Lyon, ultimately helped an outsider carry off the prize. In Lyon, as so often elsewhere in France, the victor was Robert Hersant.

## CITIZEN HERSANT TAKES ON AND BEATS JOURNALISTS AND THE GOVERNMENT

In many ways, Robert Hersant (born in 1920) typifies the media mogul of the old school. Blunt in speech yet a trimmer in politics, a master in juggling the company accounts or rather in controlling the purse strings of a host of family-controlled companies, Hersant is also an adventurer and empire-builder who embarks on costly excursionss into new territories (Spain, Portugal, Belgium) or new media (the French commercial channel, la Cinq, in 1987). He epitomizes in the eyes of most French journalists all that is worst in mogulry. He is too bad to be true, and refers to himself as the 'J.R.' of the French press.[14]

The sins imputed to Hersant are many and varied. Most important of all, perhaps, is the feeling that this mogul is above the law. In 1984, the socialist majority in the National Assembly passed a law that sought to implement anew the intentions of those who, through an ordinance of 26 August 1944, set out to protect pluralism and prevent the concentration of newspaper ownership.

From the moment when Prime Minister Pierre Mauroy first floated the idea to a Socialist party congress in October 1983, the bill was portrayed as intended primarily to break up the Hersant empire.[15] Journalistic hostility towards Hersant dated from at least 1972, when he added his first major regional daily (*Paris-Normandie*, the leading title of his home town, Rouen, and region) to his existing stable of provincial papers and consumer magazines. It intensified in 1975–8, when Hersant acquired three Parisian dailies – *Le Figaro*, *France-Soir* and *L'Aurore* – out of the ten (non-specialist) titles then extant. It was exacerbated by the strident right-wing polemics of Hersant's leading national title, *Le Figaro*, both in 1978 when the left seemed likely to win parliamentary elections, and in 1981, when a Socialist President and a Socialist–Communist government indeed acceded to power. Opposition to Mauroy's 1983 bill came from the parliamentary right, from newspaper publishers of all persuasions, and even from journalists sympathetic to the left but critical of the iniquity of the measure – of an unjust law *ad hominem*. Hersant defeated the government. The law ultimately passed in October 1984 was a much watered-down version of the 1983 bill. It did not oblige Hersant to divest himself of any of his existing print media interests. Furthermore, Hersant rode roughshod over its provisions. Hersant group dailies accounted for 38 per cent of the total circulation of national newspaper titles and approaching 20 per cent of provincial daily sales. The law, whose provisions were not retrospective (and respected existing market shares), stipulated that no group or person should control above 10 per cent of the total circulation of national dailies and above 10 per cent of provincial dailies. Nonetheless, in January 1986, Jean-Charles Lignel sold *Progrès*, the Lyon-based group, to Hersant. Hersant coolly observed: 'I merely anticipate the next law' ('je suis en avance d'une loi'). So it proved. In March 1986, the Socialists lost their parliamentary majority; the centre-right Conservative government of Jacques Chirac subsequently promoted legislation whose provisions governing the concentration of media – indeed multi-media – ownership, were liberal in the extreme.[16] Hersant triumphed.

Thus, the ordinance of August 1944, intended to prevent the concentration of newspaper ownership, was flouted by Hersant (and others); the Socialist attempt, forty years later, to tackle the issue anew failed ignominiously. Under the Conservatives (the Chirac government, 1986–8), Hersant, who already controlled

30 per cent of the circulation of the French daily press, successfully tendered for the fifth TV channel, la Cinq (1987). The acquisition of the largest shareholding and operational control of 'la Cinq' – shared with Silvio Berlusconi (each, initially, had 25 per cent, the maximum authorized shareholding), was accompanied by expansion into one of the most lucrative markets of magazine journalism – TV magazines (1988). Hersant continued to pick up newspapers, big and small, in France and abroad, to develop his magazines, broadcasting (radio and television) and, above all printing and advertising interests. The Socialist (minority) government of Michel Rocard, in office after May 1988, did not reopen the Hersant dossier – or, at least, did not embark on a frontal assault. It was left to the new audio-visual regulatory authority, the Conseil Supérieur de l'Audiovisuel (CSA) to call la Cinq to task for failure to meet its programming obligations.

By 1990, it was less measures taken by the government or the CSA that made Hersant abandon his position as owner-operator of la Cinq than the sheer scale of the channel's losses and the boardroom battles that ensued. In 1988 and 1990, la Cinq's annual losses were in the region of 800 and 600 million francs. The ambitions and disquiet of major shareholders other than Hersant, erstwhile partners but longstanding rivals, meant that there were, as the French say, too many crocodiles in the muddy pool. In late 1989, Berlusconi and Jérôme Seydoux, two of the main shareholders when the company to which François Mitterrand initially awarded the franchise for la Cinq (November 1985) was formed, attempted to wrest control from Hersant by acquiring the stock of small shareholders, and thereby to control more stock than Hersant and his allies. Hersant beat off this threat. In May 1990, a third major communications group, Hachette, became a significant minority shareholder (22 per cent) of the loss-making company. A disenchanted Hersant reportedly wanted to pull out completely from broadcasting: 'There are only two good moments in television – the day you acquire the channel and the day you sell it'; in September he sought CSA approval for a change in the ownership structure of la Cinq. Hachette, with 25 per cent, became the 'owner'-operator; Berlusconi, with 25 per cent, stated 'I'm a romantic' and announced his willingness to work with Hachette, 'a European major', in the French TV channel with which he had been associated from the outset (1985) and for which he was the chief supplier of programmes – mostly US-made programmes for which he had European distribution rights. Hersant's stake fell to 10 per cent – he reportedly would have pulled out completely but this might have led the CSA to withdraw the licence to operate the franchise issued to the consortium that he headed in 1987.[17]

Hersant displayed contempt for the law, for journalists, for politicians and, at times, for the French nation as a whole. Other French media moguls of the old school did likewise; summary judgements, born of a certain world-weariness and the belief that every man has his price, go hand-in-hand with a delight in the exercise of power. The megalomania of Bunau-Varilla is echoed in this self-analysis by Hersant:

> I brook no opposition – am self-confident beyond reason. Some say I am driven by the thirst for power. I don't deny it. One must know one's weaknesses – and how to use them.
>
> Often, I do not share the collective judgements of the French people. You don't have to be a genius to make your mark in France. . . . At the age of twelve, I knew that I would never work for, or be indebted towards, anyone, and that no one would ever have any hold over me.
>
> During my 23 years as an MP, I ladled out decorations to all and sundry. You can hardly imagine that I can possibly dream of wanting to receive such an honour myself.
>
> If I had thought it necessary, I would be a candidate for any post that was going.
>
> All things considered, I don't think much of my success. I'd hoped for more and thought I was worth more. I am disappointed – in myself. The only people who have really profited from my success are the 10,000 journalists, printers and company employees who have exploited me over the past thirty years. It is the exploitation of man by man. Not in the way that Marx put it, but the exploitation of a man who has some creative imagination by all those who have none and who milk him dry.[18]

The way in which, in 1944, some Frenchmen climbed on the bandwagon of the Resistance, claiming to have been active opponents of Germans and the Vichy authorities, 'inspired in me an immense feeling of disgust and loathing. . . . I realised then how low man could sink.' The contempt shown towards journalists and print workers stems from their apparent indifference to the fact that Hersant has provided them with gainful employment when hosts of newspapers have folded, and to the fact that he considers many journalists left-wing:

> For me, pluralism does not mean a diversity of political views within a particular newspaper. If a journalist joins *l'Humanité*, it is to produce a newspaper that tallies with the wishes of the Communist party. The press, by its very nature, has to make policy choices and journalists must choose to work for newspapers that accord with their political views.
>
> Those who are forever talking of the freedom of expression of journalists in fact have only one aim: to destroy the freedom of the press.[19]

Hersant uses politics and politicians to protect his media interests. As an MP (1956–78) and MEP (since 1984), he profited from the immunity conferred on parliamentarians from certain types of legal proceedings. On acquiring *France-Soir* in 1976, Hersant was cited by journalists' unions on charges of violating the press ordinance of August 1944, relating to the concentration of ownership; investigations, appeals and counter-appeals lasted for eleven years until with the passage of the liberal communications legislation under the Chirac government of 1986–8, the lawsuits lapsed. Hersant renewed a practice dear to many a press baron of the Third and Fourth Republics (1870–1940 and 1946–58) – the control over parliamentarians who advance his interests with their colleagues. In the 1986–8 National Assembly, some twelve MPs at least worked for the Hersant group in some capacity. Inn 1975, Valéry Giscard d'Estaing, the then president of the Republic, and Jacques Chirac, his Prime Minister, did not oppose Hersant's acquisition of *Le Figaro*, even though there were other candidates. In 1988, the politician Michel d'Ornano, one of Giscard's closest lieutenants, entered the Socpresse, the major Hersant holding company, with a watching brief over the group's relations with parliamentarians.

At the head of 'empires' whose products help fashion public opinion day by day, week by week, press barons and media moguls believe themselves to be more influential than most politicians. Not without reason. In the jockeying for position between leaders of the French right – Giscard, Chirac and Barre – from the mid-1970s to the late 1980s, the assiduous courting of Hersant, and of the support of his media interests, involved the offer of many a *quid pro quo* – including, possibly, the franchise to run a new

TV channel. As noted, in 1987, the regulatory body set up by the Chirac government, the CNCL (Commission Nationale de la Communication et des Libertés), awarded Channel 5 to the Hersant–Berlusconi-led consortium.

## HERSANT II: FROM PRESS BARON TO MEDIA MOGUL

The Hersant 'group' is something of a misnomer. Robert Hersant is at the head of some 200 companies. Only he and his closest henchmen apparently understand the intricacies of their financial structure; under the Socialist governments of 1981–6 the tax authorities reportedly tried but failed to unravel the minutiae of the cross-holding and subsidiary interests. This opacity is occasionally, and partially, broken by investigative journalists. The general consensus is that Hersant controls the financing of his print media activities via a company, Socpresse, in which he alone has 60 per cent of the shares and his family approximately another 25 per cent. The secrecy of the finances of the group is a trait that has characterized French press barons of the past; the tight family control is reminiscent of that exercised by Rupert Murdoch via the Cruden Company in Australia, and by Robert Maxwell through a company registered in Liechtenstein.

Of all contemporary French media tycoons, Hersant alone is the mogul writ large. From socially humble beginnings, he built up, in the 1950s and 1960s, a career in consumer magazines (*L'Auto-Journal*, 1950, etc.) and in provincial newspaper printing and publishing, while pursuing the political career deemed necessary to protect his media interests. The lower middle-class family with roots in western France (Vertou, near Nantes, and above all Rouen, the capital of Normandy) and the small group of close associates, formed in his late teens and early twenties, are sometimes cited as indicators of Hersant the outsider, set on getting his own back on society – a goal partly reached in 1972 when he acquired *Paris-Normandie*, his first major regional daily, that of his home town, Rouen.[20]

The political millstone around Hersant's neck dates from the dark years of 1940–4: in June 1940, the Germans occupied Paris; Hersant, at the age of twenty, was involved in a fascist movement, Jeune Front, and published an anti-Semitic newspaper. Later, in Vichy France, Hersant headed a youth camp committed to a curious mixture of boy-scout values and the 'national revolution' ideology dear to the collaborationist authorities. These 'errors' of youth blighted Hersant's subsequent career. In the short term, during the Liberation, he was imprisoned and lost the right to vote and stand for election; in the long term, opponents exploited these errors throughout Hersant's career. Many media moguls have had to overcome major obstacles encountered at the outset of their careers. In the case of Hersant, his politics of 1940–4, and his subsequent violation of the provisions of the August 1944 ordinance intended to protect pluralism and diversity of ownership, illustrate the interdependence of the Press and politics in France that long circumscribed the freedom of manoeuvre of media moguls.

In Paris and the provinces, many newspaper titles were launched in 1944–5 and newspaper circulations increased apace. But, by the late forties, the reverse trend had begun – newspapers and circulations declined. In the 1950s and 1960s, the trend was even more marked among Parisian popular daily titles than in the regional press. Parisian newspapers, with but few exceptions, ceased to be distributed nationwide; their major sales area was the Parisian region.[21] Consolidation and the concentration of ownership occurred anew. The Hersant 'group' was still small in scope compared to some of the major print media companies of the time (Amaury or Hachette, for example). Hersant picked up small provincial titles that might otherwise have gone under. He even bailed out Socialist provincial papers – *Nord Matin* in Lille (19667) for instance. To be saved by the 'collaborationist' Hersant added insult to injury for such as Pierre Mauroy, the future mayor of Lille and – later still – the Prime Minister behind the 1984 press law.

Just like Rupert Murdoch, but on a smaller scale, Hersant built his newspaper career mainly by buying up titles in difficulty (declining sales and advertising revenue, high production costs) and turning them around. His group created few new titles. *France-Antilles*, in the French West Indies (1964) was a rare exception; it was launched partly to cement ties with some of the Gaullist ministers of the period – some of whom, such as Alain Peyrefitte,[22] would later work for Hersant.

In July 1975, Hersant bought *Le Figaro* from the nonagenarian Jean Prouvost, a press baron of the previous half-century (*Paris-Midi, Paris-Soir, Match, Marie-Claire, Télé-7-Jours, Paris-Match*).[23] In August 1976, Hersant bought *France-Soir* from the Hachette group, in association with Paul Winkler, a septuagenarian.

Thus, Hersant took on board two leading titles of the Parisian daily press, situated respectively in the quality and popular markets, and both of which operated at a loss.[24] The formerly prestigious, but then moribund *L'Aurore*, fell to Hersant a year later. At a presidential press conference, Giscard d'Estaing answered at length a question on the Hersant menace to pluralism; Hersant, assailed by journalists' unions and left-wing politicians alike, had 'arrived'.

*Le Figaro* became the centrepiece of the Hersant empire. The quality daily proved a launching pad for a range of satellite publications; by late 1988, there were twelve *Le Figaro* titles. To the daily itself (circulation 400,000) was added a series of regional editions, supplements – some weekly, some thematic – and magazines. Two with the most appeal for advertisers and readers were *Le Figaro Magazine* (launched in 1978) and *Madame Figaro* (sold together with the Saturday edition of the daily (circulation: 618,000)). In politics, *Le Figaro* trimmed as and when needed: following the re-election of President Mitterrand in May 1988 and appointment of a (minority) democrat Socialist government, Hersant even imported an editor-in-chief from the left-wing news weekly *Le Nouvel Observateur*.

*Le Figaro* is the centrepiece of the group's printing strategy. Hersant has often been in the forefront of the modernization of printing and production plant – unlike other Parisian newspaper publishers. In the mid-1970s, he opted for facsimile transmission, photocomposition and offset printing; he sought to decentralize the printing of the provincial editions of his Paris-based title, with a grandiose scheme for regional printing plants across the country – seven were indeed created and produced, in addition, some of his seventeen provincial dailies.[25] In the late 1980s, Hersant revised his printing strategy: he invested 700 million francs to create an ultra-modern printing plant near Roissy Charles-de-Gaulle airport, from which to despatch copies by air across France. In his way, Hersant 'did a Wapping', without the labour conflicts with the print unions that bedevilled Murdoch, Maxwell and Eddie Shah in Britain. Unlike rival French publishers, such as the Amaury group (*Le Parisien*) Hersant enjoys tolerably satisfactory relations with the print unions, including those affiliated to the Communist Party. And Hersant, the 'high-tech' printer, has sometimes won the custom of rival groups; the Socialist *Le Matin* (1977–88) printed the copies distributed in western France on the presses of Hersant's *Presse-Océan* in Nantes.

Hersant takes risks. Not for him the generally prudent·financial strategy followed by provincial press owners. The latter often enjoy a quasi-monopoly situation in their main catchment-area. Hersant likewise, but for different reasons. In the late fifties, when he first cobbled together a regional daily (*Centre-Presse*) out of a series of disparate local titles, Hersant set up shop in one of the few areas in which a regional daily did not enjoy a dominant position: the region involved, covering areas of central-western France, had few attractions in sales and advertising revenue potential. In much of provincial France, there were tacit agreements between newspaper publishers not to compete on the frontiers of their respective territories. The more aggressive-minded Hersant does not act thus: in recent years, he has even been seen as a marauder by France's most successful regional daily, *Ouest-France*.[26]

Hersant practises economies of scale and rationalization of costs; he transfers funds (and staff) from one group company to another. But, in developing multi-media and transnational strategies, he runs up massive debts – as does Rupert Murdoch elsewhere. Here also, Hersant appears a media mogul of the old school. The opacity surrounding media finances has a long history: even today, only a few newspapers, such as *Le Monde*, publish their accounts annually, as required by the 1944 ordinance and the 1984 Press law. The Hersant line of reasoning appears to be: 'my degree of indebtedness is such that my creditors have gone beyond the point where they could pull out'. His group's debts in 1988 allegedly exceeded 1.5 billion francs in 1988 and between 1.3 and 2.1 billion francs in 1989.[27] It is reckoned that up to twenty banks – including nationalized and private sector banks (Parisbas, Crédit Lyonnais, Société Générale, and the Banque du Marais headed by Jean-Marc Vernes) support the Hersant group. Christian Grimaldi, the group's head of finance, is a past master in negotiating and rescheduling bank loans. A necessary skill: save for *Le Figaro* and (especially) its satellite publications, some of Hersant's specialist-interest or consumer-oriented magazines,[28] and possibly some of his provincial titles and the horse-racing tipsters' bible, *Paris Turf*, Hersant's print and – especially – broadcasting media run at a loss.

Hersant, like his friend and associate in la Cinq, the banker J.-M. Vernes, is reckoned to be one of the top ten most wealthy French families. He is supported by what used to be termed *le mur de l'argent* – the monied interest. One well-informed right-wing observer even claims that it was because Hersant, as of July 1981, could rely on the support of bankers throughout the first Mitterrand presidency that he had merely to bide his time and profit from the tactical errors made by the Socialists in their parliamentary and other attempts to unseat him.[29] The latter do not appear to have used their influence on the heads of nationalized banks to curtail Hersant's credit.[30] Hersant's financial risk-taking therefore, is also reminiscent of media mogulry of the old school; it rests on the collusion between the monied and political interests of the establishment (for services rendered). Socpresse, the holding company which controls most of the Hersant empire, is itself controlled by the Hersant family. Hersant rarely appeals to outside investors or floats company shares on the stock market. In the 1960s and 1970s, Hersant acquired control of provincial newspapers by buying up the small shareholdings taken up by idealists who, following the Liberation of France, had pledged their support of the local paper with little hope of financial gain. In 1989–90, as noted above, he beat off attempts by even such as Berlusconi to wrest control of 'his' TV channel, before choosing to throw in the sponge, and call in Hachette.

It is perhaps as a media and advertising broker that Hersant has maintained his position as the communication industry mogul *par excellence*. From the early days of *Centre-Presse*, Hersant practised the maximum possible unification of available resources (be they journalists, printing plant, or the cash flow), and the maximum standardization of news/editorial and advertising content. Later his news and features agency AGPI provided copy and journalists from his print media to run the news bureaux of the TV channel. Advertising considerations are paramount. Hersant's losses on la Cinq were partly offset by his control – jealously preserved – of the management of the channel's advertising budgets. In 1989, four Hersant ad brokerage companies controlled the ad spaces in the group's national and provincial paid-for titles, its freesheets, and its radio stations.[31] Hersant centralizes control of the ad space of the various media of the group and sells media packages containing several media targeting the same given audience. In the Rhône-Alpes region, where Hersant controls all the major Lyon and Grenoble-based titles, the advertiser has no choice but to place, via Hersant's Publi-Print Régions, his ad in all the Hersant titles . . . and to pay a hefty rate. Rival media brokers note that Hersant companies even seek to control ad space of media that do not belong to the group. In 1990 Hersant titles accounted for some 40 per cent of the total advertising income of the national daily Press; advertising represented 70 per cent of the income of the Hersant group flagship, *Le Figaro* and 54 per cent of that of the group as a whole.

Mogulry *à la* Hersant presupposes unremitting expansion – planned and, more often than not, unplanned. Via la Cinq, Hersant planned to tap regional TV advertising potential. In a related sector, his proven success with magazine supplements was extended to TV programme listings magazines. In France, as elsewhere, this is one of the most lucrative (advertising and sales) categories of the periodical Press; the market leader, *Télé-7-Jours*, is the major money-spinner of the Press division of the Hachette group (3.3 million copies weekly). In October 1988, Hersant's *TV Magazine* had a circulation of four million; it was included as a supplement in twenty-three dailies distributed across the country; these included provincial titles – the Toulouse-based *Dépêche du Midi* for example – from outside the Hersant group. *TV Magazine* claims to be the highest circulation weekly magazine in Europe.

In October 1990, as noted, Hersant lost his position as 'owner-operator' of la Cinq. Yet, despite the continued losses of many of his print media interests, he continued to expand his newspaper and magazine publishing, printing and advertising 'empire' – within France and across Europe. In April 1991, his group reportedly accounted for 35 per cent of the circulation of the national daily Press and 18 per cent of that of the regional daily press. This was before his acquisition, in March 1991, of the Dijon-based daily *Le Bien public*. . . .[32]

## CLASSIFYING MOGULS: FROM HERSANT, THE LAST DINOSAUR, TO HACHETTE, THE ETERNAL OCTOPUS

A media mogul of the old school, Hersant diversified from the Press into broadcasting. He differs in this from some of the moguls who emerged in the 1980s – Francis Bouygues and Patrick le Lay of the construction group Bouygues and, subsequently, TF-1; Jean-Paul Baudecroux of the music and news radio station NRJ (pronounced *énergie*) or André Rousselet, for forty years the friend of François Mitterrand, to whom he owed his first chairmanship of (the then state-controlled) Havas, the advertising, media and tourism combine, and later that of Canal Plus, now Europe's premier subscriber pay-TV channel. Other French print media tycoons lack some of the quintessential characteristics that mark the metamorphosis from press baron into media mogul. Hersant bears comparison with the foreign nationals operating as media moguls in France. Hersant appears singularly homespun in such company – whatever his group's interests in Belgium (*Le Soir* etc.), Portugal and Spain and eastern Europe. Jean-Luc Lagardère and Daniel Filipacchi, of the Hachette and Filipacchi groups, both born in 1928 and jointly responsible for the press division of the Hachette group, cross swords with Hersant in magazine and even daily newspaper publishing.[33] In Hachette, they control a group with a print media tradition of over 150 years standing, and which they have developed internationally – significantly more so than the Hersant group. Yet, of the present vintage of French media moguls, none like Hersant (with the partial exception of Baudecroux) has renewed the megalomaniac tradition of the past – defying, and indeed defeating, the government of the day.

Judged in terms of turnover and workforce, the Hersant and Hachette-Presse groups dominate rival print media organizations (see Table 7.1).

Of course, the classification of communications groups poses all manner of problems. Some relate to availability of data, and to their presentation, interpretation and comparability. Diversification and internationalization strategies compound the problem. In the 1980s, groups based primarily in one medium or range of media accelerated their diversification into other media. Transnational groups increased their presence in the French media – not only moguls like Berlusconi and Maxwell, but also 'Corporation men', such as Bertelsmann's (via Gruner and Jahr and Prisma Presse) Axel Ganz – or the representatives in France of the British Pearson–Longman and the American Dow Jones groups. Furthermore, French industrial, financial and service industry conglomerates increased their communications industry presence: Editions Mondiales, the print media group, ranked number three in 1988, is 100 per cent controlled by the Cora Revillon (consumer goods distribution) group. In addition, many a multi-media group has a stake in what ostensibly appear rival concerns; Berlusconi in 1989–90 held shares in TF-1, while remaining one of the chief shareholders of its competitor, la Cinq. For decades, Havas has had a stake in Audiofina, the holding company controlling 54.6 per cent of the Luxembourg broadcasting company, CLT – both the CLT

*Table 7.1*   The top five print media groups (newspaper and magazine publishers)

| Rank | Name | 1987 | | |
| | | Turnover '000 francs | Profit/loss '000 francs | Employees |
| --- | --- | --- | --- | --- |
| 1 | Hersant group[34] | 6,500,000 | −250,000 | 9,800 |
| 2 | Hachette-Presse[35] | 4,411,000 | +179,025 | 5,100 |
| 3 | Editions Mondiales[36] | 1,650,000 | not available | 1,100 |
| 4 | Publications Filipacchi[37] | 1,591,145 | +100,549 | 705 |
| 5 | Editions Amaury[38] | 1,557,000 | + 49,500 | 1,600 |

| Rank | Name | 1988 | | |
| | | Turnover '000 francs | Profit/loss '000 francs | Employees |
| --- | --- | --- | --- | --- |
| 1 | Hachette-Presse[39] | 8,375,000 | +272,000 | 7,210 |
| 2 | Hersant group[40] | 7,200,000 | −400,000 | 9,800 |
| 3 | Editions Mondiales[41] | 2,000,000 | not available | 1,080 |
| 4 | Ouest-France[42] | 1,777,300 | + 60,480 | 2,499 |
| 5 | CEP Communication[43] | 1,761,000 | +155,000 | 1,450 |

*Source*: *L'Expansion* (December 1988) 'Les 30 premiers groupes de presse'; *L'Expansion* (November 1989) 'Les 30 premiers groupes de presse'.

and Havas were candidates in 1987 for the franchise to operate a private sector TV channel.[44] The age of the 'Franco-French' media mogul – like Hersant in the 1960s and 1970s – is passing away.[45]

French media magnates of the 1990s include a growing number of people (overwhelmingly male) with no actual journalistic or production experience, but with proven financial acumen and management skills. Throughout the communications industry, the old guard of seasoned professionals who often fashioned the empire they now relinquish, make way for the (generally better – or more formally – educated) younger generation. In October 1987, the 81-year-old Marcel Bleustein-Blanchet formally stepped down as head of Publicis in favour of his chosen successor (and fellow Jew) Maurice Lévy; the successful pioneer of radio advertising in the 1930s and the founder of an advertising group that competes for first place in the rankings with the 150-year-old *grande dame* of French advertising, Havas, made way for a 45-year-old who had joined Publicis as a computer programmer and had risen through the company ranks largely through his management skills.[46] In 1987, the Bouygues construction group led the consortium that successfully bid for the franchise for France's leading, and privatized, TV channel, TF-1: in 1986, aged 65 and in ill-health, Francis Bouygues ensured that Patrick le Lay, one of his 'Bouygues boys', succeeded him as Chief Executive of TF-1 (despite the opposition of the second biggest TF-1 shareholder, Robert Maxwell). Previously in charge of the group's diversification strategy, le Lay, like Bouygues himself, had no experience of the audio-visual sector prior to 1987. He had difficulty in ridding himself of the group image of bulldozers and cement, especially as privatized TF-1 was acutely audience ratings-conscious (with the previous day's viewing figures hung up in lifts and on office doors alike); its dominant market-share – 54 per cent of TV advertising revenues, and 41 per cent of the audience in 1989 – made it the channel to beat, and, it claims, Europe's leading private broadcaster and advertising medium. The scenario at TF-1, with a hardened technocrat and manager seconded by a seasoned broadcasting professional – Etienne Mougeotte – in charge of programmes, is often repeated in other French media groups. As is the ascendancy enjoyed by the advertising supremo – Bochko Givadinovitch; at 6.2 billion francs, TF-1's gross advertising in 1989 was almost three times that of France's number two national advertising medium – la Cinq.

French media moguls seek to 'keep it in the family', or at least, to transfer the management of their company to the chosen heir. Thus did Bleustein-Blanchet confer that of Publicis on Maurice Lévy. So, likewise, did Francis Bouygues ensure in 1989 that the mantle of his throne passed to his 38-year-old son, Martin (whose studies stopped with the school-leaving exam, the *baccalauréat*). So, above all, has Jean-Luc Lagardère (born in 1928) prepared his son Arnaud (28 years old in 1990).

As Chief Executive of the Hachette and Matra groups, Lagardère is redolent of both the new and old schools of media moguldom; Hachette, alone of French communications groups, figures in the world's top ten media corporations. An engineer by training – and a product of Supélec, one of the leading private sector training schools – Lagardère first worked (for ten years) in the Dassault aviation company. He is part of the French political–industrial establishment. He heads an armaments and military communications group, Matra, with interests in civilian communications which allegedly dovetail with his chairmanship of France's leading print media communications company. Some argue that Lagardère is the only true link between companies as different as, first, Matra – ranked number thirty-five among French industrial groups in 1988 (5,468 employees, interests in defence and space, telecommunications and information technology, automobiles and transportation systems); second, Hachette – the printing, publishing and print media distribution and newsagent group (24,640 employees, ranked number twenty-eight among French industrial groups and with 48 per cent of its turnover generated outside France); and third, Europe I – one of France's leading commercial radio stations of the past thirty years (acquired by Hachette when the state sold its majority shareholding in 1986).[47]

Lagardère's own direct experience of media management dated from 1977–81: as Chief Executive of Europe I, he made – unsuccessfully and illegally – the first serious attempt to launch a private commercial TV channel (Télé Monte-Carlo). He has experienced several failures as a would-be broadcasting entrepreneur. After years of preparing to enter the audio-visual sector, Hachette was beaten in 1987 by Bouygues for the franchise for privatized TF-1; paradoxically, perhaps, it was following this failure that Hachette accelerated the international expansion of its print media interests (newspapers, magazines, directories and distribution) while biding its time to compete anew for a French TV channel franchise; in June 1990, it acquired a significant minority stake in the Hersant-Berlusconi-led, and loss-making, la Cinq and, in October obtained CSA authorization to up its stake to 25 per cent and become the 'owner'-operator. Yet Lagardère, 'manager of the year' in 1979, sells himself above all as an engineer, a boss, a businessman whose entrepreneurial spirit never flags. He denies that he heads a 'Lagardère group', yet the companies' headquarters, Place de l'Etoile, house executives who attend concurrently to Matra, Hachette and the banking division ARJIL (formed in 1989–90):[48] 'as we occupy a leading role in publishing, in finance and technology, it is only appropriate that our chief staff – fifteen or so top executives – have a vision (and an eye for an opening) of and for the group as a whole.'[49]

'If you're involved in advanced technologies, you have no choice but to diversify.' At Matra, where Lagardère held top management posts between 1963 and 1978, the company diversified from its military base into the manufacture of civilian equipment (vehicles, computers, TV sets). Diversification did not always pay off – in 1975, for instance, when Matra failed to acquire a significant stake in the French market for TV sets. As noted, Lagardère – *un gagneur*, 'a leader of men' – has had his fair share of reverses and defeats. Various factors contribute to his survival. Not least is the role of his mentors, and to his ability, like them, to have appropriate friends in high places. This contributes to Lagardère's abiding positive image in French political, economic and media circles.[50]

Lagardère readily recognizes his debts to his mentors – Marcel Chassagny, the founder of Matra, and Sylvain Floirat, Chassagny's associate from 1957; Floirat also owned an aviation company and, above all, owned Europe I, where, as noted, Lagardère gained his first experience of media management. Personal connections matter: in early 1989, Patrice Pelat, a close friend of President Mitterrand, a walking companion in the streets of Paris, was associated in an insider trading scandal; Lagardère recalled how Pelat had befriended him thirty-five years earlier when, as a young engineer working for Dassault, Lagardère was a nobody. Lagardère has been photographed with all the Presidents of the Fifth Republic (four since 1958) and was made an officer of the Legion of Honour by Mitterrand in 1985. Years of experience at Matra in negotiating contracts with French and foreign governments testify to an ability to combine political prudence, an eye for the main chance, and the image of a forward-looking chief executive who mobilizes a staff of financial, industrial and communications specialists. With the possible exception of André Rousselet,[51] Lagardère symbolizes more than any other French communications mogul the convergence of state and private sector capital, of industry and media, of high technology and commerce.

In late 1980 – or so Lagardère later recounted – a banker proposed that he purchase 41 per cent of Hachette; Matra had already acquired, at Sylvain Floirat's suggestion, Europe I in 1978; in April 1980, it had bought the book publisher Aristide Quillet and the regional daily newspaper, *Les Dernières Nouvelles d'Alsace*. The Floirat–Lagardère friendship explained the Europe I operation; the acquisition of Hachette, however, occasioned several raised eyebrows. Lagardère himself, at a general meeting of Matra shareholders in 1981, hardly provided a convincing explanation of how Hachette fitted into Matra's diversification strategy. Known as 'the green octopus' (*la pieuvre verte*), Hachette was France's leading book publisher, book seller and distributor of print media (via a 49 per cent holding in the Nouvelles Messageries de la Presse Parisienne). Management of the 150-year-old concern was generally on the defensive when criticized for the company's overweening position.

The Hachette operation was concluded through an association with Daniel Filipacchi (born 1928). Back in the 1960s, the flamboyant Filipacchi (with a fellow journalist and jazz fan, Frank Ténot) launched a magazine under the same title as one of Europe I's star pop music programmes – *Salut les copains*. Filipacchi and Ténot subsequently launched other titles aimed at the same or similar 15–34-year-old target markets. In 1976, the flashily-dressed Filipacchi bought *Paris-Match*, the news magazine (from the same Prouvost group from which Hersant acquired *Le Figaro* in 1975).[52] Thus, in 1981, Filipacchi, the proven magazine manager-operator and strategist, joined forces with Lagardère and Floirat to buy Hachette. The Filipacchi Publications group, owner of five weeklies, including *Paris-Match*, and ranked number eight among French print media groups,[53] continues independently of Hachette-Presse. But the interests of both groups are intertwined and Filipacchi is the 'p.-d.g.' of Hachette-Presse as well as of Filipacchi Publications.

We noted above how Hachette responded to its failure to obtain the franchise in 1987 for France's premier television channel, TF-1; it bought control of (more) French regional dailies and, since 1988, has established a major international presence (notably with Diamandis and Grolier in the United States, and in Spain and Latin America).[54] Hachette is reportedly the world number six multi-media group and Europe's number two (after Bertelsmann); present in at least fifteen different national markets (including the US), *Elle*, the women's magazine, symbolizes this expansion. About half of Hachette's turnover now comes from abroad.

In the 1990s, Hachette, more than Hersant or other French media groups, appears set to be France's major international communications group. Between 1985 and 1990, its turnover tripled; its employees worldwide increased from 12,500 to 30,737. In the print media – book, newspaper and magazine publishing – the German-based Bertelsmann is its sole European rival, with 41,000 employees in 30 countries. Hachette argues that it alone of French communications groups is equipped to survive against opposing international multi-media groups – such as Time–Warner, Bertelsmann and Capital Cities; in fourth place (1989 ranking) is Hachette itself. Such self-serving rhetoric was used when, in

September–October 1990, the French regulatory authority examined Hachette's bid to become the owner-operator of France's fifth TV channel. In France, Hachette is the premier book and magazine publisher, print media distributor and printer. Assistant Communications Minister Catherine Tasca argued that even if, by becoming the lead operator of la Cinq, Hachette did not violate French legislation on the concentration of (media) ownership, the tentacular presence – 'la présence multiforme' – across the French communications landscape of the 'green octopus' was such as to cause disquiet.[55] But it may be recalled that Parliament had already debated Hachette's 'abuse' of its 'monopoly' position in the 1890s.

André Rousselet, the man who launched Canal Plus, France's first subscriber TV channel, and made it succeed when many doubted, heads what is potentially France's communications group most likely to succeed internationally, after Hachette.[56] Rousselet is indisputably one of France's most successful modern media moguls: yet he owes his opportunity to his friendship with François Mitterrand. In 1954, during the Fourth Republic, Mitterrand was Minister of the Interior; Rousselet – born in 1922, and six years younger than Mitterrand – became the latter's *chef de cabinet* or Chief of Staff. When in May 1981 Mitterrand succeeded in his third attempt to become President of the Republic, he appointed Rousselet, who had remained a close confidant throughout the previous quarter-century, *directeur de cabinet*. In between these two dates, Rousselet succeeded as a businessman – at the head of a Parisian taxi-cab group – and failed in his ambition as a newspaper publisher (*Sports Magazine*). According to one well-informed journalist, Mitterrand and Rousselet had already agreed, in May 1981, that Rousselet would first act as the president's media strategist or 'Mr Media', before moving to the chairmanship of Havas, the (then) state-controlled advertising, media and tourism combine.[57] In short-term media strategy, discussed on occasion during one of the many Monday morning rounds of golf between the President and his adviser, Rousselet was not always successful; Hersant succeeded in getting the better of him, and did not carry out the promised sale – to a Socialist-leaning businessman – of the Parisian popular daily, *France-Soir*.[58] But he realised two mid- or long-term aims, despite substantial opposition from others close to the President: the creation of private TV channels, intended to shake public service broadcasting out of its lethargy;[59] and the creation of what has been called

'France's biggest audio-visual success' of the past forty-five years[60]
– Canal Plus. Rousselet, in short, is one of a host of figures –
industrialists and financiers, media professionals and politicians,
based in France or across Europe – who advised Mitterrand on
communications policy; he succeeded in becoming a mogul in
his own right, at the head of Canal Plus (launched in November
1984), because he retained the confidence of the President when
all appeared to be turning against him. In July 1985, Canal Plus
hhad substantially fewer subscribers than had been anticipated and
there were many (including the Prime Minister, Laurent Fabius)
who argued that the programming formula (and signal encryption)
should be abandoned. After a row with Fabius, and a heart-to-heart
discussion with Mitterrand (10 July), Rousselet obtained a stay of
execution. Canal Plus (with three million subscribers in 1990) went
on to become Europe's leading subscriber pay-TV channel, with
imitators and subsidiary interests in Belgium, Spain and Germany,
and with a market capitalization higher than that of the company
that sired it – Havas.

Frank Ténot, a Filipacchi man and the head of Europe I since
its outright acquisition by Hachette in 1986, is of a generation
that prefers the phrase 'a successful blending of radio with the
print media' to the term 'multi-media'.[61] Born in 1946, Jean-Paul
Baudecroux has no such reservations. He presents the success of
his FM radio network, NRJ, between 1981–8 as 'the greatest
audio-visual success of the [first] Mitterrand presidency', along with
that of Canal Plus.[62] This brash claim is a facet of mogulry that
Baudecroux shares with Hersant; so, likewise, is his willingness
to ride roughshod over rules and regulations. Mogulry, in the
1980s and 1990s, as earlier, involves bending, if not transgressing,
existing media legislation. Baudecroux fashioned an FM radio
network, with a music and news programme format and funded
by advertising, that beat the competition for its target audience, the
young. He did so *despite* Socialist ministers (like the Premier, Pierre
Mauroy, 1981–4) opposed to the rise of *radios-fric* (commercial
radio): on liberating the airwaves in 1981–2 from the state
monopoly of programming (and, in 1986, of transmissions), the
Socialists had encouraged the emergence of non-commercial (local,
minority interest, etc.) radios. Baudecroux, with socialist party
members on his board of directors, promised they might control
NRJ's news-content – a vacuous promise given the sparse news
flashes on what is above all a music station. And Baudecroux

mobilized his audience against the authorities; on 8 December 1984, over 100,000 young demonstrators, many of them at high school, took to the streets in response to the NRJ appeal 'hands off our radio'; NRJ was threatened for the umpteenth time with the confiscation of its transmitters for violating frequency arrangements – at one time NRJ was transmitting at eighty times the power authorized by the law.

For much of the 1980s, Baudecroux cultivated the 'pirate' image. When NRJ began transmission, with a tiny studio located in a modest garret in the unfashiionable Belleville district of Paris, Baudecroux's model was Radio Caroline, the British archetype of pirate offshore stations. With a background in the hotel business and catering, he launched NRJ with family savings, and – like many another mogul-in-the-making – with a small number of close associates. Baudecroux created an FM radio empire. He did so despite the government and the broadcasting regulatory authorities (la Haute Autorité de la Communication Audiovisuelle, 1982–6; la Commission Nationale de la Communication et des Libertés, 1986–8), and despite the opposition of groups that had previously dominated commercial radio in France – RTL, Europe I, and RMC. Baudecroux, in short, became the broadcasting millionaire of the 1980s, by seizing the commercial possibilities of the liberalization of the airwaves and the technical opportunities (quality of reception) of FM radio. The aggressive methods of the pirate radio captain of the early 1980s and the hard-nosed entrepreneur of later years, frightened rival commercial stations and record publishing houses alike. Baudecroux now seeks respectability, and group diversification possibilities – primarily, but not exclusively, in radio and in France.

The overlap of media ownership is easier in France, say, than in Britain, which has contributed to the expansion of existing empires and the emergence of new moguls; thus two of the leading members in the consortium operating the sixth TV channel between 1986–7 were NRJ and the advertising group Publicis. In France, unlike Britain, advertising agencies are not precluded from part-ownership of television stations. France has little anti-trust legislation in general; periodically there occur scandals or protests at what is known as 'the abuse of a dominant position';[63] but legislation concerning multi-media ownership is liberal. As already noted, the Communications Minister François Léotard argued for very liberal limits (in what became the law of 27 November 1986) so that French groups would not be penalized in competition with their European counterparts.[64] At the national (as opposed to the local) level, a group may own terrestrial television, radio and cable interests as well as daily newspapers; the audience of the radio stations, terrestrial TV and cable channels, however, must not exceed respectively 30, 4 and 6 million inhabitants; as to the Press, the self-same multi-media group must not publish titles whose combined circulation exceeds 20 per cent of the total circulation of all daily newspapers. These restrictions do not appear to have hindered the media diversification strategies of the Maxwell or Hachette groups in France: with a 10 per cent stake in TF-1 (later rising to 12.6 per cent), the majority shareholding in the second French news-agency, ACP (until he closed it down in 1990), and various printing and publishing interests in Paris and the provinces, Maxwell in 1987 tried to buy the leading Marseille newspaper group *Le Provençal*, only to be bested by Lagardère's Hachette.[65] Some experts suggest, however, that Hersant currently develops his newspaper acquisition strategy *outside* France (Spain, Portugal, Belgium and eastern Europe), partly because the circulation of his French (Parisian and provincial) titles exceeds the maximum tolerated level.[66] This does not convince.

In conclusion, it should be recalled that France is also the home of the *anti*-mogul. Hubert Beuve-Méry, the chief founder of the respected daily *Le Monde*, inculcated during his stewardship (1944–69) a respect of pluralism and a detestation of all kinds of dependence – political, economic or other; his oracular editorials following Charles de Gaulle's presidential pronouncements (1958–69) epitomized what was best in the French journalistic tradition. Under 'Beuve', *Le Monde* journalists were poorly paid and advertising revenue tightly controlled. By 1990, *Le Monde* was a major print media group operating in a capitalist and competitive environment; successive directors – while experiencing contrasting fortunes at the head of France's leading quality daily – succeeded in avoiding mogulry *à la française*. A final irony, however, is worth noting: *Le Monde* was created (in December 1944) partly because the then head of government, Charles de Gaulle, wanted France to have a newspaper with international prestige;[67] his motive was little different from that of King Louis XIII and Cardinal Richelieu, who in 1631 authorized the creation of the first major periodical publication in France, *La Gazette*.

# Chapter 8

# Media moguls in Italy

*Gianpietro Mazzoleni*

The term 'mogul' is not so familiar to Italians as the more common 'tycoon'. Leading home-grown representatives of industrial and financial mogulry are known as 'magnate', 'king', 'baron', 'steam-master' and the like. The reference is often personalized, in the form of nicknames that draw on individual or corporate idiosyncrasies. Thus, Giovanni Agnelli is 'The Lawyer', Carlo De Benedetti 'The Engineer', Raul Gardini 'The Farmer'. Or again, expressions like 'financial raider', 'construction king', 'finance magician', 'knight', 'boyard', 'Number One' and similar epithets are applied to Italian moguls and tycoons.

The same is true of Italy's media moguls: the powerful press groups are best identified and known via the names of the families who founded and/or control them.

The rare use of the word mogul, in addition to its exotic origin, is possibly due to the fact that in Italy, the overwhelming majority of firms and businesses are much smaller than the typical US, Japanese, British (and other foreign) giants and multi-nationals. This is particularly true of Italian media corporations: none of them figured in the 1988 classification of the world's ten biggest communications empires.

If, however, from a comparative and international perspective, there are no major Italian media tycoons, the same is not the case when one adopts a strictly domestic viewpoint. The print media industry in Italy since 1945 has witnessed the establishment and strengthening of several economically and politically important publishing oligopolies; these long dominated the domestic media scene.

First (in time) came the Mondadori, the Rizzoli and the Rusconi groups. All three were based in Milan. They gradually acquired control of more than 90 per cent of book publishing and of the weekly magazine industry. The latter is a distinctive feature of the Italian press, and carries considerable influence; for decades the circulation of Italian daily newspapers was very low – below five million copies for a population exceeding fifty million – whereas the circulations of periodicals were high (when compared to consumption rates per capita in other developed countries). None of these top three *editori* or publishers owned a national or a regional daily. Traditionally, daily newspapers were controlled by 'non-publishers': the owners of the *Corriere della Sera, La Stampa, Il Messaggero* and other leading titles were industrialists and finance moguls who found it in their interest to control newspapers; see figures 8.1 and 8.2.

Accordingly, in the debate over the control of the media in Italy, a distinction is often made between 'pure publishers' as opposed to 'impure publishers'.

In the last fifteen years, the separation – which was previously clear-cut – between these two categories and their ownership of various media, gradually disappeared. In 1974, the Rizzoli Editore bought the daily with the highest circulation, the *Corriere della Sera*. In 1976, Eugenio Scalfari, a respected and influential

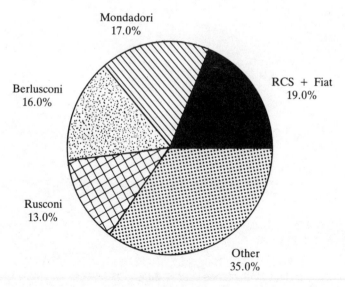

*Figure 8.1* Total weekly Italian magazine circulation, 1989
*Source: Ordina-Tabloid* (January 1990)

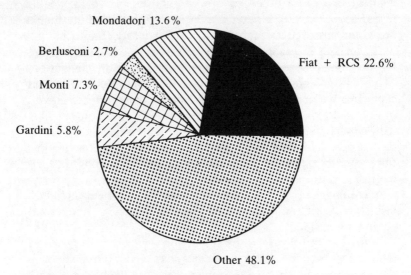

*Figure 8.2* Total daily Italian newspaper circulation, 1989
*Source: Ordina-Tabloid* (February 1990)

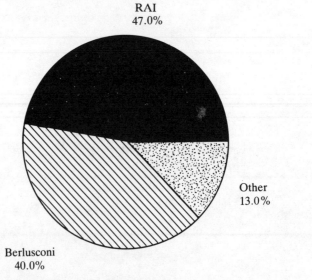

*Figure 8.3* Italian TV audience shares, 1989
*Source: Ordina-Tabloid* (February 1990)

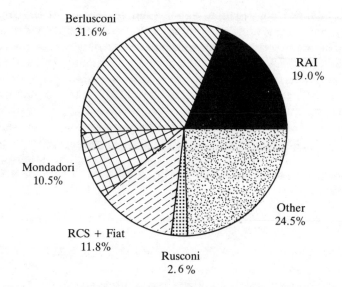

*Figure 8.4* The controllers of Italian Press and TV advertising, 1989
*Source: La Repubblica* (7 December 1989)

journalist, founded a new daily, *La Repubblica*: 50 per cent of
its shares were held by the Arnoldo Mondadori Editore, which
subsequently launched its own chain of provincial newspapers.

The Rizzoli venture into daily newspaper publishing ended in
bankruptcy (1984); both the publishing house and the *Corriere* were
taken over by a consortium of financiers, banks and industrialists
(Gemina). The Mondadori–*La Repubblica* story ended differently:
in 1989, it merged with Editoriale L'Espresso. This expansionist
publishing group owned the prestigious news-weekly *L'Espresso*
and a chain of local newspapers; it was controlled by De Benedetti,
an 'impure publisher'.

The crossholdings between the media and industrial or financial
groups are not limited to publishing (books, newspapers and
magazines). In the late 1970s, the celebrated – or infamous –
'television revolution' in Italy saw the end of the state monopoly
of broadcasting exercised by the RAI, a public company (whose
top appointments were mostly controlled by the leading political
parties). In 1976, the Italian Supreme Court ruled that RAI
had no monopoly on local broadcasting; private entrepreneurs
were free to enter the broadcasting sector.[1] Silvio Berlusconi,

a little-known construction tycoon (and real estate developer), along with the leading publishing groups – Rizzoli, Mondadori and Rusconi – went into television; each company first opened a (commercial) TV station in Milan, and subsequently established nationwide networks. The absence of clear rules and regulations – Parliament debated broadcasting bills from 1975, to little or no avail – and the bitter fight for market share (audience and advertising revenue) resulted in the defeat of the three publishing groups, and the emergence of a victorious Berlusconi. He eventually acquired Mondadori's Rete-4, and Rusconi's Italia-1. Bloody, but unbowed (and aggressively expansionist) he continued to battle with the RAI channels.

## MAPPING THE MOGULS

This brief historical outline sketches in some of the features of the map of Italian media moguls.

From Table 8.1 it is clear that Berlusconi group interests and assets cover the entire media spectrum (save for book publishing); it is present in the print media, satellite broadcasting and advertising (and related interests: in 1988 it acquired the Standa supermarket chain). The Mondadori and Agnelli groups come a good second, even though their activities are centred on the print media. The five remaining groups appear 'baby' moguls by comparison; either they only have interests in a smaller number of media fields, or their corporate turnover is significantly lower than that of the Berlusconi, Agnelli and Mondadori groups. Some of these baby moguls are giants in their principal area of activity or sector (Gardini and ENI in

*Table 8.1* Map of Italy's media moguls, 1989

|  | TV | Dailies | Periodicals | Books | Film | Advertising | New media | News agencies |
|---|---|---|---|---|---|---|---|---|
| Berlusconi | X | X | X |  | X | X | X |  |
| Mondadori |  | X | X | X |  | X |  |  |
| Agnelli |  |  |  |  |  |  |  |  |
| +RCS |  | X | X | X |  | X | X |  |
| Rusconi |  | X | X | X |  | X |  |  |
| Gardini |  | X |  |  |  |  |  |  |
| Monti |  | X |  |  |  | X |  |  |
| ENI |  | X |  |  |  |  |  | X |
| Parretti | X |  |  |  | X |  |  |  |

the chemical industry and agribusiness, for instance); but their stake in the media industry is not comparable to that held by Berlusconi or Agnelli.

In early 1990, there occurred what promised to be a major change in the ownership of the Italian media; Berlusconi appeared poised to snatch the control of the Mondadori group from De Benedetti – following a complex manoeuvre involving Mondadori shareholders, including members of the original family firm, the Mondadori and Formenton families. De Benedetti resisted fiercely, and successfully; there was general Press and political condemnation of the Berlusconi mega-media group that would have emerged if the 'construction king' had added Mondadori to his existing media empire.

## BEHIND THE MYSTIQUE: CHARACTERISTICS OF MEDIA MOGULRY

The important role of 'impure' interests in the ownership of the Italian media makes it very difficult to pinpoint the distinctive features of Italian media moguls. Initially, the moguls come to public attention as the *condottieri* of non-media empires – as 'captains of industry', to use a nineteenth-century phrase. Their public images are suffused with the trappings of industrial and/or financial power. The media-related imagery comes later, just as their stake in the media sometimes appears secondary to their main sector of activity.

Thus, references to Agnelli are grounded in his mystique as Fiat's (and Italy's) 'lord and master', even when it is his media policy that is under discussion. Almost the same can be said of the public images of De Benedetti and Gardini. Berlusconi is the exception; despite his 'impure' origins, he was first – and remains best – known as a media entrepreneur, as 'Mr Broadcasting' (*Sua Emittenza*).[2]

Nonetheless, the following characteristics appear to be valid for most Italian media moguls:

1 The print media were *not* the power-base of most moguls. As already noted, the majority of today's moguls bought into the media with money acquired elsewhere. The daily Press, in particular, has always been considered a strategic investment by ambitious industrial groups; this was possible because of the traditional subservience of the Press to the political and

economic establishment in Italy. Accordingly, the wielding of political influence is the major reason why an industrial or business tycoon seeks to acquire media interests: public visibility and private (and public) influence count for more than return on investment.

This explains why industrialists did not get rid of their newspapers even when their circulations were in decline. Nowadays, the publishing industry is, broadly speaking, in a better financial state; the electronic and print media are sometimes sources of high financial return. Moguls accordingly have additional incentives to stay in the business and expand further.

2 Most media moguls are more concerned with owning (than with running) the media. In the period when the Mondadori Editore and Rizzoli companies were still under family control, 'own-and-operate' remained the dominant attitude. But today, after the takeovers, mergers and concentration of ownership mentioned above, ownership alone is the dominant concern. The only 'own-and-operate' media magnate is Silvio Berlusconi. His empire is largely his own creation and he personally supervises its daily management and masterminds its long-term strategy: he is actively involved in running his various companies, and, above all, his TV channels.

Other moguls – such as Agnelli, Gardini and Parretti – limit the exercise of their control to ownership and to appointing loyal executives to manage their media interests.

This attitude is consistent with the 'impure' nature of ownership of Italian media. Industrialists and financiers are generally unfamiliar with the ground rules and lack the necessary know-how to be directly involved in managing a newspaper or a broadcasting organization.

3 The economy, the media and politics are closely intertwined in Italy. The rise and fall of the captains of industry can often be explained in terms of their political ties. Political parties are extremely sensitive to the role of the media. They either seek to control directly the editorial policies of dailies and news magazines by owning shares in media organizations or by running their own newspapers; or else they seek to condition and influence media owners indirectly, in all manner of ways. All the media moguls, albeit in varying degrees, are connected with the political establishment. None of them can operate without

paying homage to one or more actors on the complex Italian political scene. The moguls support – sometimes financially – the politicians, and the latter favour the expansionist strategies of the moguls.

Italian media moguls, like their foreign counterparts are often controversial figures. Four of the eight – Agnelli, Berlusconi, De Benedetti, Gardini – are much in the public eye. They pronounce upon a host of issues; their deeds are the subject of biographies, articles, television specials; their faces adorn the front covers of high-circulation magazines. Many like to see their own, or their family's, idiosyncrasies given prominence. Whenever they are criticized or attacked, Italian moguls strike back with considerable effrontery; it is not unknown for them to cancel the advertising budget planned for the media employing the offending journalist or writer.

## SILVIO BERLUSCONI OR 'MR BROADCASTING'

Born in 1936, this self-made man is the media mogul *par excellence*. The public immediately associates him with television, much more so than it does Agnelli and De Benedetti with publishing and newspapers.

As mentioned above, he struck gold in the construction business. But it is his subsequent media empire, which he built from nothing, that has led him to be known as 'Mr Broadcasting'. Today, Berlusconi is one of the wealthiest men in the country. He owns 100 per cent of Fininvest, his empire's holding company. *Fortune 1989* ranked him thirty-sixth in its list of the world's richest men, and credited him with a personal estate of $2.8 billion; this placed him far ahead of Agnelli, who ranked seventy-seventh.

Fininvest's assets are not confined to the media. Its interests range as widely as construction, retail, insurance and football. The media (and related activities), however, are the jewels in Berlusconi's crown. In 1987, they accounted for 84 per cent of the consolidated revenue of the group. In 1988, following the takeover of Standa, the supermarket chain, the media-generated proportion fell to 43.8 per cent.

Berlusconi has a highly diversified range of interests in almost all the sectors of the media:

Through the subholding RTI SpA Berlusconi has effective monopoly control of Italian commercial (private sector) television.

His most cherished network, Canale-5, alone commands 20.7 per cent of the prime-time national audience, ranking second after RAI-1 (1988 Auditel data). When this is combined with the audience of Berlusconi's other networks, Rete-4 and Italia-1, the audience share rises to 39.7 per cent (the RAI channels total 46.7 per cent). RTI also controls Berlusconi's television assets abroad – including the stakes in la Cinq in France, Telefunf in Federal Germany and Telecinco in Spain.

The Fininvest subsidiary, Reteitalia, oversees Fininvest's activities in cinema, show business and sports. Berlusconi controls the complete cycle of the fiction industry: from production, through distribution, to the movie theatres (310 in 1988). His avowed ambition is to become a 'European major' of the cinema industry. He may well succeed, if his negotiations with Italy's Cecchi Gori (controlling much of the distribution of feature films in Italy), France's Pathé Cinema – which another Italian media mogul, Giancarlo Parretti sought to acquire in 1990[3] – and Germany's Leo Kirch end positively.[4]

Berlusconi's interests in sport stem from the belief that in Italy public relations are advanced considerably by sponsoring a football team. This way, one is guaranteed daily media coverage. Agnelli owns Juventus, a top European team. Berlusconi bought Milano, which subsequently won the league championship. This proved a masterly coup; Berlusconi became one of the country's beloved heroes.

Like other media and financial magnates, Berlusconi wanted to control a daily newspaper. He has 82 per cent of *Il Giornale Nuovo*, an influential conservative daily based in Milan and which has a national readership. 'Mr Broadcasting' has stakes in both publishing and printing. Along with *Il Giornale Nuovo* he owns *Sorrisi e Canzoni TV*, a television weekly, the major money-spinner of his Press division. Furthermore, he has a number of printing plants strategically placed throughout the country. As a result of the anti-trust provisions of the 1990 media law, however, Berlusconi will have to sell his interests in *Il Giornale Nuovo* within two years if he wishes to continue to own three TV networks.

Last but not least, Publitalia 80 is easily the most successful of all his companies – a veritable goldmine. This agency grew by leaps and bounds during the hectic years of the birth and expansion of private sector commercial television (late 1970s and early 1980s). It is responsible for the amazing increase in advertising expenditure that benefited all the Italian media during the 1980s, but particularly television.[5] The first, of course, to profit from this boom was – and is – Berlusconi's television empire. He controls 32 per cent of Italy's total advertising spend and 70 per cent of television advertising expenditure.[6]

What most strikes analysts and observers is Berlusconi's skill in promoting his various domestic interests and in scouting for new business opportunities on the international market-place. No other Italian media mogul is as aggressive in the attempt to diversify and to expand his stakes abroad. Temporary set-backs do not appear to dishearten him. His entrepreneurial risk-taking is acknowledged by friend and foe alike, and is undoubtedly one of his most distinctive traits.

Berlusconi's strategy throughout western and eastern[7] Europe is to be constantly on the watch for media opportunities; he establishes countless contacts and concludes all manner of deals, joint-ventures and buy-outs, most of which prove successful.

Berlusconi has much in common with other multi-media moguls. Like Maxwell, he does not love the stock market. Like Murdoch, he knows how to generate profits so as to fuel his next move. He resembles Hersant (and Murdoch) in his ability to buy up media in difficulty and turn them round. To succeed in the media business, he believes it is essential to recognize its multi-media and multi-national dimension.

Accordingly, he strives to overcome political resistance at a supra-national level. In June 1989 he became chairman of a body set up to defend private television industry's interests in the European Community's single market. He pledged that this lobby, the Association of Commercial Television in Europe (ACT) would defend the cause of free competition in broadcasting as well as the improvement of quality: 'every product is improved by competition,' he claimed.[8]

As mentioned above, Berlusconi is a truly 'own-and-operate' media mogul. He is surrounded by a talented and efficient management team, but all are overshadowed by his dominant personality. The image conveyed by the news media is that Berlusconi is very much in direct control of each of his myriad companies.

In the Milan football team saga, he even seems to be involved emotionally. He loves stepping out from his helicopter in the middle of the stadium just before the game starts. He does not hesitate to appear on RAI TV sports programmes to discuss the performance of his team.

For all this show-biz approach, Berlusconi keeps a tight personal watch over his businesses. He has always done so. At the outset of his career as a property dealer and building contractor, he chose his associates from within his family and close friends. He was reputedly the most cunning, the most ambitious, and the most cynical of the lot.

Of middle-class origins – his father was a Milanese bank official – Berlusconi graduated with honours in law from Milan University with a dissertation on 'The newspaper advertising contract' – a striking omen of his future fortune. Like many self-made men, he had a varied and colourful early manhood. He once made his living by singing in a music group on boats cruising the Mediterranean. His piano partner, Fedele Confalonieri, is still his most trusted *alter ego* – in work, as in play.

With the help of his father's contacts in banking circles – and (according to hostile biographers[9]), of mysterious Swiss financiers – Berlusconi first struck gold when he won the contract to build an entire village complex, in northern Milan. He has never looked back: Milano-2, Milano-3, Telemilano, Canale-5, Fininvest, Publitalia '80, Milan Club, Standa, Mondadori.

Despite (or because of) his rapid financial success, Berlusconi, like De Benedetti and Benetton, was long snubbed by the 'old guard' of the exclusive club of Italian high finance.[10] He does not seem to show regret or resentment about this. He discreetly weaves his web of contracts with the financial establishment; he exchanges compliments with Agnelli, and avoids stepping on his and others' strategic interests. The end result is the image of a tycoon gradually gaining acceptance by Italy's corporate establishment – some of whose members, however, perhaps secretly enjoy the Berlusconi – De Benedetti struggle over Mondadori, as the come-uppance of rival upstarts.

Berlusconi, however, has substantially more opponents within the political establishment. For all his attempts not to irritate the 'anti-Berlusconi faction', he has failed to soften its stance. The Communists and Christian Democrats combat 'Mr Broadcasting's' broadcasting policies and, indeed, his presence in television. Neither party has forgiven his destruction of the monopoly of public service television. The Communists, especially, bitterly oppose the commercialism of private sector television channels, and the possible emergence of a Fininvest–Mondadori group. Berlusconi sought to overcome this hostility by cultivating his long-standing friendship with a key figure in Italian politics, Bettino Craxi, leader of the Socialist Party and former Prime Minister (1983–7). It was under the Craxi government that 'Mr Broadcasting's' empire was rescued from various judicial enquiries and legal proceedings. The Parliamentary opposition of the time referred contemptuously to the 'Berlusconi decree'.

In the spring of 1990, Berlusconi appeared to have more enemies in Parliament than friends. Parliament debated a broadcasting bill, first mooted in 1987, and presented by the Post and Telecommunications Minister, the Republican Oscar Mammi: none of the provisions of its thirty-nine articles (anti-trust arrangements, the incompatibility of ownership of both national and local TV channels, etc.) exactly favoured Berlusconi. In March, the Senate or upper house examined the Mammi Bill's proposals concerning advertising – an hourly limit or ceiling varying from 10 per cent to 18 per cent, depending on whether the broadcaster was a public or private channel. Unexpectedly, the left wing of the Christian Democrat Party supported the amendment presented by the Communist Party, banning 'natural breaks' and advertising spots during the transmission of a feature film, a play, opera or ballet. Were the amendment to be adopted by the lower house, the Chamber of Deputies, and become law, it was claimed that Fininvest would lose up to a quarter of its advertising revenue. The unexpected support for the amendment of Christian Democrat senators appears to have stemmed from the hostility towards Berlusconi, engendered both by the rampant commercialism of his television programmes, and by his attempt, from January 1990, to acquire control of Mondadori; this highlighted the contradictory attitudes towards Berlusconi of the five parties that formed the government coalition – ranging from one of lukewarm tolerance (the Christian Democrat leadership) to one of enthusiastic support (the Socialists). Few dared to surmise what would happen when the bill returned to the Chamber of Deputies.

Berlusconi's intervention in the Mondadori group's affairs was made possible by a switch of allegiance by members of the formerly dominant family (the Mondadori-Formenton). Berlusconi thus touched upon the raw nerves of corporate Italy and provoked a reaction in many circles – political and cultural, as well as financial.

## CARLO DE BENEDETTI, THE CANNY FINANCIER

In 1988, on winning the hard-fought battle to gain control of Mondadori, 'The Engineer' was asked why he had embarked on the enterprise: 'because it is a good company' was his reply. A year later, at the climax of the talks about a merger between Mondadori and L'Espresso, De Benedetti was questioned about the risks to Press freedom presented by the new combine. He replied: 'I'm neither a journalist nor a politician, so I look at the profit margins.'

These remarks encapsulate the entrepreneurial spirit of Carlo De Benedetti, undoubtedly the most extraordinary Italian financial mogul.

The boldness and shrewdness of his business methods have made De Benedetti a European celebrity and the subject of continual controversy within Italy. He is little loved by either the 'old guard' of Italian finance – whom De Benedetti once called a 'historical monument' – or by other figures of the 'new financial order'.[11]

His foes consider him something of a bore, a lone wolf who only makes alliances for the immediate, short-term advantage they can bring. Berlusconi, his antagonist in the bid for the control of Amef, the holding company controlling a bare majority of the shares in Mondadori, described De Benedetti's methods as 'cannibalistic': '[he] specializes in buyups and mergers, with the sole purpose of impoverishing someone to his own advantage.'[12]

'The Engineer's' financial strategy is applied to a wide range of interests: car components, computers, the media, insurance, banking, food, and pure finance. As an entrepreneur, he is clearly an 'owner', but not an 'operator'. Unlike Berlusconi, his personal identification with any of his various assets is fairly weak. The media interests are no exception. He did not immediately put his imprint on Mondadori–L'Espresso for example.

De Benedetti entered the communication sector relatively late in his career. Some argue, indeed, that this happened almost by chance.[13] In 1983, he acquired a minority shareholding in L'Espresso and thus helped strengthen the company's shaky financial structure. In 1985, he pumped fresh cash into Mondadori, at the time in dire straits, following its disastrous venture into television.[14] Thus De Benedetti's love affair with the media began by his bailing them out.

Even if he is not a mogul with a base in the print media, his knack of singling out potential winners made him appreciate the strategic importance of his initial 'casual' involvement in the media business.

De Benedetti is also convinced of the worldwide challenges and opportunities in the information sector. Anything but parochial, he speaks and operates in global terms:

> I believe that I've established, through Olivetti and my publishing interests, an extraordinary platform for the construction of an 'information industry' capable of standing up to international competition. No other European group is in a comparable position.[15]

The Mondadori–L'Espresso group, however, is far from being a multi-media company. Its interests are primarily in traditional or mainstream publishing: books, magazines, daily newspapers, papermills, printing plants. Under De Benedetti, the group considered it necessary to diversify into commercial television: here, however, it ran up against Berlusconi. A previous Mondadori venture into television in 1982–4 was not a success, possibly because of the company's unfamiliarity with a sector where, at the time, the law of the jungle prevailed.

On merging with Mondadori (1989), L'Espresso brought with it SPER, one of the major national radio networks. Radio, however, was not considered then a major growth sector, partly because of the impending likelihood of severe broadcasting regulation.

Nor does the group have much of an international presence. This is largely limited to interests in Spanish book publishing and in Dutch stationery businesses.

The Mondadori–L'Espresso group, nonetheless, enjoys an excellent financial situation (US $1.8 billion in sales in 1988) and generates high profits; its stock is much sought after by investors. The daily newspaper *La Repubblica*, in particular, is a highly successful newspaper, both economically and journalistically. In addition many of the group's weeklies and local papers are the leading titles in their respective market sectors.

At one stage in the Berlusconi–De Benedetti battle for control of Mondadori, it appeared the group might be split up. There might be a return to the *status quo ante*, of prior to the Mondadori–L'Espresso merger; Berlusconi was to control Mondadori Editore, still Italy's leading publisher, and De Benedetti would control L'Espresso group. This solution appeared likely to satisfy in part some of the most resolute critics of Berlusconi's concentration-of-ownership policy; these included the editorial board of *La Repubblica* and *L'Espresso*, which were close to the opposition parties. But by mid-1990 it appeared that De Benedetti was well-placed to regain control of Mondadori, following a decision by a special arbitration panel in his favour. In classic mogul fashion, 'The Engineer' and 'Mr Broadcasting' gave one another a good run for their money, before the likely agreed compromise.

In politics, De Benedetti, like other Italian media moguls, is finely-tuned to changes in the political mood. He manages to keep on good terms with all the parties and, indeed, exercises something of a fascination over the Communist Party (PCI) and its progressive elements (whose influential mouthpiece is *La Repubblica*). He is seen as the personification of enlightened capitalism. His positive image among the left doubtless stems from the praise that De Benedetti has given, publicly and repeatedly, in the process of democratic evolution within the PCI. Like Agnelli, 'The Engineer' likes to play the thinker and the sage when fashioning his public image.

## GIANNI AGNELLI: 'THE LAWYER'

'The raw power of the Agnelli empire is masked in many ways. The man himself seems at times to be a royal figure; indeed the House of Agnelli in Turin is in many ways a natural successor to the Turin-based Royal House of Savoy. . . . When . . . the monarchy was abolished just after the Second World War, the Agnelli family almost immediately took [its] place. It is sometimes hard for non-Italians to understand the aura that surrounds the Agnelli family. To challenge the House of Agnelli is virtually unthinkable. . . . This is why De Benedetti [and others] are so unusual in recent Italian history. They did mount a challenge, each in his own way. When their techniques – modern Wall Street methods such as hostile takeover bids or public share offers – are employed in the Italian business world, the tendency is to be suspicious and to search for 'motives' behind each deal, as though the quest for corporate assets and profits were not sufficient motive in itself.

In the 1980s . . . Gianni Agnelli, the unquestioned *Numero Uno* of the nation, was still using the language of the Medici to describe 20th century business transactions. 'We have annexed a weak province,' he proclaimed in 1986 when he took control of

Alfa Romeo. It was 'heresy' to suggest that the Italian Press was not totally free, said the man who in 1988 controlled two of the three leading newspapers in the country.'[16]

The 'Agnelli saga' is an integral part of the history of Italy in the twentieth century. Fiat – Fabbrica Italiana di Automobili Torino – was founded in 1899; from Gianni's grandfather – Giovanni, born in 1866, a founder shareholder and the managing director of Fiat in 1899 – to the 69-year-old Gianni (born 1921), successive generations of the Agnellis, the Turincsc automobile dynasty, have been closely associated with many of the major political, economic and cultural events in Italy.[17]

One might expect that a group that has established such a network of power and intrigue would be viewed critically. The contrary is the case; in Italy, Gianni Agnelli enjoys a positive image, is revered by the Press, is reckoned the most prestigious ambassador of Italian enterprise, has the ear of many politicians, and gets his way on most issues – from Alfa Romeo (which the Craxi government initially had the temerity to intend to sell to Ford, the world number two automobile concern) to the rejection of proposals for anti-trust legislation.

Agnelli, of course, promotes the family legend, and is personally assiduous in self-promotion. The one-time rake and socialite, who was already aged 45 when he took personal charge of Fiat (1966), today delivers speeches to the Trilateral Commission and lectures in prestige university campuses around the world. Much more than De Benedetti, Agnelli sedulously cultivates the image of the industrialist as philosopher. He plays the role of a new Maecenas, patron of the arts.

Constantly under public scrutiny, Agnelli appears to enjoy his popularity and, indeed, sometimes plays to the gallery. The most often quoted examples of his 'coquetry' are the wristwatch laced over his cuffs and the tie that adorns his waistcoat. The pictures portraying 'l'Avvocato' ('The Lawyer' – he never actually practised) in quality and gossip magazines are always extremely stylish; he is seen sitting among other VIPs attending an official ceremony or skiing at St Moritz or at the helm of his luxury yacht. In a word, he cultivates the image of the irresistible power-broker, at work and at play, for fellow-Italians and foreign observers alike.[18] Observing Agnelli stepping out of his jet, an American tycoon reportedly 'had the impression of watching a celestial apparition'.[19]

And Agnelli is associated with more 'popular' sports. In Italy, football reigns supreme, and the media industry – there are three daily newspapers solely devoted to sports (with a total circulation of two million) – manufactures countless stars and gossip. Even Agnelli finds it wise to maintain the family association with Juventus, built up by his father, Eduardo, into a major football team. Gianni Agnelli therefore owns a Turin-based team that has won countless Italian, European and international trophies: 'la Juve' is 'the team of the heart' – the team with which the Italians have the greatest sentimental ties.

The Agnelli interests and assets in communications followed, as a matter of course, the expansion of the Fiat-based empire; they appear part and parcel of its public relations' strategy. The Turin daily, *La Stampa*, has been Agnelli-controlled since 1920:[20] their ownership has never been challenged, whereas most of the other major newspapers have frequently changed hands since World War II. Through Gemina – a finance company indirectly controlled by Fiat – Agnelli and his allies have since 1984 had a majority stake in the *Corriere della Sera* (Milan), one of the most influential Italian newspapers and a title with a long and prestigious history.[21]

The *Corriere* is part of the Rizzoli–Corriere group, RCS, the second major publishing concern in Italy (1988 turnover: 1,489 billion lire); in 1984, the Rizzoli–Corriere newspaper and publishing concern was reportedly Italy's biggest. In early 1990, RCS published titles that accounted for over 16 per cent of the total circulation of weeklies, and owned the fourth biggest advertising-selling or media brokerage agency (RCS Pubblicita). In book publishing, it ranked second – after Mondadori. In February 1990 the Gruppo Editoriale Fabbri, which controls several medium-sized but prestigious publishers (Bompiani, Etas, Fabbri, Sonzogno, Adelphi), was sold to RCS by Agnelli.

The best indicator of Agnelli's power in the communications sector is the advertising expenditure which his group controls. The sheer scale of his financial and industrial assets makes him by far the country's biggest advertiser. The allocation – or withholding – of advertising budgets gives him vast influence over the media.

The range and scale of Agnelli's interests in the communications industry has occasionally been the subject of judicial investigation. The Press Guarantor – a body overseeing the concentration of newspaper ownership, set up by the 1981 press law – ruled that Fiat exceeded the authorized limit of the control of titles accounting for

20 per cent of total circulation, through its ownership of *La Stampa*, the *Corriere* and other Rizzoli newspapers. Cesare Romiti, Fiat's chief executive, fought the ruling. The case was brought before a Milanese judge; in December 1986, he acquitted Fiat, arguing that it did not control Gemina, the investment company which led the consortium that acquired a majority stake in Rizzoli–Corriere between 1984 and 1985. Whatever the technical and legal niceties – there exists no such group as Fiat–RCS, but cross-ownership between myriad companies – political and cultural circles were alarmed at the apparently ever-increasing power of Fiat in the print media and publishing.[22]

The story of how Agnelli acquired control of the Rizzoli–Corriere group illustrates the policy and attitudes of 'impure' publishers towards media ownership.[23] In late 1984, Agnelli imputed to noble motives the actions of the consortium led by Fiat, organized to save the venerable but nigh bankrupt 'declining-and-falling' *Corriere*: 'We took part in the operation in order to disinfect and purify.' The 'cheap' acquisition of Rizzoli–Corriere (now RCS) proved a financial success. In 1987, it was reckoned that Rizzoli might be worth ten times what the original consortium had paid. The group expanded internationally – significantly more so than Mondadori. It swapped shares (10 per cent) with Hachette, and is present in the US. It aims to buy publishing houses and magazines when and where they become available.[24]

RCS, however, has little broadcasting presence. In 1987, Romiti announced RCS had an option to buy 50 per cent of Télé Monte-Carlo, an Italian-language network based in Monaco, and therefore beyond the reach of Italian law. Agnelli, however, allegedly killed off incipient attempts to enter television, apparently so as to secure the good offices of Berlusconi, whom he stated was the only television mogul in Italy.[25] Observers have pointed out that Berlusconi remained quiet when in 1986 Fiat succeeded, despite considerable parliamentary and press hostility, in acquiring Alfa Romeo.[26] Parliamentary critics of Fiat's potential control of a television channel – and thus of news programmes – included Gianni de Michelis, the then Socialist leader in the Chamber of Deputies: 'it is more typical of Malaysia than an advanced industrial nation that a single group should control everything from industry and banks to insurance, newspapers and television.'[27]

The Agnelli family's involvement in politics extends back to the founder of the dynasty; Giovanni Agnelli was close to the leading

Liberal Prime Minister of early twentieth-century Italy, Giovanni Giolitti, and in 1914 supported a rising young politician called Benito Mussolini. In the late 1970s, Giovanni's brother, Umberto, was a Christian Democrat Senator; his sister, Susanna, was still a Senator of the (small but influential) Republican Party in 1990, and has been Undersecretary of the Ministry of Foreign Affairs. Gianni himself has avoided a parliamentary career; his Fiat empire power-base is more than sufficient to enable him to deal as a power in the land, with Italian ministers, Prime Ministers and Presidents. His control of influential newspapers is his chief instrument in the hurly-burly of daily politics.

More so, it seems, than De Benedetti or Berlusconi, Agnelli basks in power for its own sake.

## THE 'BABY' MOGULS

The media empires of Agnelli, Berlusconi and De Benedetti are by far the largest in Italy. There exists, in addition, a series of small, but expanding, media groups, from whose ranks there may shortly emerge new moguls. Raul Gardini, whose varied interests include a burgeoning media group, is one such possibility.

To call the chairman of the Ferruzi group a 'baby' mogul may sound a little odd. As noted earlier, he heads a multinational corporation with interests in chemicals (Montedison), cement, sugar (Béghin–Say) and agriculture (Central Soya). Nonetheless, his stake in the print media, although significant, is still too limited for him to merit inclusion with the leading media moguls. He owns the leading Roman newspaper *Il Messaggero* – this was already part of the Montedison group when Gardini acquired control of the latter in 1987 – and, until 1990, controlled the small financial daily, *Italia Oggi*. In addition, Gardini is a minority shareholder in the Gemina investment company (which controls RCS) and in the Editoriale SpA (which controls a number of leading regional newspapers).

Gardini is reportedly eager to expand his media interests. In 1990, he acquired the Italian-language channel of Télé Monte-Carlo, which as a company transmitting from outside Italy can, unlike Berlusconi's channels, broadcast 'live' programmes. Gardini is set to join the exclusive club of Italian media moguls. He already has all the other hallmarks – wealth, idiosyncrasies, aggressive business methods, the necessary political connections. Like Agnelli and De

Benedetti, Gardini is an 'impure' publisher: he owns newspapers primarily because of the influence and pressure they can wield, and only secondly because of the profits they may generate.

The Rusconi group is possibly the only surviving 'pure' publisher of any significance. Its founder and chief executive Edilio Rusconi was born, and has remained, a print entrepreneur. For some thirty years, his publishing company was generally associated with the troika – Mondadori, Rizzoli and Rusconi. While the first two founding families lost control of their companies, Rusconi succeeded in keeping the majority of shares within the family.

His medium-sized empire had a total turnover of 430 billion lire in 1987. It has stakes in newspapers (100 per cent ownership of *La Notte*, a Milan afternoon daily), periodicals, books and advertising: it controls 13 per cent of the circulation of weekly titles, and ranks fourth after Mondadori, RCS and Berlusconi.

Rusconi is basically a print media 'baby' mogul of the own-and-operate category. His attempt to create a commercial television group, after initial success, foundered against Berlusconi's ever-expanding empire. Unlike Mondadori, Rusconi was clever enough to sell off his TV assets before incurring losses that would have seriously damaged his finances and image.

Attilio Monti, a former petrol tycoon who moved into publishing, is at the head of the above-mentioned Editoriale, the parent company of Poligrafici, a medium-sized group of regional and provincial newspapers. In addition 'The Knight' owns the Spe, an advertising-space sales agency.

The Monti group assets are often the subject of the attention of financial raiders. Monti recently tried to resist such pressures by exchanging shares with the German group Springer: Springer acquired 10 per cent of Poligrafici and Monti 10 per cent of Axel Springer Gesellschaft für Publizistik. Through this strategic alliance, the Monti group was launched onto the international stage.

As regards advertising agencies, nearly all the leading agencies are subsidiaries of US, British and French groups. The few all-Italian agencies, such as Armando Testa, have not bred any mogul-like figure. This is somewhat surprising: a media system as dynamic and lively as the Italian one might have been expected to generate a strong indigenous advertising industry.

The main reason why this did not happen stems perhaps from the variegated nature of the media in Italy. The information media (press, TV, radio) have a high political profile and as such have always been coveted by Italian industrialists and closely monitored by politicians. Commercial communication (advertising) has no such significance; the moguls were uninterested in the investment necessary to acquire control, and the politicians simply disregarded it.

## CONCLUSION

This brief account of the characteristics of Italian media moguls, and of the context in which they operate, indicates the precarious, fast-moving nature of the relationship between the media, politics and big business. Two facets of this precarious situation are the fluid structure of domestic media empires, and the changing nature of public policies towards the media.

As indicated earlier, the scale of the media assets of Italian moguls is quite small compared to that of Bertelsmann or Murdoch (or even Hersant) interests. Even were the Berlusconi and Mondadori–L'Espresso merger to occur, the result would still remain relatively small-scale. In June 1990, the Agnelli group controlled 20 per cent of the circulation of weekly titles and 22 per cent of that of daily newspapers; Berlusconi already controlled 50 per cent of the TV market (three of eight major channels; Publitalia, his advertising sales arm, sells airtime for a number of other commercial networks[28]) and 16 per cent of the circulation of daily newspapers; were he to acquire control of Mondadori–L'Espresso, he would control a third of Italy's magazines. But he would still not figure in the Bertelsmann or Murdoch category. Italy's media trusts are structurally handicapped by the Italian language and Italian culture; whatever their international appeal and aura the Italian media groups are largely confined to the domestic market. Berlusconi is probably an exception, for he is increasingly active on the international stage. But the difficulties his TV export policies (of Italian programming, and of US-bought programmes) encounter in France and in Spain testify to the in-built limits of even his empire. The next difficulty that hampers big and 'baby' moguls alike is their relatively small degree of diversification. Three-quarters of their turnover comes from the traditional print sector or, in the case of Berlusconi, from television- and radio-related activities.

The result is that Italian media moguls are relatively absent from the international market and that they are potential targets of raids and buyouts by outside investors. The financier Giancarlo Parretti, who acquired control in 1989–90 of the US Metro Goldwyn Mayer and United Artists studios, is possibly the exception that proves the rule; but by 1991 his control seemed tenuous at best.

In recent times, political parties have developed proactive media policies. They are increasingly sensitive to the issues of media ownership and influence. Berlusconi's attempt to acquire Mondadori generated considerable political disquiet, as we have seen, and a resolve to tighten anti-trust measures. The long-awaited broadcasting law passed on 5 August 1990 set limits on media concentration: the owner of three TV networks must not own a daily newspaper; the owner of two networks may control no more than 8 per cent of the total circulation of daily newspapers; he who controls a bigger percentage of the daily newspaper market may not operate a TV network. Furthermore, no one may control more than 20 per cent (25 per cent for the 'pure' publisher) of all the media (dailies, books, periodicals, advertising, television). Limits were also placed on television advertising. With effect from 31 December 1992 there will be no natural breaks in films of less than 45 minutes, and no more than three in longer films.

The broadcasting bill brings to an end the 15-year period of aregulation which began with the 1976 court ruling heralding the end of the RAI monopoly. In principle, there should be no further concentration of ownership and existing groups have two years in which to divest themselves of some of their assets. This may mean the end of the Italian media mogul story. But, somehow, one doubts this will happen.[29]

# Chapter 9

# Media moguls in Germany

*Hans J. Kleinsteuber and Bettina Peters*

Asked if we find media moguls in Germany hardly anybody in this country would answer yes. Even those who approach the situation with a critical mind most probably would prefer to say that we have a number of large media companies that more or less control the different media markets. But the label mogul does not really describe the situation well, even though Germany shows the classic feature of 'mogul-land': a high degree of media concentration on all relevant media markets. Furthermore Germany is the national base of one of the real giants on the world market, Bertelsmann. And there are other companies of international significance, such as Springer, Bauer, Burda or Kirch. But who actually owns and controls Bertelsmann? Certainly not a person who is interested in an image as a mogul.

This chapter attempts to put the concept of the mogul into a German context. The leading question is this: why is there no typical German mogul? We shall first briefly review German media history: the disaster of Fascism and the period of reconstruction after 1945 are seen as basic. After this the characteristics of Germany's new masters of the media are described. There follows an overview of the main German media companies, including their international activities and links.

## HUGENBERG: THE FIRST GERMAN MOGUL?

Major newspaper companies (like Scherl, Mosse and Ullstein) were already operating at the turn of the century. But one figure emerged just before World War I and dominated the media scene of the Weimar Republic: Alfred Hugenberg, a former director general of Krupp AG. He established a partly invisible but most influential media empire through and for the interests of German heavy industry and nationalist circles.

His conglomerate company included national and local newspapers (he bought Scherl among others), news agencies, advertising activities and film production (Ufa, today a Bertelsmann company); all his publications propagated anti-democratic and reactionary-conservative positions against the young and vulnerable Weimar Republic. He was also a major politician in a right-wing nationalist party and became Minister of Economics in Adolf Hitler's first cabinet in 1933. In short, he represented the bourgeois–nationalist forces that helped Hitler into power without being integrated into the Nazi party system. He was often described as the first German media Baron. The name Hugenberg is still related to some of the darkest aspects of German media history and it seemed clear to all in 1945 that another Hugenberg should never be tolerated. Hugenberg discredited the concept of the mogul for a long time to come.

## 1945: THE 'HOUR ZERO'

What makes the German media situation unique is the existence of an 'Hour Zero', a totally new beginning after the defeat of 1945.[1] Media policy and responsibility was taken out of the hands of the beaten Germans and transferred to the allied Occupation forces. They tried to make absolutely sure that not only the Nazis but also their supporters like Hugenberg would never have a second chance. This was true for all four Occupation zones: as the course of developments became totally different in the Soviet zone, it will not be analysed here.

In broadcasting, the allies took over the remaining stations (or what was left of them) and started new radio programmes, trying to integrate them in a policy of 're-education'. They handpicked their German co-workers and generally took care that former Nazis were not re-employed (which worked, with a few exceptions). In the late 1940s they returned the stations to German management and thereby laid the foundations of the present public broadcasting system (ARD and ZDF). The BBC was the main model, but the structure became much more decentralized, based on the federal states, the *Länder*. As the public service monopoly remained intact until the early 1980s, all commercial activities were necessarily limited to the print media.

The rebuilding of the Press took a different course. The allies began by issuing licences to Germans which allowed them to publish a certain type of paper in a defined region. Again they made sure that (with a few exceptions) former Nazis were successfully excluded from this procedure. During 1945–9 a system of licensed papers was established, based mainly on protection of the (relatively few) published papers. This was done in order to secure the survival of the newly established and vulnerable press.

In 1949 the licence system was abolished in favour of a market system, open to all, including even some of the old pro-Nazi publishers who had been able to keep their printing facilities untouched. But by 1949 the newly licensed press had become so strong that it dominated markets for years to come. A generation of publishers had been created by the licence policy that would become the backbone of the whole media system. Today the licence holders of the 'Hour Zero' have grown old, some of them have died or retired, but the system they helped to establish still lives on.

## LICENCE HOLDERS OF THE 'FIRST DAY'

All of these fortunate receivers of licences after 1945 had been screened by the allies and were considered reliable people with anti-Fascist backgrounds. Most of them had a journalistic background, some had business experience. Only one (Axel Springer) had links to a former publishing business that his father had owned. Some of the publishers of the 'first day' should be mentioned here (several of them received only shares of a licence, but gained total control later):

*Rudolf Augstein* established (and still heads) the weekly political magazine *Der Spiegel* (modelled after *Time* magazine); *Der Spiegel* is without serious competition as one of the best selling magazines and most influential political publications in the country.

*Henry Nannen* started the weekly magazine *Der Stern* (loosely modelled on *Life* magazine); this is still the most respected magazine of a politically progressive nature for a general readership. *Stern* is now part of the Gruner and Jahr company, controlled by Bertelsmann. Nannen is still alive, but has left the magazine to his successors.

*Axel Springer* received licences for the first radio programme weekly *Hör Zu*, which is still number one in this market. He gained another licence to publish the daily *Hamburger Abendblatt*, today still the leading paper in the city. In addition he was able in 1953 to buy the daily *Die Welt* (for a rather low price) which had originally been established by the British Occupation forces. Springer received more publication rights than any other German and became owner of the largest newspaper empire; the company he established was, and still is, definitely first in current publications (as Bertelsmann was strongest in books and has only recently entered the market for daily newspapers). During his reign as a successful publisher, Springer became extremely conservative and used his papers systematically to promote political causes of the right, sometimes even the extreme right. He died in 1983 after he had changed his media conglomerate into a public company. After his death, fights started over the control of the Springer company; these have been won by his heirs. But Leo Kirch is a significant shareholder (see p. 199).

*Gerd Bucerius* established *Die Zeit*, a weekly with a newspaper format that is well known for excellent journalism. Today its Chief Editor is former Federal Chancellor Helmut Schmidt, but Bucerius is alive and enjoys special writing privileges in his paper. Bucerius also owns a significant share in Bertelsmann.

This list is certainly not exhaustive. But it should demonstrate how important the years after 1945 and the 'founding fathers' of the post-war years were and still are for the media situation today in Germany.


**PUBLISHERS IN POLITICS**

Strong political links have always been a characteristic of German publishers. This long established principle was enhanced by the fact that many individuals received licences in 1945 because they represented a certain political current. The old ideological press, closely related to political parties, was purposely revived after World War II. But it had no chance on the post-war markets and any publication that did not adjust in time to a more independent approach faced extinction.

Bucerius became an MP for the conservative CDU Party, but later left that party in protest. Augstein briefly represented the liberal FDP Party in the Bundestag as a backbencher, but soon lost interest – being a political publisher offered much more power and influence. Springer was well known and often criticized for his staunchly conservative, sometimes reactionary, views and support for the right wing of the CDU/CSU. His paper *Die Welt* was his major mouthpiece and had to be heavily subsidized by other papers of his empire (especially the mass market paper *Bild*), as it never became profitable. 'Expropriate Springer' was the most popular slogan of the 1960s student movement, which saw in him a key political figure of the right. He was sometimes depicted as a 'Super-Hugenberg'.

Today most of the large publishing houses are considered to be close to the conservative political camp (Springer, Burda, Bauer, Kirch, Holtzbrinck), though simple propaganda is a thing of the past (even Springer shows liberalization these days). A certain affinity with positions of the moderate left may be found in *Der Spiegel* and *Die Zeit*. Bertelsmann has publicly declared a company policy of political balancing and – as the Social Democratic SPD Party has few partners to choose from – enjoys especially good contacts with that party.

The two major commercial TV networks, Sat-1 (media co-owners include Springer and Kirch) and RTL Plus (a joint venture mainly of CLT and Bertelsmann, also involving the WAZ group), are considered to be loosely affiliated to the two large parties. Sat-1 often received the best terrestrial TV frequencies in the *Länder* ruled by the CDU, while RTL Plus only ranks second there; in the SPD *Länder* precisely the reverse situation occurred. The headquarters of Sat-1 are in the capital of the CDU-governed *Land* of Rhineland–Palatine, whereas RTL Plus resides in Cologne in Social Democratic Northrhine–Westfalia (NRW). Obviously the major parties keep an open ear to the interests of the publishing industry, and certainly did nothing to prevent some companies from becoming world-scale enterprises, while minimizing competition within West Germany itself.

## MOGULS OR BENEFACTORS?

For some of the famous publisher-personalities of the 'Hour Zero', political and journalistic success was more important than economic growth. *Der Spiegel* has a virtual monopoly in political magazines in Germany; attempts to publish competing journals (for example by Springer) failed miserably. The product turned out to be a goldmine, but Augstein rarely expanded into other sectors (like founding a business magazine). Instead much of the money goes into maintaining an excellent staff of journalists, which has a liberal-left tendency and regularly intervenes in politics with investigative-style journalism; *Der Spiegel* has ruined more than one political career and endangered whole governments. Today employees own part of the magazine and share its extremely high profits; they probably are some of the best remunerated writers in the world.

Another post-war publisher, Gerd Bucerius, followed somewhat similar patterns. In his book *The Publisher Accused* he offered alongside an anti-trade union diatribe an amazing degree of self-criticism; he analysed his personal ambitions in a rather realistic, sometimes ironical, way. He described the licence which he had received in 1945 (on a shared basis) from the British Occupation forces as 'indeed virtually a permit to print money'.[2] The flagship of his activities, *Die Zeit*, was and is a well-written and highly influential paper. But because of the maintenance of a large staff it did not produce any surplus for most of its existence. Still, his early start as a publisher secured him an important position in the German media industry. As well as having been publisher of *Die Zeit* for a long time, he headed the board of the Bertelsmann company, in which he also owns a minority share.

But some of the other publishers who enjoyed the privilege of an early start used their profits to build considerable empires which were little recognized outside Germany. Among them are Bauer, Burda and the owners of the WAZ company; none of them showed much interest in making their financial operations known or using public relations to become publicly acclaimed figures. Bertelsmann certainly falls into this category; the company is still located in the small provincial town of Gütersloh and operates under many different names (for example, to mention an extreme, RCA, Radio Corporation of America). But this company started with book publishing and expanded into media only much later. None of these companies shows the typical signs of a business dominated by one identifiable mogul, but might still act in ways resembling Berlusconi or Maxwell.

Before giving an overview of the major companies, some more information should be given on important aspects of the framework of media policy.

## CARTEL RESTRICTIONS

Germany sees itself as having a social market economy; that is, a private enterprise system, limited by a framework of public rules. One of these is a system of regulations in a cartel law executed by a Federal Cartel Office. Although media companies were theoretically always included in the cartel regulations, in practice they usually were too small to fall within the limits of the law. During the Social–Liberal government of the 1970s, however, criticism of the increasing degree of media concentration intensified. When it became obvious that the general stipulations of the cartel law could not stop the concentration process, special regulations were introduced into the law in 1976 which required the reporting and public approval of media company mergers.

Whenever a merger enables a company to control a specific Press market or strengthens its already controlling position, the cartel office should intervene to prevent this. The regulation has been used several times and with success; it prevented Springer from conquering the Munich newspaper market. However the rule does not apply to a minority shareholding of less than 25 per cent, which has quite often been used as a loophole. Undoubtedly, this cartel law quickened the large companies' move towards international diversification. Restricting them from print markets also made them more aggressive in breaking the public broadcasting monopoly and becoming commercial broadcasters themselves, as the regulations do not yet apply to these markets.

## MEDIA AND THE TRADE UNIONS

The political culture of present-day Germany is very much determined by corporatist structures – close and constructive co-operation between capital and labour. This system arose out of the 'economic miracle' of the post-war period and some central aspects of this corporatism are relatively high wages, few labour strikes and the general acceptance of trade unions as important actors on the labour side.

This general description however, hardly applies to the relation-ships between publishers and journalists' unions which are some-times openly hostile. Journalists are organized either in an inde-pendent trade organization (Deutscher Journalisten Verband, DJV) or in two unions (Deutsche Journalisten Union, DJU, for print journalists and Rundfunk–Fernseh–Film Union, RFFU, for broadcasting) which are part of the IG Medien and as such affiliated with the main Trade Union Federation (DGB). Certainly the trade unionists of the latter two unions have been quite militant, as, to a lesser extent, have been those of the slightly more conservative DJV: all three unions have been quite aggressive in criticizing the powerful publishers' organisations, their continuous political interference and their concentration of power.

To give an example: a field of continuous conflict in the 1970s was a planned Federal Press Bill (*Presserechtsrahmengesetz*); this never became law because of fierce publishers' resistance (accordingly, laws governing the Press are entirely *Länder* law). Targets of journalists' criticism have been the unchecked concentration of media ownership and the intended destruction of the public broadcasting system.[3] What still infuriates journalists most, though, is the non-application of the German co-determination principle (*Mitbestimmung*) which is expressly excluded from media companies. Employees there may establish workers' councils (*Betriebsräte*), but they are kept from any substantial decision-making.

Journalist unions, like other organizations (such as the Protestant Church) have often criticized the 'monopoly game' which media companies are playing – but with very little effect. Their alternative proposals include stricter cartel regulations, no cross-ownership of newspapers and broadcasting stations in the same region, co-determination in all media companies and the protection and strengthening of the public broadcasting sector.

## ARE THERE ANY *LÄNDER* BARONS?

Commercial companies usually do not care much about *Länder*-boundaries; therefore in most cases they have little significance for large economic actors. There are exceptions to this rule, though. One is the newspaper chain that was erected around the *Westdeutsche Allgemeine Zeitung* (WAZ), the leading paper in the heavily populated and industrialized Ruhr region of Northrhine–Westfalia. NRW is a special case, by far the most important of all *Länder* and a long-lasting stronghold of the Social Democratic Party (SPD). When the WAZ was licensed by the British, it was already seen as a paper leaning towards the SPD without having the formal links to the party; it has been like this ever since.

Both the WAZ and the SPD were equally determined to keep Springer out of NRW and they largely succeeded. In this protected *Land*-isolation, the WAZ group grew to become a regional mini-empire and accumulated enough capital to reach out to another region with a strong Socialist background, Austria. (For more on the WAZ group: see pp. 202–3).

We are now leaving this somewhat historical and general approach to give a 'horizontal' overview of the media landscape.

## THE MAJOR MEDIA COMPANIES

Almost all of Germany's media companies were originally publishing companies. Some of them have a history that extends beyond 1945 but even for them this is the date of a new start. The seven following companies are the largest and most active on the German and international media market:

*Bertelsmann AG*: founded in 1835. Total returns in 1988 were 12,000 million DM; profits were 400 million DM.
*Axel Springer Verlag AG*: founded in 1945. Total returns in 1988 were 2,840 million DM; profits were 93 million DM.
*Heinrich Bauer Verlag*: founded in 1875. Total returns in 1987–8 were 2,000 million DM.
*Holtzbrinck-Konzern*: founded in 1949. Total returns in 1988 were 1,600 million DM.
*WAZ-Gruppe*: founded in 1948. Total returns in 1987–8 were 1,500 million DM.
*Burda GmbH*: founded in 1927. Total returns in 1988 were 1,023 million DM; profits were 18 million DM.
*Beta/Taurus Gruppe (Leo Kirch)*: total returns in 1987–8 were 600 million DM (estimated figure).

(*Source*: Muzik (1989), *Die Medienmultis*, Vienna, Stuttgart and Bern, *Neue Medien Jahrbuch* 1989, p. 210)

This analysis will focus on the Bertelsmann AG, the Springer AG and Leo Kirch's Beta/Taurus Gruppe to put the concept of the mogul into a German context. Bertelsmann is one of the world's largest media companies; it is therefore most important to see if this company operates with mogul strategies. The importance of the Springer AG lies in its second rank but also in its unique power on the German newspaper market. Leo Kirch is fairly new on the media market, but has already shown clear traits of mogulry.

## THE BERTELSMANN AG

Carl Bertelsmann, the company's founding father started with a printing press for religious scriptures, 150 years ago. After his death his son-in-law Johannes Mohn took over the family business. Today the Mohn family holds 89.26 per cent of the company's shares. The other 10.74 per cent belong to Gerd Bucerius (former publisher of *Die Zeit* as mentioned above).

After 1945 Bertelsmann's first media activities were book and record clubs, which still account for one quarter of total returns. Today Bertelsmann is a highly diversified company with strong positions in all media markets. At present Bertelsmann is one of the world's largest media companies (although this position is challenged by Rupert Murdoch and Time–Warner). The company's stronghold is the publishing business.

In Germany alone the company owns twenty book publishing companies and holds shares in another four. In magazine publishing Bertelsmann owns a 74.9 per cent interest in Gruner und Jahr. In 1987 Gruner und Jahr had total returns of 2.6 billion DM. It is one of Germany's leading publishers for magazines; the company focuses on special interest magazines, which are also increasingly sold on an international scale. In the German market Gruner und Jahr has best-selling titles like *Stern* and *Geo*. Internationally Gruner und Jahr is most successful with several special interest titles. Its women's magazine *Best*, for example, has editions in the UK, France and Spain.

The company recently entered the newspaper market by taking control of the mass market paper *Hamburger Morgenpost* and thereby challenged a traditional stronghold of the Springer company.

In recent years the company has been especially active in new media and high-tech information systems. Through its holding company Ufa Film und Fernseh Union, Bertelsmann owns 38.9 per cent of RTL Plus, one of Germany's nationwide commercial TV stations. In commercial radio Bertelsmann holds minor shares (16–24 per cent) of three (*Länder*) state-wide radio stations. The company also expanded into cable communication, video production and broadcasting rights. Bertelsmann owns 50 per cent of the Kabel–Marketing–Gesellschaft (KMG), Germany's biggest commercial cable company. It operates its own film companies, such as Stern–TV, Geo–Film, Ufa–Film and controls 90 per cent of the shares of RUFA, a news agency that produces radio newscasts and sells them to local radio stations. Most recently Bertelsmann started joint ventures with the French Canal Plus. Both companies launched a joint German pay-TV channel together with Leo Kirch's Teleclub. The new channel, called 'Premiere', received a licence in

Hamburg to start broadcasting in March 1991.[4]

In 1988 Bertelsmann bought the rights to broadcast the 'Bundes-liga' soccer games, formerly the stronghold of the public TV channels (ARD, ZDF) sports coverage. This received national attention. The company succeeded not only in outbuying the public television system, but also in demonstrating the large financial resources that RTL Plus can command.

Bertelsmann owns six companies producing digital information systems, a market where the company faces little competition. With the acquisition of RCA Music, one of the world's largest music copyright empires, Bertelsmann extended its power into the record business; the company owns another three record firms in Germany. In 1988 65 per cent of Bertelsmann's total returns came from outside Germany. On the international level Bertelsmann's main activities are in book and magazine publishing, the printing and the record industry. The company owns Bantam Books, the world's largest paperback publisher. In recent years Bertelsmann has made major acquisitions on the US market (Doubleday Bookstore Group and RCA Music). The company also owns a system of book clubs in Latin America. It has no significant international activities in electronic media.

### Bertelsmann – a mogul company?

Although some traits of mogulry can be found in the Bertelsmann company set-up (it is owned by one family which cannot be removed by other shareholders) there are several reasons why the mogul tag hardly applies to Bertelsmann's proprietor and chief executive. First, the man who owns Bertelsmann, Reinhard Mohn, adopts a low profile; his personal life-style is rather frugal and he is hardly ever mentioned when his company makes media acquisitions. Even though this might be regarded as his individual style as a media mogul, and one might think that Reinhard Mohn commands the company quietly but nevertheless self-interestedly, this does not seem to be the case. Mohn, in fact, distributes some of the profits of the company among its employees and has stated publicly that companies are no longer the private affair of the specific owner. He sees himself as a manager (not so much as a journalist or publisher) who organizes profit-making together with his employees.

Secondly, the management is decentralized; some subsidiary

companies, such as Gruner und Jahr, operate quite independently of the parent company. Unlike media moguls such as Rupert Murdoch, Reinhard Mohn is not known to intervene in management decisions of his subsidiary companies. Bertelsmann is organized in profit centres, each subsidiary being responsible for its own profits and management decisions. Reinhard Mohn's idea of organizing a company is that of a common experience, where the decision-making process is in the hands of the top managers as well as the employees. After Mohn's death the company's capital will stay with the Bertelsmann Vermögensverwaltungs GmbH, connected with the Mohn family, but a board comprising top managers, a representative of the family and a representative of the employees will decide company policy.

Thirdly, the company is not known for openly promoting a political creed in its media. The main goal seems to be business growth, and not to operate as a leader of opinion. However, while most of the large German media companies are considered to be more or less associated with the conservative party, the CDU, it seems that Bertelsmann enjoys some special ties with the Social Democrats; this impression is supported by the fact that a former top politician of the SPD (Lahnstein, last Minister of Finance of the Social–Liberal coalition) works as one of the leading managers of Bertelsmann. The fact remains though that Bertelsmann operates like a purely commercial company, demonstrating a high degree of political openness, publishing both left-leaning magazines like *Der Stern* and die-hard conservative periodicals like the business magazine *Capital*.

Bertelsmann's policy of expanding and taking over other companies is prudent rather than aggressive. It concentrates on acquiring prosperous companies rather than buying 'cheap firms'. Normally Bertelsmann does not intervene in the publishing or broadcasting of the newly-acquired firm, but changes the management (replaces executive managers) and tries to streamline production.

Bertelsmann has generally circumvented anti-cartel regulations. Its policy of diversification on the national level led to the company owning large parts of every media market, but never enough to qualify as controlling a specific market (more than 30 per cent of a given media market). Recently Bertelsmann has centred its expansion on the international level and has thus avoided legal complications with German anti-cartel regulations. In short

Bertelsmann can be presented as an 'anti-mogul' company – which does not mean that it is any the less powerful.

## THE AXEL SPRINGER VERLAG AG

The Springer company, which started as an early licence holder after 1945, remains the leading publisher in the daily newspaper market. After the death of the company's founder, Axel Springer, in 1983 a struggle for control started between the heirs of the publishing house and outside interests. (These events will be mentioned later in connection with Leo Kirch and his attempt to gain control of the company).

Today the ownership of Springer AG is:

| | |
|---|---|
| 52 per cent: | Axel Springer Gesellschaft für Publizistik (shares held chiefly by Springer's widow); |
| 10 per cent: | Leo Kirch and partners; |
| 2 per cent: | Morgan Grenfell (London); |
| 34 per cent: | divided among forty other shareholders. |

Trading in the stock of the Springer company requires the permission of the board of the company. Leo Kirch is said nonetheless to control more than his actual 10 per cent, probably another 15 per cent, through trustees.

Springer AG is mainly involved in publishing. Its mass market newspaper *Bild* alone accounts for nearly 30 per cent of Germany's total daily newspaper market. In 1988 the *Bild-Zeitung* had a circulation of 4.4 million, which made it western Europe's best-selling daily newspaper. (*Bild* means picture in German).

The company controls up to 80 per cent of the daily newspaper market in several major German cities. This is the case in Berlin (West) and in Hamburg, Germany's print media capital, where the company publishes *Hamburg Abendblatt*, *Bild*, *Welt* and other titles.

In book publishing Springer owns seven companies, one of them Ullstein, a major publishing house with a long tradition. The company also has interests in several large printing presses and marketing firms.

In recent years Springer, like most German publishing companies, has expanded aggressively into commercial TV and radio. The company holds 15 per cent of a nation-wide commercial TV station, Sat-1 and in another station Tele-5. In commercial radio Springer has interests in four radio stations in northern Germany and Berlin. With 35 per cent of the shares of Radio Hamburg, Springer expanded into electronic media in a city where the company already controls the daily newspaper market. Thus, media policy regulations in Hamburg decided upon the so called 'Lex Springer', which allows a leading publisher to own 35 per cent of commercial radio in the same given market, but forbids him to have more than 25 per cent of the company's votes. This is only one example of attempts to place regulatory controls on Springer's power in the German media market. Despite such attempts Springer is, at least in northern Germany, clearly the leading company. It continues to expand, mostly by buying minority shares (below 25 per cent in the remaining papers; this is not covered by anti-cartel rules.

After the death of Axel Springer the company expanded into international markets. So far Springer has launched special interest magazines in England, France, Spain and Italy. The company has been especially active in the Spanish market, where it publishes six weekly or monthly magazines with a total circulation of 595,000. Springer has also started to move into the eastern European media markets. So far the company has opened a subsidiary in Budapest (Hungary) and started publishing magazines. It also owns a share of the newly launched Austrian paper *Standard* and of the leading Tyrolean paper.

### Axel Springer – publishing political ideas

Springer's international activities are of relatively little importance, but at the national level, the company wields considerable power. In northern Germany especially the company holds significant shares of most leading newspapers.

Axel Springer used his publishing power to promote his conservative political ideas through Germany. He operated the company in a very centralized manner, under his personal supervision. Some of his management decisions were not financially wise, but were purely politically motivated. For instance, he moved the company headquarters to Berlin in the 1960s – right next to the Wall – as proof of Springer's adherence to the unity of the two German states and to Germany's former capital (with the reunification of Berlin the company HQ is located right at the centre of Greater Berlin).

During the student revolt in 1968 Springer was criticized throughout the country. He was often associated with Hugenberg, the anti-democratic media baron of Weimar and the beginning of the Third Reich. Since the group is the leader in the newspaper market, political and legal attention focused on the consequences of Press concentration and on the company's role as an opinion leader. Thus, Springer's media power attracted far more attention than the even greater power of the Bertelsmann company.

With the death of Axel Springer, managers with more economic motivation moved in and started operating the publishing house as a diversified media company with the former owner merely serving as an inspiration. The strongly conservative, sometimes reactionary, position of the company has softened, but – to give just one example – until August 1989 its journalists were forced to write the abbreviation of the German Democratic Republic 'DDR' in parenthesis as this country was not considered to be a fully established state.

## LEO KIRCH – AN ATTEMPT TO BECOME GERMANY'S FIRST MEDIA MOGUL

Leo Kirch is the first of Germany's major media owners who did not begin his career in publishing.

He was born in 1926 in Würzburg and studied economics. In 1954 he moved into the film marketing business, when he bought the German rights to the famous Fellini movie *La Strada*. In 1959 Kirch purchased a large movie package from United Artists and Warner Brothers for $6 million; this was the foundation of Kirch's success in the media business. To give an example: in 1959 Leo Kirch paid $3,000 for the German rights to *Casablanca*, which thirty years later he sold for 250,000 DM.

With his large fund of film material Leo Kirch, from the beginning of the 1960s until 1980, made most of his money by selling movies to the public service TV network, ZDF. Today he owns the German broadcasting rights to more than 15,000 movies, which makes him Europe's biggest film distributor.

Kirch owns two major film companies (100 per cent of both Beta and Taurus Film). In commercial TV he holds shares of Sat-1 and Eureka Television GmbH. Through his holding company (PKS), which he operates in partnership with a German bank, Kirch controls 40 per cent of Sat-1. Through his shares of the Springer AG he partly influences another 15 per cent of Sat-1.

In 1988 the major shareholder of Eureka Television sold his capital to Leo Kirch's son, Thomas. The Kirch family controls 49 per cent of

Eureka and has already started to change the former news channel into a movie programme, now called Pro-7. He is also very active in the video market (Taurus Film Video, Videobox).

More recently Kirch has started the joint operation of the German pay-TV channel Premiere, with the Bertelsmann subsidiary Ufa and the French Canal Plus. Kirch contributed his pay-TV channel Teleclub as part of the deal. Teleclub, which used to be Germany's only pay-TV programme, has been fairly successful. The programme reaches fifty-five cities and is said to have about 30–40,000 subscribers.[5] The new channel would have been a serious competitor to Kirch's programme. Since the German pay-TV market was not expected to be profitable for two channels, the three companies agreed to rule out internecine competition. They decided to operate the new channel, Premiere, together. Kirch owns 25 per cent of the shares, Canal Plus and Ufa both have 37.5 per cent. The channel received a licence in Hamburg to start operation by March 1991. Since Kirch is the major program software supplier for commercial TV and pay-TV he will probably expand even more into this field.

Kirch bought a successful book club (the Deutsche Bücherbund) from the Holtzbrinck company. He will probably not use it to expand into the book publishing business, but to boost sales of his video-cassette production.

Kirch gained extensive media coverage when he attempted to take over the Springer AG. After Springer's widow Friede Springer refused to collaborate with him, Kirch then tried to proceed against her with the other co-owners Franz and Friede Burda. Since the Burdas later changed sides, they sold their interest to the heir's 'Axel Springer Gesellschaft für Publizistik' and Kirch's attempts to gain influence in the company failed; he later compromised with the Springer family. This attempt at a hostile takeover of a somewhat weakened company clearly looks like a typical mogul strategy.

Another mogul strategy is Kirch's co-operation with the Deutsche Genossenschaftsbank (DG Bank). Some of Leo Kirch's acquisitions were financed by the DG Bank and it is said that Kirch owes about 800 million DM to this banking institution.[6] This kind of co-operation is a usual one in other European countries (e.g. Hersant and the Crédit Lyonnais or Maxwell and several European banks), but it is unique in the German media market. So far only the DG Bank operates directly in the media business; the Deutsche Bank only acts as a trustee to shares of Sat-1 and RTL Plus. The other German media companies do not co-operate with banking institutions on a large scale. Recently Leo Kirch has expanded into the international market. In film and video he owns a company in Rome and in Paris. He co-operates with Silvio Berlusconi, Jérôme Seydoux and Robert Maxwell. In the US market Kirch started a joint-venture with Tribune Broadcasting Corporation; the company will produce TV films and mini-series that will be shown on Tribune's TV channels.

Leo Kirch might well become Germany's first media mogul. He moves aggressively into the new media market and enjoys frequent news coverage. He expresses trenchant views: 'With the joint power of printing presses, data-banks, television, film and video we will break the predominance of public television';[7] he speaks disparagingly of the public broadcasting system and tries to gain publicity for his commercial approach.

Leo Kirch often uses covert or underhand methods: he buys interests through trustees or front men or tries to influence other shareholders. For years Kirch denied his interest (via PKS) in Sat-1 and only recently admitted to the actual number of his shares in Sat-1. Another mogul strategy is Kirch's co-operation with the DG Bank. The bank often merely appears as a company shareholder whereas Leo Kirch also influences the company's management decisions. In the future Kirch will probably expand more aggressively into the new international media markets, especially since the German media market is already largely divided up between the big publishing companies.

The following section briefly presents other large German media companies.

### The Burda GmbH

The Burda company grew up with fashion magazines like *Burda Moden*, which is still the publisher's leading title. Most of the Burda empire was built under the reign of the late Senator Burda. Today the company is owned by his three sons and his widow Aenne Burda.

Apart from magazine publishing, Burda is active in commercial radio (it owns 30 per cent of Radio Bayern) and video (it owns 100 per cent of PAN TV Videoproduktion), where the company concentrates on southern Germany. It also has shares of printing companies and is active in the marketing and distribution of magazines.

But Burda's main business is magazine publishing. The company sells magazines in France and the United States and its fashion magazines in particular in many other countries. In fact, Burda developed a production process which makes it possible to print the coloured pictures of the magazine first and then add the text in many different languages to adapt to local conditions. Aenne Burda succeeded in introducing the first western magazine into the Soviet market. The Russian edition of *Burda Moden* has a circulation of a million copies.

### The Holtzbrinck-Konzern

The Holtzbrinck-Konzern is a family-owned publishing house. The company holds a leading market position in newspaper and magazine publishing, especially in southern Germany. Dailies like the *Handelsblatt* (the German *Financial Times*) and the *Wirtschaftswoche* (the German equivalent of *The Economist*) are published by Holtzbrinck. The company is also active both in book clubs and in book publishing. Major publishing houses like Rewohlt and Fischer are 100 per cent Holtzbrinck subsidiaries. In recent years Holtzbrinck has entered the electronic media market. Through its holding company AV Euromedia Gesellschaft Holtzbrinck holds 15 per cent of Sat-1 and shares of eight radio stations. The company also produces programme material for Sat-1 and offers a 24-hour network programme for local radio stations.

With the selling of the Deutsche Bücherbund to Leo Kirch, Holtzbrinck now disposes of large financial resources. So far it is not clear into which media market Holtzbrinck will invest this money, but it is rumoured that the company plans to move more aggressively into the newspaper and radio business.[8]

On the international level Holtzbrinck owns two publishing houses in the United States (100 per cent of both Henry Holt and W.H. Freeman). Holtzbrinck is quite active in the Swiss media market, where the company owns four book publishing houses. There are no significant activities in video or new information systems.

### The Heinrich–Bauer–Verlag

The Bauer Company, owned 100 per cent by the Bauer family, is Europe's largest magazine publisher. In Germany Bauer, with its more than twenty magazine titles, achieved profits of 301 million DM in 1986. The company's best seller is the weekly television magazine *TV Hören und Sehen* with 2.25 million copies sold in 1987. The company is mainly active on the 'yellow press' market. With *Quick* and *Neue Revue* Bauer publishes two leading titles of this type. On the international level, the company sells women's and television programme magazines in Austria, France, the UK and Spain, and also publishes *Woman's World* in the United States.

In the past few years though, the company has seen its profits decline. Even though the yellow press titles still sell fairly well, this market is expected to diminish in the future. To strengthen business Bauer has tried to move into the market of expensive and high class special interest magazines. In 1987 the company introduced several up-market titles like *Esquire* (a fashion magazine) and *Wiener* (a 'Zeitgeist' title). Recently the company has also entered the market for business magazines with a German version of *Forbes*.

Bauer has few interests in electronic media; it has a 25 per cent holding in one commercial radio station (Radio Hamburg). Outside Germany, Bauer still concentrates on magazine publishing and has made only modest attempts to diversify its media activities.

The owner Heinrich Bauer is hardly ever mentioned in news coverage; management policy is 'low profile'. Although the company is family owned, its several editorial staffs work rather independently. While the company expanded heavily in the 1960s, today its media activities are few and show no signs of mogul strategies.

### The WAZ group

Although the WAZ (Westdeutsche Allgemeine Zeitung) was founded in 1948, it has only recently attracted public interest. The ownership of the company is:

50 per cent: Erich Brost (publisher);
50 per cent: Funke-Holding (the Funke family).

In the *Land* of Northrhine–Westfalia, the WAZ is the leading newspaper publisher, with five newspapers in the region. It might be called a '*Länder*-baron' not only because of its leading market position, but also because of its connection to the governing party in Northrhine–Westfalia, the SPD.

The company is also active in electronic media. The WAZ holds

10 per cent of RTL Plus. It owns two film companies (Allianz Filmproduktion and Westfilm Medien GmbH) and has interests in two cable companies.

Internationally, the WAZ group concentrates on the Austrian market, where it owns printing presses and is very active in magazine publishing. The WAZ group owns 45 per cent of the Viennese *Neue Kronen Zeitung* and 45 per cent of the *Kurier* (also Vienna), the two leading circulation dailies in Austria.

The expansion policy of the WAZ has been quite successful in economic terms; in 1987 the WAZ was number 109 on the list of the world's largest media companies, in 1988 it moved to number 71.[9] At least in the German market the company shows no signs of 'mogulism'. On the contrary it is known to handle its business rather quietly and carefully. Its investments are sound and there is no indication of a hazardous spending policy. Above all no one individual appears to dominate the WAZ's media activities.

## CONCLUSIONS

When the concept of the mogul became an international phenomenon, German scholars wondered what it might mean to the reality of the (West) German situation. Certainly we had media entrepreneurs in our history whom we called the 'media barons' and who, like Hugenberg, might appear to have characteristics of present-day moguls. But they were a thing of the past. After 1945, as a result of World War II, the country took a radically new course. The licence system laid the foundations for the establishment of large media companies. But the people who controlled them were primarily publishers and journalists and showed few traits of the typical media mogul. They were all highly interested in politics, but considered economics a means to strengthen their political standing.

The one exception from this rule was of course Bertelsmann, a company which has a long history in book publishing, never received a licence and followed a much more commercial course by systematically buying up media property and expanding into national and international markets. The political philosophy of Bertelsmann is one of balanced reporting – this translates into political opportunism, which helps the company in dealing with politicians. The men who control Bertelsmann adopt a low profile and are discreet in their public statements. Bertelsmann could perhaps be defined as a mogul empire without a mogul. Clearly this company reflects the post-war consensus in Germany that business is fine, but that any powerful business leader is met with understandable distrust and rejection.

Possibly this apersonal and low-profile approach to media expansion contributed to Bertelsmann's success, for the company met with very little public scepticism and resistance. If there is a lesson to be drawn from the German example it might be that, behind an apparent anonymity, firms like Bertelsmann can be just as powerful as high-profile, aggressive and publicity-seeking moguls. The social and economic consequences of media concentration are equally severe, no matter whether it is a 'high-action' mogul business or a low-profile company expanding on the media market.

But Germany is certainly not isolated from the rest of the world. Berlusconi is already present in one of the new TV channels (Tele-5). The generation of the licensed publishers is dying out, handing over their lucrative companies to more business-minded media capitalists. This new type is most clearly represented by Leo Kirch, who became famous for using all means available to expand a media empire that started with film rights. He began his career by exploiting conservative political contacts to monopolize film trading with the public service TV corporations. Having grown rich, he entered commercial TV (exercising a strong influence on Sat-1) and, with his son, now controls another commercial TV channel (Pro-7). He attempted a rather aggressive takeover of the Springer publishing company, but had to settle for a significant share in it. His activities spread all over Europe. He may become the first real German mogul in the international meaning of this word. He might not be the last, as the post-1945 generation is disappearing and is making way for new and much more aggressive media entrepreneurs. They will be supported by a recent change of tremendous impact.

With the events that started in October 1989 and ended in October 1990, unification turns out to be more and more a process of handing over the bankrupt East German economy to large West German companies – seemingly with the consent of most citizens of the (former) German Democratic Republic. West German capital tries to save the new market for itself, preventing foreign competition (with some exceptions) from entering what is now a wide-open country. Large media conglomerates of western Europe see the chance to expand with their products into a market in which the old Communist media industry proved defenceless. For example: Berliner Verlag, the largest publishing house of the old Communist Party (SED) was bought jointly by Bertelsmann and Maxwell.

Basically these conglomerates are following three strategies to achieve their goals:

1  exporting West German publications into East Germany and selling them if necessary for prices below actual costs;
2  building up a modern and effective distribution network: in fact the transitional communist government invited the four largest media companies of West Germany quickly to build up an effective distribution system; later they compromised with smaller companies;
3  starting joint ventures with East German media companies.

It is too early to give a full account of this process, but the underlying dynamic seems to be clear: West German media companies have enough surplus capital to be eager to invest in the East German economy. The losers will again be the small media producers on both sides: in West Germany because they lack the necessary financial resources to move into East Germany, and in East Germany because they will not be able to survive the strong competition from the West German media. Unification will mean an extension of the West German media system into East Germany and a further push towards more concentration on the future all-German media markets. Seen from this angle, unification will probably strengthen the largest media companies and might as such lead to some more 'mogulization' in the years ahead.

# Chapter 10

# Conclusion: Europe's future media and moguls

The 1989 adoption of the European Community's Broadcasting Directive was far from being an isolated event. The Directive was only one part in a much wider sea change affecting European media in general and American–European media relationships in particular.

1989–91 saw a strong trend away from deregulation and towards reregulation both in Europe and the US. Japanese and European interests bought key companies in Hollywood. High interest rates severely affected a number of media moguls who had financed their acquisitions and growth by bank debt. Many of Europe's new video channels, which began operations both before and during 1989–91, faced a bleak prospect of continuing losses. Meanwhile imported American TV series continued to be relegated from major European channels to new channels with low audiences.

## 1990s CONSOLIDATION: POLITICS, TECHNOLOGY, COMMERCE

The three fundamental forces in the history of the mass media have been politics, technology and commerce.[1] The future evolution and interaction of these forces are not easy to predict. Nevertheless the 1989–91 period of sea change also marked a phase of consolidation which we believe will continue through most, if not all, of the 1990s.

Through the 1980s media policy assumed an increasingly central place on the political agendas both of western Europe overall and of particular European countries. Around 1990 there was a marked move towards reregulation of terrestrial (or conventional) television. Most remarkable was the case of Italy; after many abortive attempts, the Italian legislature at last passed a comprehensive piece of broadcasting legislation. This was quickly dubbed the 'Pax Televisa' – the establishment of a regulated duopoly with the future of the public service RAI confirmed; the position of the commercial mogul, Silvio Berlusconi, was in effect accepted as a legitimate, permanent and regulated entity. In 1990 a duopoly policy was also being consolidated in France, Germany and Spain – even if the public service broadcasting sector remained on the defensive. And in Britain 1990 saw the passage of a Broadcasting Act which confirmed both the existing television duopoly and the national tradition of policy gradualism.

In terms of technology also we expect the 1990s to be a decade primarily of consolidation. We expect, for example, that there will be fairly few new channels after 1991. The main change will be an increase in consumers acquiring access to channels which already existed at the start of the decade. Most new customers for extra channels will acquire these channels via plain old cable, rather than directly via satellites and domestic dish antennae.

Ultimately, no doubt, domestic consumers will be able to choose from an *à la carte* menu of hundreds or thousands of new movies, old TV series, video specials and other services. Whatever the technology mix will be – between the super multi-purpose ISDN network, high-definition television, or enhanced capacity cable and pay-per-view – we doubt whether this technology will be in significant numbers of households until well after the year 2000. And sorting out the copyright problems may be more complex than sorting out the technology.

The commercial forces of the 1990s seem also to point towards consolidation. Around 1990 United States financial institutions began to adopt much more cautious attitudes to the kind of bank borrowing upon which the growth of the media companies depended so heavily in the 1980s. Many European TV channels and other media enterprises will continue to make losses. Consequently the emphasis on cutting costs will continue to be important for media companies in the 1990s.

## TOWARDS A WORLD MEDIA INDUSTRY

Part of the sea change around 1990 was the emergence of Japanese companies on the world media scene. The most spectacular examples were the purchase of two Hollywood studios (Columbia and MCA) by Sony in 1989 and Matsushita in 1990. This followed Sony's 1987 purchase of CBS Records. There were several other Japanese advances on the world scene – for example by Fujisankei (a TV network and newspaper colossus) and by Dentsu (the leading Japanese advertising group). NHK (the public service broadcaster) was, of course, active with Sony in the development of high definition television. These advances had one dominant theme – the marriage of Japanese hardware with American and European entertainment software.

As seen from Europe, this looked like the emergence of a American–Japanese media alliance. As seen by the rest of the world it must look more like the triad pattern – the US, Japan, western Europe – which dominates so many other industries in terms of both production and consumption.

Elements of global media can be traced back to the nineteenth century (news agencies) and early twentieth century (Hollywood). But these trends certainly advanced much further in the 1980s. The US (AP), Britain (Reuters) and France (AFP) now dominate the world flow of news; the international advertising agency scene is largely a US–UK–Japanese preserve. American (and British) book publishers have established a world presence. Well over half of world recorded music sales are dominated by six companies. Since 1990 two of these (CBS, MCA) were Japanese-owned, three (Polygram, RCA, EMI) European-owned, and only one (Warner) was US-owned.

We anticipate that in these fields this already very high level of both globalization and concentration will advance further. However in what we have called the main 'cash flow' media – newspapers and television – the situation has been quite different. Broadly the pattern has been of nationally-based ownership. There are a few examples of major European newspapers being wholly or partly foreign-owned – mainly in Austria (German interests), Belgium (French interests) and Britain (primarily Murdoch). This foreign ownership element may expand somewhat in the 1990s, and perhaps especially in eastern Europe.

In television the 1980s saw the emergence of minority foreign ownership stakes in European TV channels. The two leading examples of this were the Berlusconi–Fininvest interests in France, Spain and Germany and the Canal Plus interests in Spain, Germany and Belgium. This phenomenon is, of course, highly regulated, and will continue to be in the 1990s.

## HOLLYWOOD AND US MEDIA IN EUROPE: RETREAT AND ADVANCE

How powerful is Hollywood in relation to Europe? The answer is complicated by two paradoxes. Firstly Hollywood seems to have become steadily more powerful in the world, while becoming less American-owned. Secondly a major component of the 1990 sea change was a decline in the appeal of US TV programming on major large audience networks in Europe; however the other aspects of Hollywood influence expanded in the 1980s and may continue to grow through the 1990s.

Increasingly from about the mid-1980s onwards Hollywood series became less popular with European TV audiences. This was most notable in Italy; as the Berlusconi channels became more and more commercially successful, they increasingly used Italian-made programming. The same sequence seems to be happening in France and is likely to happen on the new commercial channels in Spain and Germany. By 1990 very few American series featured among the top ten or twenty highest rated programmes of the week – especially in the most populous European countries. But American imported programming continued to be heavily relied upon by weaker channels.

At the American end of this relationship was the ever stronger emphasis on ratings competition and the focus upon striking gold in the syndication market with a hit series of 100 or more episodes. The tug-of-war between the networks and the Hollywood production houses, as to which will control the syndication rights to networked series, seems likely to continue through the 1990s. Increasingly in the late 1980s there was a marked weakening in the syndication market's demand for the action adventure one-hour shows, which had appealed to Europeans and other foreigners. Increasingly the situation comedy, which travels less well than the cops-and-robbers shows, became the predominant Hollywood TV offering.

Although the 1990s will probably see fewer American TV series on major European channels in high audience time-slots, other forms of Hollywood influence may well increase.

First, Hollywood may increase the strength of its offerings via other 'windows'. Hollywood strength in feature films, and therefore in cinemas, shows little sign of reducing. These Hollywood feature films and made-for-TV movies will continue to be given prominence on European television. Moreover, by 1990 Hollywood movies were already earning more money through video outlets than through cinemas, both in the US domestic market and abroad (which means mainly Europe). Hollywood films also played a very prominent part in all of the European premium film TV channels, offered by Canal Plus and others. And the US–Hollywood element in music videos, and recorded music generally, remains strong.

Second, Hollywood and US interests are likely to increase their infrastructure investments in the 1990s. This will include the already successful Hollywood investment in new cinema multiplexes in Britain and Germany. Another example of investment leading to vertical integration is American involvement in European video distribution outlets. A further American infrastructural investment is by US cable and telephone companies in local cable operations in Britain.

Third, many of the most popular home-made shows on European television screens are based on American models, and some include the purchase of the local national rights. American formats like the police drama have become universal. The situation comedy format has made steady progress. So also the chat show, and the home-made soap opera, while game-quiz shows are perhaps the most successful format export of all.

Fourth, a whole range of commercial broadcasting practices – including, but not limited to, advertising – have been imported into Europe. One crucial example is the art of commercial scheduling – in pursuit of audience maximization throughout the broadcasting day. Europe's most successful commercial channels – such as Canale Cinque in Italy and TF-1 in France – explicitly and self-consciously adopted American scheduling and competitive practices, such as eliminating less popular programming and buying up the ratings stars from the public service channels.

However the full significance and cultural impact even of directly imported programming is far from clear. Still less clear is the significance of these indirect forms of influence. A game show like *Wheel of Fortune* (born 1975) may indeed be American, but when it has been translated into French or Spanish and peopled with local citizens, how American does it remain? As time goes by, the locals start to invent their own game shows. Some Fininvest game shows can make the Hollywood offerings seem tame by comparison.

Perhaps this indicates that European and American popular cultures have become indistinguishable. But perhaps not. Under European reregulatory conditions such cheap formulae in effect make profits, some of which are used to cross-subsidize less market-oriented programming.

## EURO-MEDIA, EURO-PUDDING AND EURO-SOAP

In Chapter 2 of this book we have given a critical account of the development of European broadcasting policy in the 1980s. The whole *Television Without Frontiers* exercise, we believe, actually added to – rather than reduced – United States media influence in Europe.

Nevertheless the final 1989 Broadcasting Directive marks the birth of an effective EC media policy. A new Brussels offering, MEDIA,[2] went through a trial phase in 1989–90 and was then extended for five years. Rather than the grandiose, legalistic, and somewhat naive beginnings of the earlier policy, MEDIA has a much more targeted and hands-on character. It deals with television and film distribution, production and training. To quote just two examples from the twelve separate programmes within MEDIA: SCRIPT gives loans for writing screenplays and for pre-production of film and TV fiction. A second example is CARTOON which – against the background of US–Japanese domination of animated film – seeks to create 'pods' of animation studios across Europe; the assumption is that animated film is a relatively expensive form but one which offers most of the potential benefits, and few of the drawbacks, of Europe-wide co-production.

We believe that MEDIA, not least because it is swimming with the tide and involves media professionals, may – despite very modest funding – be quite effective at encouraging Europe-wide co-operation. But there remain enormous problems – some of which are well represented by the term 'Euro-pudding'. Co-productions across several European countries have indeed often been bland, lowest common denominator, offerings. Even some of the apparently easiest television fields – such as sports channels – have been less successful than might have been guessed.

But the biggest challenge occurs in fictional programming, the high-cost field in which American imports are especially strong, while even the most expensive European fictional programming is relatively weak outside its home country.

Nevertheless we believe that progress will be made in the 1990s in producing fictional programming made in Europe and acceptable to audiences across Europe. One source of such programming is the major European countries and their networks. There are many co-production efforts varying from two networks co-producing one or two programmes to a club of networks planning co-operative efforts over a period of years. The problems of different languages, different cultures, different practices and different regulations are indeed formidable. But the experience is cumulative and some modest progress has been made.

We believe that the emergence of more and stronger independent producers across Europe will deliver other Euro-wide successes in the 1990s. Independent producers' numbers, variety and financial motivation will be compelling spurs to co-production achievement.

Then there are the Euro-soaps. Around 1990–1 there were major new attempts to develop Euro-wide daily soap operas. These efforts involved not only European networks but American advertising agencies (such as Interpublic) and also soap companies (such as Unilever) – a strong echo of the 1930s origins of United States radio soap operas. The involvement of advertising and soap adds an additional commercial dimension to the existing mix of public service and commercial co-production efforts. Another important aspect of this Euro-soap element is the inevitable heavy emphasis on research across a number of European national markets.

This Euro-team of would-be Euro co-producers may seem a somewhat motley collection. But we believe that several components – Brussels-based MEDIA, network combines, independent producers and advertising-initiated soap operas – may add up to more than the sum of the parts. Amongst all of these we believe that the independent producers may provide not only the most energy and variety but also the greatest success; this is an opportunity for some independent producers to become Euro-moguls.

## MOGULS, DEBT AND REREGULATION

The sea change around 1990 had both negative and positive implications for the successful media moguls of the 1970s and 1980s. Debt was the most obvious and difficult problem for a number of media moguls. Given that we have included rapid growth (usually by acquisition) and personal control as part of the definition of moguldom, it follows that heavy bank debt was also a common mogul problem. Financial pundits and other commentators throughout the 1980s pointed to the high risks involved in funding acquisition via debt, rather than by issuing shares. The moguls took the risks in order to retain the control.

Murdoch, Maxwell, Hersant and Berlusconi were amongst those who had major debt problems. However their problems should not be exaggerated. Each of these moguls owned enormously valuable assets. They were not in the position of the new Italian mogul, Giancarlo Parretti, who, in struggling to acquire the Hollywood studio MGM–UA, seemed to sell off most of the assets in advance. Nor were mogul-companies alone in having debt problems. Many American companies and media companies in particular had such problems. The champion media-debtor was perhaps the Time–Warner giant.

While the period around 1990 exacerbated mogul debt problems, it also offered some of the same moguls the benefits of reregulation. The most remarkable example of this was the Italian Broadcasting Act of 1990. It contained many detailed provisions, several of which were clearly intended to clip Silvio Berlusconi's wings. In particular there was a provision on cross-media ownership, aimed at making Berlusconi sell his daily newspaper, *Il Giornale*, and give up many sports channel interests. There were various cutbacks on the showing of 'adult' films on television before the late evening, a reduction in the amount of advertising allowed within feature films, and a complete stop on advertising within cartoon programmes. There were several constraints on Berlusconi's advertising sales company, Publitalia; it would only be allowed to sell advertising for the three Fininvest TV networks and not for other TV networks and radio networks.

However, balancing out these losses were several Berlusconi gains. In particular Berlusconi's control of three national television networks was confirmed and regularized. Second, Berlusconi would now be allowed for the first time to carry live programming, including news. Third, Berlusconi's Publitalia was allowed to continue, with its dominant position in Italian TV advertising only slightly diminished. Indeed, fourth, the provision preventing Publitalia from selling the advertising of other TV channels would weaken those channels as commercial competitors. Fifth, Berlusconi was allowed to retain his commanding position in film industry production, distribution and exhibition. Finally this regularization of Berlusconi's position at home *de facto* confirmed him as the representative of Italian broadcasting across Europe and especially in France and Spain. The Italian law confirmed and strengthened the existing duopoly – placing a private citizen's three channels on an equal footing with the three TV channels of RAI, one of the world's leading public service systems.

Through reregulation Berlusconi was confirmed as the leading broadcasting mogul, not only in Europe but in the world.

## NEW CONDITIONS, NEW MOGULS

The relative decline of public service broadcasting and the rise of more commercial forms of broadcasting opens up opportunities for entrepreneurs as station owners, channel owners or part-owners, and as programming suppliers. This will occur in countries such as Spain and Britain in which the commercial element in broadcasting will expand substantially in the 1990s. German moguls especially will assume a higher profile as they look east and cease to look backward. New media moguls will appear in the smaller population countries – in Greece and Portugal, in Scandinavia, and not least in eastern Europe. But even in Italy and France – already far advanced down the commercial path – new regulations, new policy and new commercial trends may well throw up new apprentice moguls.

An example of an apprentice mogul with a distinctive pattern of success is Joop van den Ende of the Netherlands. The Dutch broadcasting system has traditionally relied on programming provided by national associations and a distinctive form of independent producer. In this system Joop van den Ende by the late 1980s was the agent for many of the Netherlands' leading performer-talents. Initially he had hoped to launch his own TV channel (TV-10). In January 1990 he decided to abandon this plan and to join the rival (Luxembourg-based) RTL-Véronique. This leading mogul position within a dominant commercial TV channel could become a pattern which is repeated elsewhere. In a number of other European countries the small population and the restricted quantity of public service output have confined the main national entertainment talent to quite small numbers of key people. An entrepreneur – whether as agent or otherwise – who can deploy much of this leading national talent must be on the path to national media moguldom.

Magazines have been a common launching pad for both moguls and media innovation in the past. This may well continue, as the major magazine companies seek to diversify in a cash flow direction. One major 1980s trend which will surely continue is the strong march from magazines, via professional and business publications, into on-screen data. This was a route taken in the 1980s by Thomson (legal and medical) and Maxwell (Official Airline Guides). Reed International (of Britain) also focused in the late 1980s on travel industry data. And the huge price paid by Murdoch's News Corporation for the American *TV Guide* was based in part on an assessment of its database, electronic publishing, potential. All four of these magazine-data strategies were focused on the United States. European publishers, such as Elsevier, can be expected to follow the same path in the 1990s.

Another major trend of the late 1980s was the launching of multi-national editions of consumer magazines. Leaders in this strategy included Bertelsmann and other German publishers, as well as the French Hachette. These national launches became enormously expensive – with, for example, the first issues being given free to retailers.

High-priced and/or high-technology practices of this sort may distract the attention of the big companies from more modest areas of magazine innovation. This may leave the way open for apprentice moguls to enter new magazine fields. Moreover the traditional mogul path of magazine-to-newspaper-to-broadcasting may be modified in the 1990s. With more 'themed' TV channels, as well as more independent TV production, magazine publishers may be well placed to carry their magazine expertise directly into specialized television series.

We also anticipate major developments in the old field of newspapers. In most countries there is a strong provincial daily Press, with each provincial market typically dominated by a single ownership. All European nations also have some national newspapers, with the bulk of the national sales and prestige belonging to a very few titles. But this does not preclude change and the emergence of new Press moguls. Indeed Robert Hersant emerged from a provincial Press dominated by monopoly dailies with large regional circulations. Hersant was able to buy up and turn around selected provincial and national dailies. He then introduced major cost savings within his growing group.

The national newspaper presses within Europe are highly varied and we anticipate major changes as innovations, already present in some countries, become more prevalent across Europe. These innovations include the transformation of separate local titles into a standard group product with local editions; the spread of free publishing from small local weeklies into larger newspapers; the expansion of Sunday and seven-day-a-week publishing in a number of countries where newspapers are largely a six-day-a-week business; multi-centre printing of national titles; increasingly sophisticated editorial and advertising use of high quality colour printing.

The largest newspaper changes may occur in southern Europe. Newspaper sales per population are highest in Scandinavia and lowest in Italy, Spain, Greece and Portugal. In these southern countries we anticipate increased sales of daily newspapers and hence opportunities for new moguls specializing in the newspaper turnaround art. Also during the 1990s, Scandinavian and other northern newspaper circulations may well fall − not least because of competition from more expensive and more commercial video offerings for both audience time and advertising revenue.

The move of certain press groups into commercial television, as it spreads across Europe, will have consequences not only for television but also for all newspapers. Some press groups will be successful in television (and/or satellite-and-cable), and will soon come up against regulations preventing further television investment; such press groups may then invest further in newspapers.

We also anticipate that stronger European daily newspapers will offer increasing numbers of pages and sections along American lines. Such a trend will put pressure on weaker newspapers. Another consequence of the multi-section newspaper is the emergence of magazine and other sections which may be saleable with different titles. Moreover, since women's magazines editionized across several European countries have succeeded, there may be opportunities for similar Euro-sections within a single multi-section newspaper package.

## MORE NATIONAL AND LOCAL MEDIA, AND MORE MOGULS

Most Europeans will continue to consume a primarily *national* diet throughout the 1990s. But with the media continuing to grow faster than the economy generally, there will also be an expansion in both local–regional media and at the international–world levels.

Below the national level, most European countries have small community and city-based, as well as regional, media. Radio stations and local newspapers will continue to be important launching pads for new entrepreneurs. But regional television may be still more important. Germany and Britain already have a strongly established regional system; France and Italy have less well financed regional channels. Spain has given greatly added emphasis to regional television. The combination of these regional channels, plus the Europe-wide requirements for independent production, present opportunities for new patterns of finance and co-production, and hence for new moguls to appear.

However the bulk of the media action will continue to be at the national level. Most of the political power and regulatory control, the finance and subsidy, the language and tradition, is at the national level. National and semi-national newspapers will continue to accompany powerful regional groupings (which may in turn become more semi-national). Radio, including much supposedly local radio, will be (as in France) primarily national in terms of ownership and content. Indeed the stitching together of local media into various types of national combine, company or network, will continue to be a classic field for the emergent mogul.

Television will remain a primarily *national* force across Europe, while including as before regional and international elements. Many predictions have pointed to the decline of the broadcast licence fee and the decline of public service broadcasting. The licence fee will certainly constitute a declining fraction of total broadcasting finance. But this does not mean the end of public service broadcasting. Elements of PSB have long been advertising-financed, a tradition which the Italian and British broadcasting legislation of 1990 duly confirmed.

Despite anxiety across western Europe as to the inadequacies of finance for all of the channels, we believe that more finance will continue to flow. The numbers of channels already available in 1991 will not significantly increase; but combined licence fee and advertising finance will increase, while video–cable–satellite finance across Europe will certainly advance.

However this range of screen finance – state licence fee, advertising, subscription (TV and cable), rental and purchase (video) – will continue, under evolving national and European regulation, to make for volatile conditions.

Already common by 1990 was the pattern of a national media company with minority foreign participation. This pattern can be expected to increase in the 1990s. American, Japanese and other non-Europeans are, and will continue to be, hesitant about buying European media companies outright. European political, regulatory and cultural sensitivities compel caution. A familiar business strategy is for an American, Japanese (or Australian or Brazilian) company to buy a large minority slice (say 25 per cent or 35 per cent) of a European company. A Japanese company, when acquiring part of a European music company may offer access to the domestic Japanese music market. An American company when acquiring a slice of a European TV independent producer, may offer finance, possible access to the US market and perhaps distribution in other national markets. But such arrangements are notoriously volatile; this has been true even of such prominent and regulated examples as the foreign participation in French television channels. While such national–international linkages do not result in stability, they may still breed new media moguls. The European media entrepreneur may see the US or Japanese giant as the potential financier of his rise to mogul status. Meanwhile for the large non-European company it may be a case of Spot The Future European Mogul.

## MULTI-NATIONAL MEDIA COMPANIES, BARONS AND MOGULS

Despite the national level being likely to remain dominant, we believe that there will also be an expanded world media industry element. As with other industries, this will largely consist of a smallish number of 'multi-national companies', which usually means, of course, companies based in, or dominated by, a single country, although operating in several or many others. Some of the companies – including some of the fastest changing and most volatile – will be controlled by moguls; others, also as before, will be run by managerial barons.

If multi-national companies continue to dominate the world media industry, it follows that other possible types of organization are less likely to prevail. One such category is the public service broadcaster – this type of organization seems fated to remain basically at the national level (despite export programming sales).

The media co-operative is a second type of organization which seems suitable for only a rather modest role on the world scene. The limitations of the co-operative may be less evident, especially since the Associated Press is one of the most venerable of world media players and its history is as a co-operative of US newspapers. However, the more dynamic half of the AP–Dow Jones partnership in recent years has been the Dow Jones/*Wall Street Journal* side of the partnership. Reuters has been the most dynamic agency in recent decades (see Chapter 3) and its new-found dynamism involved moving from a co-operative to a more conventional company structure.

Media companies which lack a dominant ownership also seem to be quite volatile. This has certainly been the case with the French commercial TV companies. To involve several major companies, each with only a maximum 25 per cent ownership share, can be a recipe for managerial conflict.

On the other hand control of a 25 per cent or other minority slice can be a significant challenge to an aggressive media mogul. Silvio Berlusconi's Fininvest faced this particular challenge in Spain and appeared to take more than a 25 per cent interest in programming, scheduling and the selling of advertising.

An ambiguous case occurs when two companies share control. An interesting example is the German movie channel, Premiere, launched in February 1991 as a merger between two previously competing enterprises. The French Canal Plus and the German Bertelsmann each had 37.5 per cent of Premiere, while the Kirch Group (with its treasure trove of German movie rights) had 25 per cent.

However, even company alliances which give one company over 50 per cent, and hence control, can still remain volatile in terms of the ownership of minority slices. Media moguls have already shown themselves to be hyperactive shufflers of such minority slices, sometimes looking for a quick, arbitrageur, profit. But even if a quick profit is not the motivation, minority investors will often merely be getting a foot in the door (or a director on the board) in order to take a look at a new field, or new company. This will probably continue to be a standard mogul tactic; the mogul – having taken his look – is likely to seek either to eliminate, or to expand, his stake. Volatility and mogul tactics will again feed on each other.

## ADVERTISING AGENCIES – POWER AND VOLATILITY

Among the slowly growing elements of a world-wide media industry, a handful of advertising agencies are prominent. These agencies will probably handle an increasing share of world advertising, and they will become more powerful in other ways. But they will also remain highly volatile. Table 10.1 shows 'billings' (advertising expenditure) figures for 1990.

The situation of the leaders of world advertising has marked similarities to Hollywood world leadership in electronic entertainment. This is another case of getting 'more powerful, but less American'. Of the two double agencies – WPP and Saatchi and Saatchi – which topped the world league table, three of the four constituent agencies were really American; both groups were British owned and both were also highly indebted and suffering severely on the stock market.

As with Hollywood (Los Angeles), we have here a world industry heavily focused on the US domestic market and based in a single American city (New York). But the ownership by 1990 was highly international. Following the British takeovers of the 1980s, the Japanese, led by Dentsu, were moving out onto the world scene. The other rising advertising power was France (which unlike Germany and Italy had retained control over much of its own advertising agency sector). Of the 1990 top twenty billing advertising agencies, nine were based in the US, seven in Europe (France four, Britain three) and four in Japan. Given the enormous volatility of the advertising world, any precise prediction would be rash indeed. But during the 1990s more of the largest advertising agencies may come to be based in Europe.

As we showed in Chapter 4, the advertising industry has already been highly successful at Brussels lobbying. The Economic Community's 1989 Broadcasting Directive largely reflected, and accommodated, the views of the advertising lobby. The advertising lobby in Brussels in the 1980s combined a well-considered general strategy with a command of Europe-wide detail.

These latter strengths have also been evident in the advertising agencies' everyday business activities. One key example of a broad strategy has been the large agencies' use of media buying subsidiaries; through this specialized subsidiary the mega-agency can channel all of its own purchasing of media time and space – thus targeting its negotiating power and earning the maximum discounts.

Table 10.1  Advertising agency worldwide capitalized billings, 1990

| Agency | HQ | Agencies include | 1990 billings $ millions |
|---|---|---|---|
| 1 WPP | London | Ogilvy and Mather, J. Walter Thompson | 18,095 |
| 2 Saatchi & Saatchi | London | Saatchi & Saatchi, Backer, Spielvogel, Bates | 11,862 |
| 3 Interpublic | New York | McCann-Erikson, Lintas | 11,025 |
| 4 Omnicom | New York | BBDO, DDB, Needham | 9,700 |
| 5 Dentsu | Tokyo | Dentsu | 9,672 |
| 6 Young & Rubicam | New York | Young & Rubicam | 8,001 |
| 7 Eurocom | Paris | Eurocom | 5,066 |
| | 7 agency total  = | | $73.421 billion |

Source: Advertising Age (25 March 1991)

Meanwhile the Europe-wide advertising agency is geared up to handle the almost infinite variety presented by specific European markets in terms of available media, customer taste, local language, national regulation and so on.

Advertising agencies are also especially well placed to initiate and/or to support Euro-wide programming. The strength of advertising agencies, the increased centrality of advertising finance, and the continuing demand for attractive and modestly priced programming, will mean that advertising agency involvement will not be confined to Interpublic and Euro-soaps.

## EUROPE: THE WORLD LEADER IN NEWS

During the 1980s and into the 1990s the Atlanta-based Cable News Network (CNN) and its media mogul, Ted Turner, have been the champion self-publicists of international news. They have also made real advances in the live coverage of major news events.

One of the unintended consequences of CNN's self-publicity achievements has been to distract attention from a significant change in world news leadership: during the 1980s Europe took over from the United States as the world leader in news. In the 1990s we expect this leadership to be more widely recognized.

During the 1980s the UPI agency really ceased to be either a genuine world agency or a United States company. Despite AFP's difficulties, AFP remains a world agency and the lone American AP is now outgunned by European Reuters and AFP; other major European agencies (such as the German DPA and the Spanish EFE) increased their international significance in the 1980s. Meanwhile, in the field of photo news agencies, Paris is the world capital (Gamma, Sygma).

Europe's team of major daily newspapers also grew impressively in the 1980s. No other continent – certainly not North America – has either the same number of, or the same variety in, prestige daily newspapers, as does western Europe. The 1990s may see additional developments of this kind not only in eastern Europe, but also in southern Europe.

We are somewhat sceptical as to whether the European Broadcasting Union, or some other Euro-cooperative, can go much further in the supply and exchange of video news.

Of the two major international film agencies, WTN (formerly UPITN) is now dominated by the ABC television network of New York. But Visnews has clearly consolidated its position as the leading video news agency. Significantly Reuters has a controlling interest but Visnews also has access to the entire news output of the BBC and the American NBC network. Visnews' daily satellite news feeds are seen on nearly all of the world's television screens. In the 1980s the exchange of video news across the world achieved new levels of speed, sophistication and complexity. As with the traditional news agencies, the major video news organizations in the world in effect are members of a club who swap material between each other. Whatever happens to the EBU and other Euro-news initiatives in the 1990s, Europe in general and Visnews in particular seem likely to confirm that in the world news club, Europe is the first among equals.

1989 saw the launch of the Murdoch/News Direct-to-Home Sky, four-channel, satellite service. One of the channels was Sky News, Europe's first 24-hour all-news TV channel. The channel (both in its Sky and later its later BSkyB forms) has depended heavily on Visnews material. But while Murdoch thus became Europe's first 24-hour video news mogul, he will not be the last. Europe already generates most of the necessary video news material; the task of a new all-news video mogul is merely to put together a channel.

# Notes

## 1 INTRODUCTION

1  Els de Bens (1989) 'Dallasification as a result of increasing TV channel competition', unpublished paper, University of Ghent.

## 2 WESTERN EUROPEAN TELEVISION AND THE NORTH ATLANTIC SETTING

1  Home Office (1981) *Direct Broadcasting by Satellite*, London: Her Majesty's Stationery Office.
2  EC (25 March 1983) X/12/83 COM(83), Brussels, 229 final.
3  Ernest Eugster (1983) *Television Programming Across National Boundaries*, Dedham, Mass.: Artech House, pp. 133–64.
4  EC (23 May 1984) *Television Without Frontiers* 8827/84, COM(84), Brussels, 300 final.
5  EC (March 1986) *European Broadcasting*, 6739/86 COR 1 (COM(86) 146), Brussels.
6  *Variety* (18 April 1984) 'Not-so-innocents abroad: US webs in Italy', pp. 113, 136.
7  See the monthly publication *Cable and Satellite Europe*, London.
8  Mary Kelly (1989) 'The television programme market in Europe', unpublished paper, University College, Dublin.
9  Els de Bens (1989) 'Dallasification as a result of increasing TV channel competition', unpublished paper, University of Ghent.
10  Lawrence Cohn (4 May 1988) 'Unbearable lightness of being in foreign film production', *Variety*, pp. 59, 203–27.
11  William Phillips (17 March 1989) 'Leaning on Hollywood to prop up the ratings', *Broadcast*.
12  *Variety* (27 April 1988) Tenth Anniversary of Reteitalia issue.
13  *Variety* (19–25 April 1989) 'Fininvest webs passing RAI as Italo gameshow giant', p. 177.
14  Kenneth Dyson and Peter Humphreys (1988) *Broadcasting and New Media Policies in Europe*, London: Routledge.
15  William Rowland and Michael Tracey (Autumn 1988) 'The breakdown of public service broadcasting', *Intermedia* vol. 16, no. 4–6, pp. 32–42; James McDonnell (1991) *Public Service Broadcasting*, London: Routledge.

## 3 NEWS AGENCIES AND THE DATA BUSINESS

1  *Business Week* (21 December 1987) 'Reuters after the crash'.
2  Reuters Holdings plc Annual Reports 1989–90; Products and Technology 1989, 1990; Reuters Registration Statement to US Securities and Exchange Commission for fiscal year ended 31.12.90.
3  M. Palmer (January 1976) 'L'Office Français d'information', in *Revue d'histoire de la deuxième guerre mondiale*, no. 100, pp. 19–40.
4  McLean Ewing of the *Glasgow Herald*, deputy chairman of Reuters (1939) and chairman of the PA (1935–6, 1941–2).
5  Cf. M. Palmer (1976) 'L'Agence Havas et Bismarck; l'échec de la Triple Alliance télégraphique (1887–1889)', in *Revue d'Histoire diplomatique*, nos 3 and 4, pp. 321–57; G. Storey (1951) *Reuters' Century*, London: Max Parish, pp. 113–15.
6  J. Lawrenson and L. Barber (1985) *The Price of Truth*, Edinburgh: Mainstream Publishing Company, p. 86. The historian D.M. Read is currently preparing an official history of Reuters.
7  G. Feyel (1976) 'Les correspondances de presse parisienne des journaux départementaux 1825–1850', *Documents pour l'histoire de la presse nationale aux XIXe et XXe siècles*, dir. P. Albert, Paris: CNRS; P. Frédérix (1959) *Un siècle de chasse aux nouvelles: de l'agence d'information Havas à l'Agence France-Presse*, Paris: Flammarion.
8  C.F.M. Bell to D. Dalziel, 12 February 1892. MLB 5 *The Times* archives.
9  F. Hardman to M. Morris, 18 August and 15 October 1870. Hardman papers, *The Times* archives, quoted in M. Palmer 'The British Press and international news, 1851–99', in G. Boyce, J. Curran and P. Wingate (1978) *Newspaper History*, London: Constable, and Beverly Hills: Sage, p. 209
10  Havas-Paris to its London correspondent, Mercadier, 14 May 1909, quoted in M. Palmer (1983) *Des petits journaux aux grandes agences*, Paris: Aubier, p. 240.
11  Originally plural; later changed to singular.
12  G. Storey, op. cit., p. 180. See also W.J. Baker (1970) *A History of the Marconi Company*, London: Methuen, pp. 228–31.
13  Quoted in G. Storey, op. cit., p. 2.
14  J.L. Kieve (1973) *The Electric Telegraph*, Newton Abbot: David and Charles, p. 51.
15  G. Storey, op. cit., p. 15.
16  C.-L. Havas to widow de Roure, 16 January 1832, quoted in P. Frédérix, op. cit., p. 20.
17  Reuter, quoted by James Grant, editor of the *Morning Advertiser*, quoted in G. Storey, op. cit., p. 14.
18  G. Storey, op. cit., pp. 15–16. In Reuters' archives there survive copies of agency telegrams, dating from 1858, the year when London newspapers began subscribing to the agency. The very first begins thus: 'The following telegram was received at Mr. Reuter's Office, 8th October, Berlin, 8th October 4.7. PM. "The official Prussian

Correspondence announces that the King . . ." etc.' *Punch*, of 27 November 1858, poked fun at the dutiful way in which Reuter relayed news from official sources. See M. Palmer, op. cit., p. 374.

19  H. Pigeat (1987) *Le nouveau désordre mondial de l'information*, Paris: Hachette, p. 181.

20  *The Times* (6 July 1980) 'Reuters: all the news that's fit to be computerized'.

21  Reuters Holdings plc Annual Report 1980.

22  *Reuter Alert* (1987) 'The Reuter package', vol. II.

23  J. Lawrenson and L. Barber, op. cit., pp. 127–34.

24  ibid., p. 132.

25  ibid.

26  Reuters Holdings plc Annual Report 1986.

27  See ibid., and company data for 1987–90.

28  Many banks find it galling that they have to pay – heavily – for their own data to appear in Reuters' services.

29  H. Pigeat, op. cit., p. 76.

30  J. Lawrenson and L. Barber, op. cit., p. 134.

31  Quoted in *Business Week* (17 June 1985) 'Reuters starts to let its customers talk back'.

32  Reuters Holding plc Annual Report 1986, 'Managing Director's review', p. 7.

33  *Business Week* (21 December 1987) 'Reuters after the crash'.

34  N. Goodison (20 January 1988) 'How October's storms were weathered', *Financial Times*; *Financial Times* Survey (13 November 1987) 'Singapore', p. 5.

35  B. Riley (7 October 1985) 'Where the Stock Exchange draws the line', *Financial Times*.

36  This order entry system handled 2–3 per cent of all equity trading in the US (dealing in 1,000 equities and options in 1985; and 8,000 in 1986). Founded in 1969, it reported revenues in 1985 of $7.6 million, and was acquired outright by Reuters in May 1987, when it was valued at $119 million. Volume of trading on Instinet quadrupled, 1986–90.

37  *Financial Times* (21 May 1985) 'SE set for battle with Reuters'.

38  P. Benjamin, special projects manager of Reuters Europe, quoted in 'Reuters peace bid on share dealing', *Sunday Times* (26 May 1985).

39  Quotron, founded in 1957, was the first company to offer electronic stock quotations. The Dow Jones Company, publisher of the *Wall Street Journal*, and joint owner with the US agency AP of the AP–Dow Jones wire service, has a major stake in Telerate.

40  *Financial Times* (28 October 1987) 'Big-hearted visions of integrated trading'; N. Goodison, op. cit.

41  *Financial Times* (28 October 1987).

42  *Financial Times* Survey (13 November 1987) 'Singapore', p. 5; *Financial Times* (23 October 1987) 'Mixed response to black box trading'.

43  By the end of 1990, Globex, the computer-based system developed by Reuters and CME, was due to operate outside the regular trading hours of the open outcry market. It would provide 24-hour trading

of CME products and was to include European instruments, when the Paris-based MATIF, the leading European futures and options exchange, joined Globex.
44  *Financial Times* (29 October 1987) 'A program for distress'.
45  *Reuter Alert* (1986) vol. III, p. 11.
46  C. Chapman (1987) *How the New Stock Exchange Works*, 2nd edn, London: Hutchinson, p. 9.
47  Reuters Holdings plc: Offer for Sale by Tender by S.G. Warburg & Co. Limited and N.M. Rothschild & Sons Limited, 1984; J. Lawrenson and L. Barber, op. cit., pp. 156–7.
48  J. Lawrenson and L. Barber, op. cit., pp. 145–6.
49  See above, p. 57.
50  See J.-N. Jeanneney and J. Julliard (1979) *'Le Monde' de Beuve-Méry*, Paris: le Seuil; J. Thibau (1978) *Le Monde*, Paris: Jean-Claude-Simeon; L. Greilsamer (1990) *Hubert Beuve-Méry*, Paris: Fayard.
51  See O. Boyd-Barrett and M. Palmer (1981) *Le trafic des nouvelles*, Paris: Alain Moreau, p. 120.
52  C. Martial-Bourgeon (1976) unpublished, quoted in O. Boyd-Barrett and M. Palmer op. cit., p. 119.
53  H. Pigeat, op. cit., p. 70. Pigeat overstates the case when he argues that an agency has never prospered solely through general news: between 1882 and 1916, the dividend from a share in the news-division of Havas was higher than that from its advertising division (*branche*). But, as the renaissance of Reuters showed, his general point is valid.
54  J. Cluzel 'Communication', in Annexe no. 8, *Rapport général . . . sur le projet de loi de finances pour 1987, Sénat, annexe(s) au procès-verbal*, 17.11.1986, 16.11.1987.
55  H. Pigeat, op. cit., p. 180. In January 1987 the Minister of Culture and Communication, François Léotard, declared that 'our aim is to reduce "public service" subscriptions to 50 per cent of the total': if AFP were considered to be a state agency it would lose credibility in the international market-place.
56  H. Pigeat, op. cit., pp. 111–12.
57  Such as J.-F. Kahn, director of the weekly news-magazine *L'Evénement du Jeudi*, quoted in *Libération* (18 December 1986).
58  H. Pigeat, op. cit., p. 176.
59  Guy Petit, quoted in O. Boyd-Barrett and M. Palmer, op. cit., n. 123, p. 133.
60  See H. Pigeat, op. cit., pp. 174–6. Regional newspaper publishers point out that AFP subscription rates in France are higher than those of its competitors. François-Régis Hutin, the 'p.-d.g.' of *Ouest-France*, the French daily with the highest circulation, argued during the 1986 crisis that the Press *does* pay heavily, despite what is often said; but that, while having a majority on the board of directors, it has the semblance – not the substance – of power. See *Ouest-France* (20 December 1986) 'Crise de l'AFP'.
61  O. Boyd-Barrett and M. Palmer, op. cit., pp. 124–6.
62  Paillet, with a Trotskyist reputation when he entered the agency in the late 1940s, later wrote one of the modern classics on agency

journalism (1974, *Le journalisme*, Denoel) and was responsible for *Le manuel de l'agencier* (1982, AFP). In 1981 he left AFP when proposed as one of the three nominees of Mitterrand of the Haute Autorité de la Communication Audiovisuelle. He is portrayed by M. Cotta, the President of the Haute Autorité in (1986) *Les miroirs de Jupiter*, Paris: Fayard, pp. 86–7.

63  In 1968, AFP launched the SET – 'service économique par télé-scripteur'; this was one of several attempts to provide interpretative prices on financial and economic trends in France, the EEC and abroad. See O. Boyd-Barrett and M. Palmer, op. cit., pp. 382–3. Pigeat and others believe that AFP missed out, in the mid-sixties, on a golden opportunity. It chose not to invest in the development of financial and economic news, at a time when Stock Exchange trading began to change with the advent of computerization. During Pigeat's 'reign', over five years were spent on inconclusive negotiations to interface the computers of AFP with those of le palais Brogniart, situated across the street.

64  H. Pigeat, op. cit., pp. 136–7.

65  AFP revenue in 1982: 488 million francs. Turnover doubled between 1980 and 1984 (it was 750 million francs in 1984).

66  Pigeat argues, pertinently, that the Press refused to invest in AFP in 1957, when the statute was voted, partly bacause, although they had a majority on the board of directors, newspaper publishers had failed to secure that AFP became a co-operative owned by them; they considered that the state and the nation should pay for the international organization of AFP. H. Pigeat, op. cit., p. 175.

67  H. Pigeat, op. cit., p. 139.

68  F. Colombier, interview with H. Pigeat, in *Le Quotidien de Paris* (10 June 1981).

69  Defferre was also a newspaper publisher (*Le Provençal*, the leading daily of Marseille, of which he was mayor), and the 'p.-d.g.' of ACP, France's second most important news agency, and a rival to AFP, notably for the custom of provincial newspapers.

70  As in 1979, when he was first elected, thirteen out of fifteen members of the board voted for him; on all three occasions, the two representatives of AFP personnel did not participate in the vote.

71  *La Correspondance de la Presse* (1 February 1983, 5 January 1984); *Le Monde* (22 December 1982, 1 February 1983, 27 November 1983).

72  H. Pigeat, op. cit., p. 151. In October 1982, Pigeat argued that subscription rates in 1983 should rise to 22 per cent; the Ministry of Economy and Finance refused to entertain a rise of over 8 per cent.

73  Number of days lost in strikes: 1,161 in 1985; 4,025 in 1986. The July strike was not confined, as usually happened, to the services distributed to clients in France; services aimed at clients abroad were also affected.

74  H. Pigeat, quoted in *Le Monde* (27 November 1983); speech to the International Association for Political Science (10 August 1982) Rio de Janeiro; op. cit., p. 67.

75  This was one of the reasons why some provincial newspapers deserted

AFP for ACP in the 1970s. In May 1987 – after Ian Maxwell (son of Robert) had acquired ACP – the latter's general news wire contained 60,000 words. AFP recovered the custom of some provincial newspapers which had deserted it. But ACP had preceded AFP in some of the 'customized' services proposed to French subscribers: the formating of services, which required no rewriting or reprocessing and could input direct for reproduction as such by clients who were offered, in addition, various selection facilities. In July 1982, AFP replaced two text services, 'Paris' and 'Provinces', with three more targeted services – AFP-Générale (120,000 words), AFP-Sélection (66,000) and AFP-Evénement (10,000 words) (*Correspondance de la Presse*, 28 June 1982). In 1990 Robert Maxwell closed down the loss-making ACP, and France all but lost its second general news agency. See below, n. 85.

76  H. Pigeat, op. cit., pp. 89, 185.
77  UNESCO, *Statistical Yearbook*, 1984; *Le Point* (25 January 1988) 'Presse: la crise des quotidiens'.
78  The deficit for 1986 was 149 million francs, more than double that of 1985.
79  The maintenance of a German-language desk had long been considered a luxury, given AFP's poor results in German-speaking countries. Pigeat proposed that it be transferred to Bonn – whereas the financial commission of AFP urged its abolition. The refusal of the journalists to leave Paris was the spark that ignited the November 1986 conflict.
80  H. Pigeat, op. cit.
81  *Rapport général fait au nom de la Commission des Finances . . . annexe no. 8, annexe au procès-verbal de la séance du Sénat du 16.11.1987.*
82  In the US, where competition for the supply of all categories of real information is at its most intense, Reuters' principal competitor is Telerate, controlled by Dow Jones. Within Europe, the German agency DPA increasingly challenges the Reuters–AFP ascendancy in media services.
83  In 1987, the agency launched the Reuter News picture terminal: subscribers (newspapers and news agencies) can interface with Reuters and a variety of photo-agencies, and can process photographs as part of their computerized page make-up system.
84  *Financial Weekly*, quoted in *Reuter Alert* (1987) vol. II, p. 30.
85  Within France itself, AFP was perturbed by the reinvigorated presence of 'Anglo-Saxon' competitors. The American agency, AP, had long been present; in 1987 it claimed to have 200 correspondents or informers in Paris and the provinces. The second major French agency, ACP, had long been money-losing, but in 1987 developed anew when acquired by Ian Maxwell (son of Robert Maxwell); however Robert Maxwell closed it down in 1990. The agency was relaunched under different management and with more modest ambitions later that year. From the mid-1980s, moreover, Reuters has reorganized and intensified its news-collection and distribution operations in France; in western France, for example, the 1985 launching of the agency's news picture service appears to have signalled an increased market presence (it even sold services to free sheets); in 1986, it launched a

TV service (programme schedules, news, features) in France. Eighty journalists were then based in 'Reuters France'.
86 English, French, German, Spanish and Arabic. In 1990 Reuters produced news services in eleven languages.
87 *Reuter Alert* (1987) 'Foreign intelligence', vol. II, pp. 24–5. Reuters Holdings plc Products and Technology 1989–90.

## 4 EUROPEAN MEDIA LOBBYING

1 F. Burkhardt (27–28 October 1983) 'Electronic media – an overview', XIth Management and Marketing Symposium, FIEJ, Marseille.
2 In 1983, it published a seminal work in this regard: *Newspapers and Electronic Media* (Darmstadt: IFRA, 1983). Based in Darmstadt, and led in the 1980s by the ubiquitous and pithy Friedrich Burkhardt, IFRA acts as the European counterpart of the R. & D. technical centre of the American NPA, the ANPA, based in Reston, Virginia.
3 FIEJ (1978) *La liberté de la presse est la liberté du citoyen*, Paris: FIEJ.
4 Ogilvy and Mather (1984) *Europe: The New Media Review*, London: Ogilvy and Mather Ltd.
5 Ogilvy and Mather (13 April 1984) *Les nouveaux média en Europe*, Conférence de presse.
6 Michael Palmer, one of the co-authors of this book, was technical adviser of the FIEJ and served on CAEJ–FIEJ committees during the period under review.
7 *The Economist* Intelligence Unit, Foreign Report no. 2, 'The outlook for newsprint in the EC, 1984'.
8 *BDZV–Nachrichten* (November 1983); *Handelsblatt* (11 November 1983); *Paper* (5 December 1983); 'Newsprint' (March 1984) *FIEJ Bulletin* no. 138.
9 The *Guardian*, 30 November 1983; BDZV, 16 December 1983.
10 In March 1984, the BDZV stated that latest figures indicated that Germany had paid duty on at least 35,000 tonnes (0.5 million DM).
11 The Advertising Association (AA) and European Advertising Tripartite EAT (December 1988) *The European Advertising and Media Forecast (EAMF)*, vol. 3, no. 3, pp. 3–10.
12 At market prices, ranked by 1988 percentage (listed in AA and EAT (February 1990) *EAMF*, p. 77)
13 ibid., p. 202
14 See also A. Mattelart (1989) *L'Internationale publicitaire*, Paris: La Decouverte, pp. 135–41; A Mattelart and M. Palmer (February 1990) 'Europe sous la pression publicitaire', in *Le Monde diplomatique*; A. Mattelart and M. Palmer 'The conquest of space', in *Media, Culture and Society*, to appear in 1991; M. Palmer (May 1990) 'Les industries publicitaires, commanditaires de la recherche', in Société Française des Sciences de l'Information et de la Communication, *Congrès Inforcom 90: La Recherche en information-communication – l'avenir* (Université Aix-Marseille).
15 See R. Rijkens and G.E. Miracle (1986) *European Regulation of Advertising*, Amsterdam: Elsevier.

16  The Federation of Associations of Periodical Publishers in the EC (FAEP); the European Federation of External Advertising (EDMA), the European Group of Television Advertising (EGTA).
17  The one-time President of the Advertising Industry Group, Roger Underhill, was one of the leading lobbyists for the European advertising industry, and did much, in the 1980s, in Brussels and elsewhere, to help the industry get its lobbying act together. Three other prominent Britons in this regard are Ronald Beatson, the EAAA Director-General; Alastair Tempest, EAAA Director of External Affairs and EAT Secretary-General, and Mike Waterson, the Advertising Association's Research Director.
18  Commission of the European Communities (23 May 1984) *Television Without Frontiers, Green Book*, 8827/84, COM(84), 300 final. See Chapter 2.
19  Dr Ivo Schwartz, the main author of the green book, headed the legal affairs division of D.G. III, which is in charge of competition policy.
20  Commission of the European Communities (17 July 1986) *Proposal for a Council Directive on the co-ordination of certain provisions laid down by law, regulation or administrative action in Member States concerning the pursuit of broadcasting activities*.
21  During the same period, the mid-1980s, Mike Waterson, Research Director of the AA, and Alastair Tempest, Secretary-General of the EAT, spearheaded Herculean attempts by Europe's advertising industries to put their own methodological house in order. From 1985, the AA and EAT published *The European Media and Advertising Forecast* (*EAMF*), hailed as the 'first, albeit faltering, attempt to provide comparable figures for the major European markets' advertising nations, Japan and the United States' (*Marketing Week*, 23 May 1986). In an industry obsessed by data and the reliability of forecasts or informed 'guesstimates', the methodological variables country by country (and sometimes survey by survey, or from one market research body to another) cause considerable disquiet. The difficulties were analysed in an EAT symposium on Advertising Statistics, held in Rome in December 1986.

    In the December 1989 issue of *EAMF*, the necessary and courageous methodological introduction to EAT expenditure statistics continues to run to five pages, highlighting 'some of the major problems that arise in the compilation of international advertising statistics'. See also M.J. Waterson (1988) 'European advertising statistics', in *International Journal of Advertising*, no. 7, pp. 17–93.
22  EAT 'Explanatory Summary': Council of Europe draft Convention on transfrontier television, 29 August 1988.
23  EAT 'Explanatory summary' and EAT lobby brief: Council of Europe draft Convention on transfrontier television, 29 August 1988.
24  The EC Commission green book, *Television Without Frontiers*, quoted and endorsed by the AA, in 'Direct Broadcasting by Satellite and Cable Television: The Advertising Association's Commentary to the House of Commons Home Affairs Committee', 28 January 1988.
25  Both the Convention and the Directive state that advertising

should not exceed 15 per cent of daily transmission time or twelve minutes per hour. To exceed the latter figure is generally considered counter-productive (by advertisers, agencies, as well as by programme-schedulers).

26  In Britain it was reckoned that this would heavily penalize Channel 4, which screened some seventeen films a week.

27  'That means no centre breaks for either *Coronation Street* or *Brookside*. Even the advertising nirvana, the centre break on *News at Ten*, would be no more.' *Campaign* (21 October 1988) 'How the ad break war threatens TV'.

28  ibid.

29  Institute of Practitioners in Advertising (IPA) *Bulletin* no. 210, July 1988.

30  'Broadcast advertising shall not interrupt coherent programme items. Interruptions are, however, permissible where they do not constitute unreasonable interference because the advertising coincides with a break between distinguishable parts of the plot, story or presentation of the programme, or do not detract from the integrity, value and natural continuity of the programme.'

31  ibid.

32  This was backed by Germany, Belgium, Greece, Portugal and the Netherlands.

33  IPA *Bulletin*, op. cit.

34  'By way of illustration, a company which is brand leader in the partwork market and a significant advertiser in many world markets, has six comparable partworks (on Do-It-Yourself, Great Composers, Great Artists, Story-telling, and two on Cookery) which it advertises in a "natural break" country and a "block" country (Partwork is the selling of books in a series of separate parts or instalments weekly or monthly). The company's experience is that the average sales in respect of the "block" country were 42 per cent less than those in the "natural break" country.' EAT lobby brief: Council of Europe draft Convention on transfrontier television, 29 August 1988.

35  In 1988, Germany had a maximum of twenty minutes a day of TV advertising – scheduled around the news breaks. In 1987, the annual advertising spend on TV was $900 million, compared to the UK's $3.06 billion. (In Germany, the giant publishing groups long succeeded in ensuring that the growth of TV advertising remained restricted.)

36  EAT lobby brief (29 September 1988), op. cit.

37  A group of advertisers commissioned a separate study from the consultant firm of Booz Allen & Hamilton: this claimed that the COE draft Convention's proposals would have aggregate costs for the European economy totalling $800 million of restrictions.

38  *International Advertiser* (March–April 11989).

39  *Media International* (January 1989) 'Euro broadcasters reach compromise'.

40  Both the EC Directive (adopted October 1989) and the COE Convention (adopted April 1989) allow the insertion of advertising breaks between and during programmes. (The French-language

version of article 14 of the COE convention states, curiously, both
that advertising must (*doit*) be inserted between programmes and
that it may (*peut*) also be inserted during programmes. *European
Convention on Transfrontier Television* (article 14).

41  Quoted in 'European broadcast measures', in *International Advertiser*,
(March–April 1989).
42  'The EC Commission has . . . introduced a terrifying virus into the
system which could easily be used to pick off advertising, sector after
sector. In addition to the tobacco sector (. . . which is not one of the
larger categories of advertising expenditure) . . . the EC has started
in other areas (eg pharmaceutical) to base its proposals for controlling
advertising on the need to create an internal market.' EAT and AA
(February 1990) *EAMF*, pp. 20–2.
43  ibid.
44  See Charles Miller (1987) *Lobbying Government*, Oxford: Blackwell;
P. Hennessy (1989) *Whitehall*, London: Martin Secker & Warburg.
45  In its Annual Review for 1987–8, the Advertising Association
writes: 'the consumer movement used to harbour worrying suspicious
about advertising. However, there have been encouraging signs in
recent years that bodies like the National Consumer Council now have
a much more positive awareness of the role of advertising, thanks in
part perhaps to the AA's Public Action Programme. We value our
close association with the leading consumer organizations, and will
. . . co-operate with them when policy and objectives coincide (as in
the long term they usually do).'
46  See *Material for a European Media Concept*: Reports submitted to
the Committee of Ministers by the Committee on the Mass Media,
Strasbourg: Council of Europe, 1980.

## 5 EURO-MEDIA MOGULS

1  See Chapter 8, where Gianpietro Mazzoleni dintinguishes between
'pure' and 'impure' publishers in Italy.
2  Edwin Emery (1972) *The Press and America*, Englefield Cliffs, NJ:
Prentice Hall.
3  Paul Chadwick, 'Rupert Murdoch, News Unlimited and Australian
politics', paper presented at the conference on News Unlimited –
Journalism and Global Ownership, University of Sydney (8–10
February 1989).
4  From September 1990 to January 1991, 'the future of News Corporation
hung in the balance as its 146 bank lenders were parlayed, chivvied
and strong-armed into a debt restructuring'. Mr Murdoch finally
emerged with $7.6 billion of debt restructured over three years,
due for repayment by February 1994. Stephen Fidler (4 April 1991)
'Operation dolphin saves Murdoch', in the *Financial Times*.
5  A perfumier of Corsican origin, François Coty sought to develop a
French newspaper group (*L'Ami du Peuple*, *Le Figaro*, *Le Gauloise*,
etc., 1922–33) to further his political career.
6  *Economist* (11 March 1989) 'Meet the new media monsters'.

# 6 MEDIA MOGULS IN BRITAIN

1  Alan J. Lee (1976) *The Origins of the Popular Press, 1844–1914*, London: Croom Helm.
2  *Royal Commission on the Press, 1947–1949 Report* (1949) London: HMSO, pp. 14–19; Viscount Camrose (1947) *British Newspapers and their Controllers*, London: Cassell.
3  Hunter Davies (1981) *The Grades: the First Family of British Entertainment*, London: Weidenfeld & Nicolson.
4  Lord Thomson of Fleet (1975) *After I Was Sixty*, London: Hamish Hamilton; Russell Braddon (1965) *Roy Thomson of Fleet Street*, London: Collins.
5  Susan Goldberg (1985) *The Thomson Empire*, London: Sidgwick & Jackson.
6  David Owen (16 March 1989) 'Thomson merger creates group with $5 billion sales', *Financial Times*.
7  *Sunday Times* magazine (2 April 1989).
8  Tom Bower (1988) *Maxwell: The Outsider*, London: Aurum Press, pp. 35–46.
9  Maxwell Communications Corporation plc, *1987 Reports and Accounts*; Maxwell Communications Corporation plc, *Results for the Twelve Months to 31st December 1988*.
10  Michael Leapman (1983) *Barefaced Cheek: Rupert Murdoch*, London: Coronet, pp. 24–32; Simon Regan (1976) *Rupert Murdoch: A Business Biography*, London: Angus & Robertson.
11  Harold Evans (1983) *Good Times, Bad Times*, London: Weidenfeld & Nicolson.
12  See Glenda Korporaal, 'The financing of News Corporation' and J.W. Shaw, 'Mr Murdoch's industrial relations'. Both were papers presented at the conference on News Unlimited – Journalism and Global Ownership, University of Sydney (8–10 February 1989).
13  *UK Press Gazette* (22 August 1988) 'The thoughts of Chairman Murdoch', p. 20.
14  Michael Leapman, op. cit., pp. 224–34.
15  *Business Week* (Europe) (22 August 1988) 'Murdoch adds a few megatons to his arsenal', p. 39.
16  Jeff Ferry (7 January 1990) 'The decline and fall of the house of Saatchi', *Sunday Correspondent* magazine, pp. 24–9; Anna Foster (April 1988) 'Saatchi's isn't working', *Management Today*, pp. 38–44.
17  Tom Lloyd (1–7 December 1989) 'WPP plays the brand name game', *Financial Weekly*, pp. 28–33.
18  *Guardian* (6 April 1989) 'The other Green revolution'; Anna Foster (April 1989) 'Behind the Carlton screen', *Management Today*, pp. 52–6.
19  Mick Brown (1989) *Richard Branson: The Inside Story*, London: Headline.
20  *Variety* (4–10 October 1989); *Financial Times* (3 October 1989).

21 Peregrine Worsthorne (9 May 1983) 'Lord Hartwell: the voice of the silent majority', *The Times*; Maggie Brown and Clive Sanger (17 June 1985) 'Canadian capers in Fleet Street', *Guardian*; Raymond Snoddy (14 December 1985) 'From generation unto generation', *Financial Times*; Max Hastings (15 December 1985) 'Dynasty', *Sunday Times*.

## 7 MEDIA MOGULS IN FRANCE

1 Fictional representations of Hersant include Henri de Grandmaison's 1976 novel *Le Papivore* (Paris: J.C. Lattes) and the Patrice Chereau film, *Judith Therpauve* (1978).
2 See M. Palmer and J. Tunstall (1990) *Liberating Communications*, Oxford: NCC Blackwell; M. Palmer (1983) *Des petits journaux aux grandes agences*, Paris: Aubier.
3 The Haute Autorité (1982–6), the CNL (1986–8), the CSA (1989).
4 A. Raffalovitch (1931) '. . . *L'abominable venalité de la presse . . .*', Paris: Librairie du Travail.
5 *1981–1988: Bilan du septennat* (1988) Paris: *Le Monde*, Dossiers et Documents, p. 127.
6 In which the French Havas and Hachette groups themselves had stakes.
7 Quoted in J.-M. Quatrepoint (1986) *Histoire secrète des dossiers noirs de la Gauche*, Paris: Alain Moreau, p. 145.
8 Interviewed in *Le Monde* (15 September 1987).
9 Many a journalist has written of 'Citizen Hersant'; when the owner of the construction company Bouygues became a household name following his successful application as head of a consortium bidding for the privatized TV channel, TF-1, his biographers had a ready-made title: 'Citizen Bouygues'. See E. Campagnac and V. Nouzille (1988) *Citizen Bouygues, ou l'histoire secrète d'un grand patron*, Paris: Belfond.
10 On Bunau-Varilla, see M. Palmer, op. cit., and P. Albert *et al.* (1972) *Histoire générale de la presse française, t.iii: de 1871 à 1940*, Paris: P.U.F.
11 See A. Harmsworth (January 1901) 'The simultaneous newspaper', *The North American Review* (Boston); M. Palmer (January 1990) 'Newspapers in chains', *Revue Française de civilisation britannique*, Paris, pp. 23–41; R. Pound and G. Harmsworth (1959) *Northcliffe*, London: Cassell, p. 293.
12 Owner-operators closely identified with the establishment – Jean Dupuy was once Minister of Agriculture – the Dupuys are one of the few dynasties of Press barons to have been fully researched. See F. Amaury (1972) *Histoire du plus grand quotidien de la IIIe République: 'Le Petit Parisien', 1876–1944*, Paris: P.U.F., 2 vols.; M. Dupuy (1959) *Un homme un journal: Jean Dupuy*, Paris: Hachette.
13 See Cl. Hisard (1955) *Histoire de la spoliation de la presse française*, Paris: La Librairie française.

14  A reference to J.R. Ewing, an obnoxious character in the American soap *Dallas* (which had high audience ratings in France for most of the 1980s).

15  Previously, between May 1981 and mid-1983, Mitterrand's media adviser at the Elysée, André Rousselet – and not the Prime Minister – dealt with the Hersant issue; With little success, but at least without a glaring failure: see p. 238 n. 58.

16  See the law of 27 November 1986 on media ownership.

17  Broadcasting thereafter become secondary to Hersant's print media interests: see p. 151.

18  R. Hersant, interview in *L'Expansion*, 6 April 1984.

19  R. Hersant, interview in *L'Expansion*, November 1976. Hersant has spoken even more vulgarly of the journalists he employs.

20  The 'outsider' tag has often been used in studies of media moguls. See T. Bower (1988) *Maxwell: The Outsider*, London: Aurum Press.

21  Which contains a sixth of the French population.

22  A Gaullist minister between 1962–6 (information, education, etc.) Peyrefitte later became President of the editorial board of Hersant's *Le Figaro*. He is a member of the Académie française and a best-selling essayist.

23  See Ph. Boegner (1976) *'Oui patron . . .'*, Paris: Julliard.

24  See R. Brunois (1973) *'Le Figaro' face aux problèmes de la presse quotidienne*, Paris: P.U.F.

25  In 1987, four had circulations above 100,000 copies: the two most important were *Le Dauphiné libéré* (Grenoble: 330,000) and *Le Progrès* (Lyon: 272,000). Hersant also had a 10 per cent stake (subsequently increased) in the Montpellier-based *Midi libre* (174,000).

26  With 1989 sales of 786,463 copies, *Ouest-France*, based in Rennes, has the highest sale of *all* French dailies. In 1990, it acquired the Cherbourg daily, *Les Presses de la Manche*, partly to ensure that this title, previously a (small-scale) competitor, did not fall to Hersant and thereby serve as a Normandy beach-head from which to assault the Brittany bastions of *Ouest-France*.

27  See Th. Philippon (20 September 1988) 'Le groupe Hersant sous l'empire du passif', *Libération*; *Libération* (15 March 1991) 'Hersant, photo de groupe avec fissures'.

28  Including *L'Auto-Journal*, the longest-surviving (1950– ) consumer interest magazine of the group: from the outset, it claimed to defend the interests of (potential) car owners against those of automobile manufacturers.

29  Despite, apparently, the urging of the then socialist President of the National Assembly, Louis Mermaz.

30  S. Denis (1988) *Le roman de l'argent*, Paris: Albin Michel, pp. 44–5.

31  Hersant launched the Chic FM network in 1986. In May 1987, it comprised fifty stations. In 1987, Hersant acquired another network, Fun, with a similar number of stations. The merged network, called Fun, ran at a loss, aimed at the young, and promoted 'la Cinq'.

32  *Medias* (7 October 1988) 'Hersant: endetté, mais riche'; *Libération* (15 March 1991) 'Hersant, photo de groupe avec fissures'.

33  Lagardère is Chairman and General Manager ('p.-d.g.') of Hachette; Filipacchi is Vice-president of the company, in charge of the Press and magazine sector.
34  *Hersant* group: estimated figures. Chief titles: *Le Figaro, Le Figaro Magazine, Madame Figaro, France Soir, Le Dauphiné libéré, Le Progrès, Paris-Normandie, Nord-Eclair, La Liberté du Morbihan, Presse Océan, L'Auto-Journal, L'Indicateur Bertrand*, etc.
35  These figures relate only to the press division of the *Hachette* group: *Télé-7-Jours, Elle, France Dimanche, Le Journal du dimanche, Parents, Vital, Onze, Première*. (On the connection between Hachette-Presse and Publications Filipacchi, see p. 151).
36  *Editions Mondiales: Télé-Poche, Modes et Travaux, Nous Deux, Intimité, Tilt, Diapason*, etc.
37  *Publications Filipacchi: Paris-Match, Lui, Newlook, Photo, Femme, Pariscope, OK, Podium, Salut*, etc.
38  *Editions Amaury: Le Parisien libéré, L'Equipe, Le Maine Libre, Liberté Dimanche.*
39  In addition to the titles listed above (n. 35), these figures include data for communications assets acquired in 1987–8. In July 1987, Hachette acquired a majority holding in the companies that publish the leading regional dailies of Marseille and Nice – *Le Provençal, Le Méridional, Le Soir, Var Matin*; in April 1988, Hachette acquired – for $712 million – the seventh biggest US press group, Diamandis, publisher of popular and women's magazines, including *Women's Day*, America's second-leading title in the field; a month later, Hachette completed the acquisition of 90 per cent of shares of one of the top ten US publishers of directories, Grolier.
    As noted, Hachette-Presse is a division of Hachette: with a total group turnover in 1988 of 24,403,749,000 francs, Hachette was the twenty-eighth biggest French industrial company.
40  Estimated figures. In addition to the titles listed above (n. 34), these figures include data for assets acquired in 1988, such as the women's magazine *Jours de France*. The increased deficit was mostly due to the losses of 200 million francs incurred through Hersant's 25 per cent holding in the loss-making fifth channel, la Cinq.
41  As per n. 36.
42  The publisher of France's leading regional daily, with the biggest circulation of all French daily newspapers, figured in the top five print media groups of 1988 largely as a result of its acquisition of the major publisher of free sheets, the Carillon group (turnover: 48 million francs).
43  This division of the CEP (Compagnie Européenne de Publication), is a leading publisher of professional and trade magazines: *L'Usine nouvelle, A pour affaires économiques, Le Moniteur, OI Informatique, Industrie et Techniques*, etc. CEP Communication is Havas-controlled.
44  After 'alarms and excursions' worthy of a Jacobean melodrama, Havas finally pulled out (of a putative association with Hachette); Bouygues defeated Hachette among the consortia applying for (the privatized) TF-1 franchise; and the CLT was one of the two leading partners (with

a 25 per cent stake) in the consortium that obtained the franchise for France's sixth TV channel – M6.

45  'Franco-français' – an epithet used by those who decry (or decried) companies more concerned with the domestic, than with European or world, market(s).

46  'MBB' ensured that his family retained control of the majority of shares of his company.

47  'Les 1000 premières entreprises industrielles françaises', *L'Expansion* (November 1988).

48  ARJIL was coined out of the Christian names of *Arnaud* and *Jean-Luc* Lagardère.

49  J.-L. Lagardère interview in *L'Expansion* (2–15 March 1989).

50  Partly to keep his group's interests in the public eye, Lagardère, like other European moguls, has invested untold sums in major spectator sports: in Formula One racing cars – in the 1970s, Matra thrice won the Le Mans 24-hour race – in Racing football club – Matra pulled out of the (unsuccessful) first-division club, 'Matra-racing', in 1989; and in raising race-horses.

51  See p. 158.

52  See p. 147.

53  Turnover: 1,619,637,000 francs; 860 employees; titles include *Paris-Match, Lui, Newlook, Photo, OK, Podium, Salut*, etc. See *L'Expansion* (November 1989), 'Les 30 premiers groupes de presse'.

54  Throughout the acquisition of a controlling stake in the Barcelona book publisher, Salvat, Lagardère explained his 'global' strategy thus: 'there are 100 million French-speaking people in the world; people speaking English or Spanish total 900 million. Thus, by publishing in three languages, we multiply our (initially French) capacity by ten. This explains our US and Spanish acquisitions' policy.' J.-L. Lagardère interview in *L'Expansion* (2–15 March 1989).

55  See *Le Monde* (12 October 1990).

56  'European communications groups with the most international interests (Bertelsmann, Hachette) succeed in raising over half of their total turnover from abroad by being present in several distinct, if related, sectors. The international activities of Canal Plus may ultimately account for 40% of the company's turnover.' A. Rousselet interview in *Décisions Medias* (April 1990).

57  J.-M. Quatrepoint (1986) *Histoire secrètes des dossiers noirs de la Gauche*, Paris: Alain Moreau, pp. 21–3.

58  In late 1981, Rousselet reportedly negotiated directly with Hersant; a threatened tax inspection of the Socpresse, the Hersant holding company, would be waived were Hersant to sell the (loss-making) *France-Soir* to Max Théret. Hersant subsequently procrastinated; possibly because of the fears of right-wing leaders lest *France-Soir* fall under socialist influence, possibly because Hersant wanted to retain control of the newspaper's advertising revenues. Hersant succeeded in pulling the wool over Rousselet's eyes. And Mitterrand, whom some suspect of having protected Hersant on occasion, tried to dissuade Mauroy from proceeding against Hersant via the 1983–4 Press

bill. See J-M. Quatrepoint, op. cit., p. 23; Th. Pfister (1985) *La vie quotidienne à Matignon au temps de l'union de la Gauche*, Paris: Hachette, pp. 133–5.
59 J-M. Quatrepoint op. cit., p. 36.
60 F.-O. Giesbert (1990) *Le président*, Paris: le Seuil, p. 273.
61 Quoted in *L'Express* (18–24 April 1986).
62 J.-P. Baudecroux, interview in *Libération* (4 December 1989).
63 In February 1987, the Havas advertising group was – briefly – a candidate for the acquisition of a privatized TF-1: prominent French advertising agency figures seized on this *faux pas* to denounce Havas' 'dominant position' in several media markets – as a media owner (Canal Plus, for example) and media broker, etc. Havas allegedly controlled over 30 per cent of French advertising space. Despite the privatization of Havas (May 1987) and the holding of several enquiries, Havas' 'dominant' position still exists in 1991.
64 See p. 137.
65 Hachette accordingly controlled 9 per cent of the circulation and 16 per cent of the (non-local) advertising revenue of the regional daily Press in 1988.
66 P. Todorov (1990) *La presse française à l'heure de l'Europe*, Paris: La Documentation Française, p. 14.
67 Ch. de Gaulle, quoted in L. Greilsamer (1990) *Hubert Beuve-Méry*, Paris: Fayard, p. 239.

## 8 MEDIA MOGULS IN ITALY

1 Until the late 1970s, only two RAI channels were legally authorized to carry national advertising and programming. With the 1976 Supreme Court Decision, many hundreds of small local channels sprang up. Berlusconi subsequently launched or acquired three channels or networks: Canale-5, Italia-1 and Rete-4. He transported video tapes of programmes and commercials to many of these outlets for simultaneous transmission of this material, giving the impression of 'national' channels. These new private channels were not bound, as RAI had been, by regulations on how much advertising they should carry, or when they should carry it. (During 1987–8 the RAI recovered some of the lost ground.)
2 A play on the Italian words for 'broadcasting/transmitter', and 'excellency/highness'.
3 Despite French government resistance.
4 See P. Musso and G. Pineau (1990) *Italie et sa télévision*, Paris: Champ Vallon.
5 Of all major western European countries, Italy has perhaps the most dubious reputation for the reliability of its data on advertising spend. An executive of Publitalia once admitted that it was his company which – via its discounts on its official rates – was responsible for something like a 60 per cent discrepancy between 'official' and real advertising spend. Nonetheless, it is generally recognized that television accounted for something like 11 per cent of total advertising

expenditure in Italy in 1960 and for 48 per cent in 1988; the amount of advertising expenditure – the size of the cake – itself increases. According to UPA/I1 Millimetro, per capita advertising expenditure, expressed in constant 1985 prices, rose from 41,665 lire in 1980 to 98,253 lire in 1988. (Advertising Association (AA) and European Advertising Tripartite (EAT) (December 1989) *The European Advertising and Media Forecast (EAMF)*, vol. 4, no. 3, pp. 66–7).

6   Fininvest channels in 1989 were 91 per cent reliant on advertising and 9 per cent on sponsorship. Publitalia, Berlusconi's sales arm, also sold airtime for several other commercial networks and undoubtedly accounted for the vast bulk of the 2.3 billion lire in TV advertising expenditure not going to SIPRA, RAI's sales arm. Publitalia was expected to take 1,900 billion lire in 1989, although the 'official' figure it provided to the supervisory commission for 1988 was only 1,300 billion lire. *Source*: AA and EAT, *EAMF*, vol. 4, no. 1, June 1989.

7   Berlusconi was the first western media mogul to successfully negotiate with Gostelradio, the Soviet Union broadcasting authority, for the advertising of western products on Soviet television. In 1988, the hour-long programme *Progress, Informacija, Reklama* was shown once a month on three Soviet channels; Berlusconi provided the programme and money and in return controlled the advertising slots (and the advertising rates). Thus did Fiat, Pirelli, ITT, Volkswagen, etc. reach the 150 million Soviet households which have a TV set. Berlusconi now proposes similar programmes, and related sponsorship, to other eastern European countries.

8   Founder members of ACT: Fininvest, ITV of Britain, Sat-1 of Germany, France's TF-1, and Luxembourg's CLT. For example, one of the first ACT pronouncements, was to endorse the European Community's broadcasting directive. See *Financial Times* (30 June 1989).

9   G. Ruggeri and M. Guarino (1987) *Berlusconi*, Roma: Editori Riuniti, p. 30.

10  Alan Friedman (1988) *Tutto in famiglia*, Milan: Longanesi. Italian translation of (1988) *Gianni Agnelli and The Network of Italian Power*, London: Harrap.

11  A. Friedman, op. cit., p. 115.

12  *Fortune Italia* (September 1989) p. 32.

13  *Prima Comunicazione* (May 1989) p. 81

14  See above, p. 166.

15  *Prima Comunicazione* (May 1989) p. 82.

16  A. Friedman, op. cit., pp. 24, 236–7.

17  Giovanni Agnelli acquired a stake in *La Stampa*, the Turin daily, in 1920; Fiat bought the newspaper outright in 1926. During the war years, Fiat jumped from being the thirtieth biggest industrial company in Italy to becoming the third biggest. See A. Friedman, op. cit., pp. 31–2.

18  Marie-France Pochna (1989) *Agnelli: L'irresistible*, Paris: Lattes–L'Expansion–Hachette.

19  *Panorama* (September 1989).
20  See n. 17.
21  Established in 1876, the paper has a circulation of 650–700,000.
22  Possibly to quieten parliamentary criticism of the Fiat majority control of Gemina, Rizzoli swapped shares in June 1987 with Hachette, the French publisher, to reduce the Gemina stakes in Rizzoli–Corriere (which continued, nonetheless, to exceed 50 per cent). *Financial Times* (29 June 1987), quoted in A. Friedman, op. cit., pp. 118, 284.
23  For details, see A. Friedman, op. cit., Chapter 7.
24  *Prima Comunicazione* (June 1989) p. 52.
25  Giuseppe Turani and D. Rattazzi (1990) *Mondadori: La Grande Sfida*, Milano: Rizzoli, p. 123.
26  ibid.
27  Quoted in A. Friedman, op. cit., p. 119.
28  See n. 6.
29  See p. 213.

## 9 MEDIA MOGULS IN GERMANY

1  The same, however, is true in varying degrees of France and other 'liberated' countries.
2  G. Bucerius (1974) *Der angeklagte Verlager*, Munich. A possible reference to the celebrated phrase of Roy Thomson. See above, p. 119.
3  Jürgen Prott (1986) *Die zerstörte Offentlichkeit: Die leise Effizienz der WAZ-Politik*, Göttingen. Braunschweig *et al.* (1990) *Radio und Fernsehen in der Bundesrepublik: Erfahrungen und Ansätze für eine gewerkschaftliche Politik*, Cologne.
4  See pp.185–8.
5  Horst Röper (1989) 'Formationen deutscher Medienmultis 1989', in *Media Perspektiven*, no. 12, S. 733–44, p. 738.
6  Gerhard Naeher (1989) *Der Medienhändler: Der Fall Leo Kirch*, Munich, p. 740.
7  *Wirtschaftswoche* (22 April 1988).
8  Röper, op. cit., p. 740.
9  *Neuen Medien* (February 1989) p. 19.

## 10 CONCLUSION: EUROPE'S FUTURE MEDIA AND MOGULS

1  Jeremy Tunstall (1977) *The Media Are American*, London: Constable, pp. 263–9.
2  MEDIA = Measures to Encourage the Development of the Industries of Audiovisual Production.

# Further reading

## 2 Western European television and the North Atlantic setting

Alvarado, Manuel (ed.) (1988) *Video World-Wide: An International Study*, London: John Libbey.
Gould, P., Johnson, J. and Chapman, G. (1984) *The Structure of Television*, London: Pion.
Locksley, Gareth (1988) *TV Broadcasting in Europe and the New Technologies*, Commission of the European Communities, Brussels.
National Telecommunications and Information Administration (1990) *Comprehensive Study of the Globalization of Mass Media Firms*, Washington, DC: US Department of Commerce.

## 6 Media moguls in Britain

Bower, Tom (1988) *Maxwell: The Outsider*, London: Aurum Press.
Braddon, Russell (1965) *Roy Thomson of Fleet Street*, London: Collins.
Brandon, Piers (1982) *The Life and Death of the Press Barons*, London: Secker & Warburg.
Brown, Mick (1988) *Richard Branson: The Inside Story*. London: Michael Joseph.
Camrose, Viscount (1947) *British Newspapers and their Controllers*, London: Cassell.
Chester, Lewis and Fenby, Jonathan (1979) *The Fall of the House of Beaverbrook*, André Deutsch.
Davies, Hunter (1981) *The Grades: The First Family of British Entertainment*, Weidenfeld & Nicolson.
Evans, Harold (1983) *Good Times, Bad Times*, Weidenfeld & Nicolson.
Fallon, Ivan (1988) *The Brothers: The Rise and Rise of Saatchi and Saatchi*, London: Hutchinson.
Goldenberg, Susan (1975) *The Thomson Empire*, London: Sidgwick & Jackson.
Grade, Lew (1987) *Still Dancing: My Story*, London: Collins.
Haines, Joe (1988) *Maxwell*, London: Macdonald.
Jenkins, Simon (1986) *The Market for Glory*, London: Faber & Faber.
Kleinman, Philip (1988) *The Saatchi and Saatchi Story*, London: Pan Books.

Leapman, Michael (1983) *Barefaced Cheek: Rupert Murdoch*, London: Coronet.

Lee, Alan J. (1976) *The Origins of the Popular Press*, London: Croom Helm.

Malvern, Linda (1986) *The End of the Street*, London: Methuen.

Munster, George (1985) *Rupert Murdoch: A Paper Prince*, New York: Viking.

Papers presented to the conference on News Unlimited: Journalism and Global Ownership, University of Sydney, 8–10 February 1989.

Pound, Reginald and Harmsworth, Geoffrey (1959) *Northcliffe*, London: Cassell.

Regan, Simon (1976) *Rupert Murdoch: A Business Biography*, London: Angus & Robertson.

Royal Commission on the Press (1949) 1947–49 Report, London: HMSO.

Thomson, Lord (1975) *After I Was Sixty*, London: Hamish Hamilton.

Wood, Alan (1965) *The True History of Lord Beaverbrook*, London: Heinemann.

## 9   Media moguls in Germany

Braunschweig, Stefan, Kleinsteuber, Hans J., Wiesner, Volkert and Wilke, Peter (1990) *Radio und Fernsehen in der Bundesrepublik: Erfahrungen und Ansätze für eine gewerkschaftliche Politik*, Cologne.

Bucerius, G. (1974) *Der angeklagte Verlager*, Munich. epd/Kirche und Rundfunk 12/90: *Kirch und Bertelsmann beim Pay-TV wiedervereint*.

Friedebold, Fritz (1988) 'Der Konzern, die Macht und die Pein', in *Neue Medien*, no. 8, pp. 15–23.

Guratzsch, Dankwart (1974) *Macht durch Organisation. Die Grundlegung des Hugenbergschen Presseimperiums*, Düsseldorf.

Hasselbach, Suzanne and Porter, Vincent (winter 1988) 'The re-regulation of West German broadcasting', in *Politics and Society in Germany, Austria and Switzerland*, pp. 48–65.

Holzach, Heidrun (1981) *Das 'System Hugenberg'*, Stuttgart.

Humphreys, Peter (1990) *Media and Media Policy in West Germany*, Oxford.

Jacobs, Hans-Jürgen and Müller, Uwe (1990) *Augstein, Springer & Co. Deutsche Mediendynastien*, Orell Füssli.

Jansen, B. and Klönne, A. (1968) *Imperium Springer: Macht und Manipulation*, Cologne.

Kleinsteuber, Hans J. (1986) 'Federal Republic of Germany', in Hans J. Kleinsteuber, Denis McQuail and Karen Siune (eds): *Electronic Media and Politics in Western Europe*, Frankfurt.

Müller, H. D. (1968) *Der Springer-Konzern, Eine Kritische Studie*, Munich.

Muzik, Peter (1989) *Die Medienmultis*, Vienna, Stuttgart and Bern: Jahrbuch Neue Medien.

Naeher, Gerhard (1989) *Der Medienhändler: Der Fall Leo Kirch*, Munich.

*Neue Medien* (January 1989) 'PRINT: Die Auslands-Power der deutschen Großverlage', p. 75.

*Neue Medien* (February 1989): 'Top 300: Die größten Medienkonzerne', pp. 17–43.

Pätzold, Ulrich (1986) 'Wer bewegt die Medien an der Ruhr? Die leise Effizienz der WAZ-Politik', in *Media Perspektiven*, no. 8, pp. 507–18.

Prott, Jürgen (1986) *Die zerstörte Offentlichkeit: Die Bundesrepublik auf dem Weg zum Kommerzfunk*, Göttingen.

Röper, Horst (1988) 'Formationen deutscher Medienmultis 1988', in *Media Perspektiven*, no. 12, pp. 749–65.

—— (1989) 'Formationen deutscher Medienmultis 1989', in *Media Perspektiven*, no. 12, pp. 733–44.

Spaeth, Andreas (1988) 'Teure deutsche Stimmen', in *Neue Medien*, no. 7, pp. 26–8.

Timpe, Wolfgang (1988) 'Bauer handelt mit Zeitgeistfrüchten', in *Neue Medien*, no. 1, pp. 14–21.

Wehling, Hans-Georg (1987): *Medienpolitik*, Stuttgart.

*Wirtschaftswoche* (22 April 1988) 'Die Erben machen Druck', pp. 58–71.

# Index